CITY OF SECRETS

Perennial

An Imprint of HarperCollins*Publishers*

CITY OF SECRETS

THE STARTLING TRUTH BEHIND
THE VATICAN MURDERS

JOHN FOLLAIN

First Perennial edition published 2004.

Designed by Gretchen Achilles

The Library of Congress has catalogued the hardcover edition as follows:

Follain, John.
    City of secrets : the truth behind the murders at the Vatican / John Follain. — 1st ed.
      p. cm.
    ISBN 0-06-620954-4
        1. Vatican City. Guardia svizzera pontificia—History—20th century. 2. Estermann, Alois. 3. Tornay, Cédric. 4. Follain, John. 5. Police murders—Vatican City—Case studies. 6. Gay men—Vatican City—Sexual behavior—Case studies. 7. Opus Dei (Society). I. Title.

    UA749.5 .F65 2003
    355'.009456'34—dc21   2002032630

ISBN 0-06-093513-8 (pbk.)

04 05 06 07 08 ❖/RRD 10 9 8 7 6 5 4 3 2 1

TO RITA

PROLOGUE

ON THE DARKEST day of the long reign of John Paul II, the rain pelts down on the statues of Christ and the Apostles that dominate the Basilica. The water slithers down the chunky bodies and worms its way into the pockmarks that age and pollution, like a sculptor portraying the ravages of leprosy, have chiseled into the righteous marble faces.

Shortly before nine o'clock on that evening of May 4, 1998, in the Renaissance-era Apostolic Palace overlooking the Basilica, the lights are still burning in the private apartments from where an elderly figure in a white robe, spiritual leader of one billion souls, blesses the faithful who twice a week gather under his window. The palace dominates the Holy City's skyline of domes, crosses, ramparts, and towers.

In the barracks of the Swiss Guard at the foot of the palace, Sister

Anna-Lina Meier of the small, two-hundred-year-old order of the Divine Providence of Baldegg, recognizable by her springy limp, scurries across a courtyard, head bowed and white coif bobbing like a dinghy in a squall. She is on her way to the home she shares with Sisters Antonina and Gregoria.

Gray-haired and heavily built, Sister Anna-Lina has been a pillar of the Swiss Guard for longer than anyone can remember, and has outlived three popes during her time at the Vatican. Despite her many years in Rome, she still prefers to speak the Swiss German of her youth rather than Italian, and the hearty, monotonous fare with which she and the other nuns feed the guards in the canteen has similarly resisted any local influence. Her voice is as familiar to them as her cooking. She sings in the choir at Sunday morning Mass in the Guard's chapel. Despite her advanced age, she has recently discovered a new musical passion and has taken to strumming a guitar.

Sister Anna-Lina bustles into the building which, of the three that form the Swiss Guard complex, is the one deepest into Vatican territory. She takes the elevator to the second floor, whose drab and dimly lit landing the nuns have tried to brighten up with a row of straggly potted plants that reach as high as the buzzer marked, in Gothic lettering, BALDEGGER SCHWERIN (Sisters of Baldegg).

She enters the apartment and leaves the door open behind her. She does so either out of absentmindedness or simply because she feels perfectly safe. The barracks of the world's oldest, and smallest, army are, after all, one of the most tightly guarded areas within the Vatican, itself accessible only through gates that are manned day and night. Some senior officers even leave their keys outside in the lock so that their children can come and go freely.

She has barely walked in when she hears a sound from the staircase. Someone with a heavy tread is making his or her way up. She retraces her steps, sees that there is no one on the landing, and this time pushes the door shut. Sister Anna-Lina thinks nothing more of the noise and prepares to settle down for the little that is left of her evening. The nuns are early bedders. They rise early every morning to prepare breakfast for the guards who return hungry after the night shift, and for those called out on duty at dawn.

Moments later, she hears loud noises coming from the apartment next door. As she will testify later to Vatican investigators, Sister Anna-Lina can't guess what the noises mean. She stops to listen more carefully, but hears only silence. It is unlike her neighbors to make a commotion. They have no children, and rarely entertain.

Her neighbors are Colonel Alois Estermann and his Venezuelan wife, Gladys Meza Romero, a former model. All day, the courtyard of the barracks has echoed to the hoarse shouts of the chisel-jawed, forty-three-year-old Estermann and the medieval clink and clank of seven-foot halberds, or pikes, as he drilled new recruits in preparation for their swearing-in ceremony in two days' time. It is one of the Vatican community's most stirring pageants. Perfecting a rite that he insists must unfold with the unerring precision of Swiss clockwork, the stern Estermann made the guards, clad in full dress-uniform, with its orange-, blue-, and red-slashed doublet and hose, and weighed down by glittering breastplate and helmet, march up to the banner of the Guard, seize it with their left hands, and punch the air with their right, three fingers extended to symbolize the Holy Trinity.

Immobile, each in turn must shout out the oath of allegiance: "I swear I will faithfully, loyally, and honorably serve the Supreme Pontiff John Paul II and his legitimate successors, sacrificing my life to defend them if necessary . . . May God and our Holy Patrons assist me!"

At noon, the *bollettino,* the bulletin of Vatican announcements, featured the pope's appointment of Estermann as commander of the Swiss Guard. On hearing the news, Estermann, whose eighteen years of service made him a veteran of the corps, confided to a friend that he saw in his promotion "the hand of God, who will help me to perform my duty well." He sees his task as guardian of the Holy City gates and protector of the pope both inside and outside the Vatican. For him, it is a religious mission. Earlier that evening, Estermann offered prayers of thanks at the Mass that he attended, as he did every day.

To all appearances, faith binds Estermann and his wife, Meza Romero—both have studied theology and canon law, the Catholic legal manual, in their spare time and both are regular chuchgoers. She earned notoriety in her native land when she ended her modeling career to take on a male-chauvinist establishment and become the country's first policewoman, and then left Latin America to settle in Rome, where she works as an archivist at the Venezuelan embassy to the Holy See. The couple are familiar fixtures at diplomatic receptions, making powerful friends among cardinals, bishops, and monsignori.

Sister Anna-Lina makes her way back to the landing once more. To her left, the door to the Estermanns' apartment is wide open. She hesitates, but still hearing nothing, bobs across the worn, grayish-brown stone floor and looks in.

It is some time before she finds the strength to make a furtive sign of the cross over the silver crucifix resting on her powerful chest. What the nun sees roots her to the spot. Dressed in the tracksuit she generally wears for household chores, Meza Romero, who is usually elegantly dressed, slumps on the floor in an ungraceful heap. Her almond eyes are closed under her pencil-thin, permanently arched eyebrows, and she looks as if she has fainted. Her back rests against the wall of the corridor, but her head lolls at a strange angle, and the raven hair that is usually tied back in a strict bun is disheveled.

The nun is too shocked to venture any farther into the Estermann flat. She can see that the lights in the sitting room beyond the corridor are on, but the only sound is that of the wind and the rain outside. She turns away and scuttles down the stairs to seek help, as fast as her limp will allow her.

Sister Anna-Lina is not alone in hearing noises. Caroline Meier, the wife of a sergeant major, has left her flat on the floor below and walked out into the courtyard to see if anyone is there. She finds no one, and is making her way back up the stairs when Sister Anna-Lina almost stumbles into her.

Breathless after her short dash, Sister Anna-Lina tells Meier what she has seen. The commander's wife has been taken ill, she says. Neither of the women dares to intervene. That task falls to Lance Corporal Marcel Riedi, the first guard of any rank whom they can find. Valued by his superiors, he has been quickly promoted since joining the Swiss Guard.

Riedi realizes instantly that if someone has harmed Meza Romero, her aggressor may still be in the flat. He decides to risk entering it on his own. As he steals up to Meza Romero to check whether she is alive, he detects an acrid smell that hangs heavily in the damp air, more heavily than any incense. He recognizes it from long hours at the firing range: the smell of gunpowder.

It is Riedi who spots the messy trail the color of altar wine that Meza Romero left on the wallpaper as she slumped to the ground, and seeing the stain across her left shoulder, he guesses that she has been stabbed or shot. He creeps farther into the cramped flat, reaches the sitting room, and another smell becomes overpowering in the small space: the stench of death.

According to an official report published months later, never had Riedi seen so much blood. To his left Estermann lies immobile, stretched out on his right side on the stone floor, blood still oozing from a hole in his left cheek, and from wounds in the back of his neck and his left shoulder. Near him, the stain-splattered handset of a telephone swings slowly from a table. Riedi wonders whether he had attempted to call for help.

A few feet away by a wooden door, in a twisted position, partly on his front and partly on his right flank, lies a guard with the same rank as Riedi, Lance Corporal Cédric Tornay. The face of the handsome twenty-three-year-old rests in a pool of blood that trickles from his mouth and from the back of his head. The door is splashed with stains and what looks like fleshy matter. Riedi thinks of the mother and sisters whom Tornay, who joined the Guard and took the oath as a recruit only three years earlier, has left behind in his Swiss mountain village, and wonders who will break the news to them.

Behind Tornay, the view from the window is virtually filled by the Bastion of Nicholas V, a medieval tower once home to prisoners detained at the pope's pleasure. Now it is the headquarters of the Vatican Bank, whose official name—the Institute for the Works of Religion—belies a scandalous legacy of dealings with Mafia financiers. High above, on the top floor of the Apostolic Palace, which overhangs the barracks like a sheer and smooth cliff, are the two windows of the pope's bedroom.

There is nothing Riedi can do for any of the victims. They are all dead. As the news spreads through the barracks and then throughout the Vatican City village, to be greeted with incredulity and invocations to the saints, the courtyard begins to fill with officers and the lowest-ranking soldiers, the halbardiers, and with many of the priests, nuns, and lay workers who reside within its walls.

No one can remember witnessing an episode of such violence inside the city-state, on whose tiny territory every aspect of daily life is as tightly regimented as Sunday Mass. Only five months earlier, there was the case of Enrico Sini Luzi, a Gentleman of His Holiness, an order whose members, in white gloves and black tails, greet dignitaries who visit the pope. He was battered to death with an antique chandelier in his home, clad only in his underwear, a cashmere scarf around his neck, apparently during a homosexual tryst with a Romanian male prostitute. But that murder was committed outside the Vatican. So was the murder, in November 1849, of Count Pellegrino Rossi, a lay prime minister serving the papal states. He was stabbed in the neck by a political opponent upon alighting from his carriage in the courtyard of the Palace of the Chancellery, across the river Tiber.

For many in the crowd, the bloodshed in the barracks carries echoes of the darkest days of the Borgia rule during the Renaissance, when in the cellars of the Apostolic Palace courtiers hired apothecaries to prepare the *cantarella,* a poison based on arsenic and putrefied viscera, destined for their rivals, and Cardinal Cesare Borgia, son of the cunning Pope Alexander VI, drew his sword to stab his sister Lucrezia's lover in the corridors of the Vatican.

The more superstitious murmur that a great misfortune was only to be expected after the bad omen a few days earlier when the pope lost his gold Fisherman's Ring while shaking the hands of the faithful at a ceremony in St. Peter's Square. The ring is a potent symbol for popes, testimony that Christ entrusted the supremacy of the Church to the Galilean fisherman Peter, the apostle whose legitimate descendants they consider themselves to be. In the form of a cross, the ring was given to the pope after his election, and its loss, albeit short-lived—it was soon found by a pilgrim—was seen as leaving him unprotected.

On the first and second floors of the soldiers' quarters, two guards light candles and place them in the windows of their rooms. For several hours to come, the pair of tiny flames will be the only sign to outsiders that anything is amiss at the heart of the Roman Catholic Church.

Sometime after witnessing the scene in the Estermann apartment for himself, Monsignor Alois Jehle, the gaunt chaplain of the Swiss Guard, picks his way through the swelling crowd in the courtyard and strides briskly up the cobbled avenue that slopes up from the barracks. He passes the tower of the Vatican Bank, the cracked stones housing a thousand mysteries glistening blackly in the rain, and the parking space where the cars' license plates are marked SCV for State of Vatican City, but which irreverent Romans say stands for *Se Cristo Vedesse* (If Christ Could See).

As he walked, Jehle would later tell acquaintances, he battled to find the right words with which to tell of the news of that night, to explain how a profane act had violated the sacred territory of the pope's domain.

With a perfunctory order to the liveried attendant at the foot of the Apostolic Palace, Jehle takes the wood-paneled elevator to the third floor. As he makes his way down the frescoed corridor, the white pleated draperies that cover the high windows to his right and run the entire length of the corridor make his waxen complexion seem paler still, and seal him off from the outside world like a shroud. The rustle of his cassock and the creak of his wet shoes on the patterned marble floor are the only sounds that disturb the stillness.

Ushered into the antechamber of Karol Wojtyla, John Paul II, by a member of the Swiss Guard who knows nothing of the events at the barracks, Jehle is greeted by a Polish fellow priest who, like himself, enjoys the title of monsignor. But there the similarities end. No one in the Vatican can rival the velvet power exercised by the pope's chamberlain and priest secretary, Monsignor Stanislaw Dziwisz.

After a quick word with Jehle, Dziwisz leaves to tell the pope of his arrival. Dziwisz has been at the pope's side for more than three decades, since the age of nineteen, when John Paul brought him to Rome for the conclave from which he emerged pope. Dziwisz is a man of silence, who can be depended on not to betray a confidence, and who is deemed so influential as a guardian of conservative doctrine that his detractors have nicknamed him Rasputin. Few can preface their instructions with as much authority: "His Holiness desires . . ." Cardinals bristle with both indignation and envy when the pope ends a discussion with the words: "We will hear what Stanislaw has to say."

It was Dziwisz, the son of a railwayman, who gave the pope the last rites as he was wheeled into an operating room after a Turkish gunman shot him in St. Peter's Square in 1981. In the years that followed the assassination attempt, as the pope became more frail, a shadow of the robust figure that the press at the time of his election had dubbed "God's athlete" because of his passion for skiing and swimming, it was Dziwisz who reached out and steadied him whenever he lost his balance. As a token of his gratitude, the pope trampled over tradition to name Dziwisz a bishop, the only time in the twentieth century when a pontiff had honored his private secretary in such a way.

That evening, the pope's seventeen-hour day—which because of his health is no longer the frenzy of work that it once was—is drawing to a close. In the Apostolic Palace he once described to a visitor as "a cage, a golden cage," he has finished his spartan supper a little earlier than usual and is celebrating Compline, the last evening prayers, with a group of nuns in his private oratory, head bent in front of the huge bronze crucifix. John Paul, who that month would become the longest serving pope of the twentieth century, had long taken to heart Saint Augustine's instruction to "work as if everything depends on you, and pray as if everything depends on God." In his younger years, he would stretch himself out on the marble floor of the chapel for long spells, his arms spread out in the shape of a cross.

When the pope, leaning on his cane and escorted by Dziwisz, enters the simple study where he writes his sermons and speeches, marking every page with the initials *A.M.D.G.* for *Ad Majorem Dei Gloriam* (For the Greatest Glory of God), Jehle kneels on the drab carpet that covers most of the marble floor. Jehle then kisses the Fisherman's Ring and fumbles for the right words. His delivery is not as smooth as he perhaps would like.

Your Holiness, he begins, something terrible has happened, something which means that we will all have to pray a great deal.

Jehle joins his damp palms together.

John Paul listens, his shoulders hunched, his head cocked to one side, waiting. Dziwisz is just as silent.

The colonel, Jehle continues, the man whom you, Your Holiness, appointed commander of the Swiss Guard only today, has been found dead in his home. He was shot dead together with his wife. A lance corporal, Cédric Tornay, has also been found dead with them in their flat, shot with his ordnance gun.

There is no outburst, no gesture of anger by the pope. Only a startled, pained look in his steely blue eyes, followed by a great weariness that seems to weigh on the shrunken frame of the seventy-seven-year-old pontiff.

For a little while, no one speaks. Perhaps the pope remembers the words of advice he gave to the Swiss Guard on the eve of the previous year's swearing-in ceremony. He had told them: "Do not fear those who kill the body, but cannot kill the soul; fear rather the one who can lead the body and soul to destruction."

No tears come to the pope's eyes. John Paul has been seen to cry only twice, when the conclave elected him to the papal throne, and when he made his first journey back to Poland after his election. When the pope does speak, his voice now slurred by Parkinson's disease, which is slowly turning his face into a rigid mask, it is to pay tribute to Estermann's loyalty. He briefly consults Dziwisz, then orders Jehle to inform the cardinal secretary of state, Angelo Sodano, the Vatican's "prime minister" in all but name.

The pope reaches for his black walking stick and moves stiffly to his private chapel lined with Carrara marble, where he is helped to his knees at the prie-dieu before the crucifix. For decades, the sections of the Gospels that seem to have preyed on his mind, prompting him to speak and write about them again and again, are those dealing with death and judgment, with paradise and the inferno.

The 264th Bishop of Rome, Vicar of Christ, Successor of the Prince of the Apostles, Supreme Pontiff of the Universal Church, is left alone to pray.

CHAPTER ONE

SHORTLY BEFORE NOON on the day after the deaths at the Swiss Guard, I left my home in the historic center of Rome and set out down the Via dei Coronari, a narrow street of ancient palaces and ocher houses with flaking facades. The street owes its name to the *coronari,* or rosary makers, whose shops once lined its sides. From these well-placed vantage points, their owners could call out to the pilgrims who flowed into the city through its northern gateway, the Porta del Popolo, and made their way down the long cobbled street to the Vatican. Now smart antique stores have replaced the rosary makers, and the only mementos of the shops' former religious vocation are a few dilapidated shrines to the Virgin on street corners.

I had learned about the shootings from the radio that morning, and found out with a phone call to the Sala Stampa, the press office of the Holy See, that there would be a press conference that day. After crossing the river Tiber, I stopped to buy the newspapers and sat down on a stone bench on the monumental avenue called the Via della Conciliazione. Flanked by imitation obelisks, the street was forged on orders from the Fascist dictator Mussolini to open up a grand perspective of St. Peter's, but at the cost of pulling down many ancient houses.

BLOOD IN THE VATICAN, headlined the newspaper *La Repubblica,* with the subheading *Thriller in the Vatican.* Even the usually staid *Corriere della Sera* announced: MASSACRE AT THE SWISS GUARD. A third, *La Stampa,* went for a more evocative title: THREE BODIES, AND A GUN, IN THE VATICAN.

The newspapers ascribed the deaths to an "act of madness" on the part of the young guard Cédric Tornay, or to jealousy and an illicit love affair between him and the commander's wife, Meza Romero. One writer referred vaguely to "peculiar aspects" of the relationships between the three; another saw the hand of a fanatical member of a sect intent on making its mark on the eve of the "Holy Year," which the pope had announced would take place in two years' time, and which would bring millions of pilgrims to Rome. In the four years I had lived and worked as a journalist in the city, no other event at the heart of the Catholic Church had prompted so many different interpretations in so short a time.

Outside the press office, television crews jostled for position to book the best view of St. Peter's Square, while in the austere lobby, journalists who were not accredited to the Vatican pleaded for admittance. Luckily, I had been through this some years earlier when I first arrived in Rome. As a correspondent for the Reuters news agency, I had been given a Vatican press card by the surly, bespectacled Sister Elisabetta, assistant to the pope's spokesman. Sitting under a framed cover of the *Time* magazine edition proclaiming John Paul "Man of the Year" for 1994, she had asked me to sign a promise to abide by "ethical standards." When I asked to see a list of these, she looked at me blankly through her heavy spectacles, saying there was no such thing. I should just sign; there was no alternative. Please bear in mind, she told me, that the way we operate is the fruit of two thousand years of history. So I signed. At least she didn't ask me for a recommendation from a clergyman, as the press office had required of journalists covering the Second Vatican Council, which overhauled the Church in the early 1960s.

There were still a few minutes to go before the start of the news conference, so from the front desk I picked up a copy of the Vatican's first pronouncement on the previous night. The statement was in slightly odd English, as if it had been hurriedly translated, and stamped with the papal tiara and the keys of St. Peter's:

> The Captain Commander of the Pontifical Swiss Guard, Colonel Alois Estermann, was found dead in his home together with his wife Gladys Meza Romero and Vice corporal Cédric Tornay. The bodies were discovered shortly after 9pm by a neighbour from the apartment next-door who was attracted by loud noises. From a first investigation it is possible to affirm that all three were killed by a fire-arm. Under the body of the Vice corporal his regulation weapon was found. The information which has emerged up to this point allows for the theory of a "fit of madness" by Vice corporal Tornay.

I checked the timing of the statement—shortly after midnight on Tuesday, May 5, 1998. Only three hours after the deaths were discovered and before any autopsies were carried out, the Vatican had identified not only the culprit but also his state of mind at the time of the murders. And it was making no secret of its conclusions.

The statement was signed by the pope's spokesman, the sixty-one-year-old Joaquín Navarro-Valls. The press office's Spanish director is a lay worker, but the absence of a weighty religious title is no indication of inferiority. A former newspaperman who wears his pink porphyry ring bearing his family's coat of arms as if it were a cardinal's seal of office, he wields more power than most princes of the Church, and carries himself accordingly. Smooth of appearance and of manner, with the rugged good looks of a Castilian nobleman, he has attracted the interest of several of the women journalists accredited to the Vatican. But he has never married, explaining curtly when asked why: "I haven't got the time."

Navarro-Valls likes to boast that 90 percent of Vatican stories in the world's media are based on information released by him. The journalists who report them, known as the *vaticanisti,* who, unlike me, are permanently based at the press office, retort that he sheds so little light on what really goes on behind the Vatican's walls that they often feel as if they're covering the Kremlin in the iciest days of Soviet rule. Life in the Holy City is cloaked in secrecy—echoed by the way Navarro-Valls orders the seats in his briefing room to be cloaked with dust covers every night.

He can be vindictive. In January 1985, Domenico del Rio, one of the Italian *vaticanisti,* dared to write an article in which he quoted theologians and priests calling the pope a showman because of his passion for foreign trips and television-friendly mass celebrations. Within hours of the article's appearance in the newspaper *La Repubblica,* Navarro-Valls banned Del Rio from the papal plane for all future trips. The *Osservatore Romano,* the official Vatican newspaper, accused Del Rio of "old-fashioned, underhand and sordid anti-clericalism."

Navarro-Valls can also obfuscate. When his superiors reprimanded him for disclosing details of Vatican diplomacy in southern Africa, he denied he was the source, and stuck to his denial even after a radio station, whose reporter had taped his comments, broadcast them.

Some time after we had crowded into the large gray room where Navarro-Valls gives his press conferences, he stepped lightly onto the podium. Perfectly groomed, his wavy hair immaculately parted, despite what must have been for him a very short night, he lost no time in demonstrating that he, speaking with the pope's full authority, knew precisely what had happened in the Estermann apartment.

"There is no mystery," Navarro-Valls announced. "The hypothesis of a fit of madness on Tornay's part is the same as yesterday evening, and today I can say that it is much more than a hypothesis." He expanded on what he called a "moral certainty": Tornay had first fired two shots at Estermann, then another at Meza Romero, and had finally committed suicide by shooting himself in the mouth. As urbane as ever, Navarro-Valls concluded neatly that Estermann's injuries had caused "in practical terms, in physiological terms, instant death."

Tornay's motive? A searing belief that his merits had not been properly recognized in the Guard, prompted by a "courteous and firm, but not harsh" reprimand from Estermann three months earlier after Tornay had spent a night outside the barracks without permission, and also by Estermann's refusal to award him the medal for three years' service. Tornay's character was to blame—"a character that accumulates things, and then explodes without logic."

Navarro-Valls, in many ways a "spin doctor," was particularly qualified to hazard a judgment on Tornay's psychology. Before his newspaper career, he had studied medicine at university and had specialized in psychiatry. He had also published a book entitled *Manipulation in Advertising*.

As he described it, there could be no greater contrast with Estermann, a loyal servant who had gone so far as to shield the pope with his body when a Turkish gunman tried to assassinate him in St. Peter's Square in 1981, and who had been rewarded with membership in the order of the Gentlemen of His Holiness.

Besieged by questions from the journalists, Navarro-Valls insisted that no one could have foreseen Tornay's reaction to Estermann's punishments, and neither the Guard nor its selection procedure could be faulted in any way. "This episode could have happened in any other community of individuals," he said. And that was that. If there were any skeletons in the closet of the Guard, Navarro-Valls would certainly not be the man to expose them. The closet door had been firmly reshut.

When a reporter asked why Estermann's appointment had been delayed for seven months, Navarro-Valls denied that it had been blocked: "The selection process is a long and complicated one, hampered by historical factors. And sometimes when you're looking for the right person, you don't even notice that the perfect candidate is right under your nose." It was a less-than-convincing explanation.

He had one final, tantalizing piece of information for his audience: shortly before his death, Tornay had written a letter to his family and entrusted it to a friend in the barracks. Although the Vatican did have a copy of the letter, Navarro-Valls refused to reveal its contents out of respect, he said, for Tornay's family. It was up to them to decide whether to make it public. What he could say was that the letter supported his diagnosis of "a fit of madness."

Of course, he said, the judicial inquiry that the Vatican had launched must take its course, but he confidently predicted that the investigators would eventually reach the conclusions he had outlined. The case would then be closed.

In the hours that followed, eminent members of the Curia, the Vatican's own court and the oldest in Europe, flocked to give their support to the official version. The Austrian Cardinal Alfons Stickler, eighty-seven years old, described Tornay to one reporter as "an individual suffering from the psychological disorder of paranoia," although Stickler had never met him. Cardinal Carlo Furno, a veteran Italian diplomat, pronounced: "The Devil is everywhere."

The official Vatican newspaper, *L'Osservatore Romano,* and Vatican Radio paid tribute to Estermann as a loyal servant of the pope. They, and Vatican officials, painted a flattering portrait of Estermann: born the oldest of five children to peasants in the Swiss-German village of Beromünster, near Lucerne in the geographical and spiritual heart of Switzerland, he had turned his back on his father's farm to join the Swiss army, and then traveled to Rome. He admired the ideals of medieval chivalry and told friends: "I have two passions—the military and the Church, and the Swiss Guard brings them together."

Estermann made brisk progress to become the pope's chief body-guard, escorting him on more than thirty journeys to meet the faithful around the globe. Estermann's private collection of photographs showed him at the side of world leaders from Ronald Reagan to Fidel Castro. When intelligence services warned of imminent threats to the pope, Estermann was even said to act as a stand-in and don the white papal cassock and skullcap. A rare honor was bestowed on Estermann when he was appointed to research the life of a nineteenth-century Swiss layman, Nicolai Wolf, so that the latter could be declared a saint.

Estermann had met his wife, Meza Romero, shortly after his arrival in Rome, when he was still learning Italian, at the language school they were both attending. Despite fifteen years of marriage, they had no children. Two years before her death Meza Romero had a miscarriage, but although she was in her late forties, she had not given up. "It is in the hands of Providence," she told friends when asked about the couple's chances of having a child.

From the men of the Swiss Guard, over whose barracks the Vatican colors of gold and white flew at half-mast, there was no reaction, no comment on the loss of Estermann or Tornay. According to Navarro-Valls, they had chosen silence in order to show their respect for the dead.

Only one churchman dared to speak out and challenge the word of the absolute monarchy that is the Vatican. Monsignor Alessandro Maggiolini, bishop of Como in northern Italy, appealed to his superiors to suspend judgment. "The clues gathered so far speak little," he told a newspaper. "I'm inclined to be wary of explanations that are too easy, too obvious. Let's not give importance to explanations which are too hasty." Even under the uniforms of the Swiss Guard, there were men of flesh and blood "with their passions and failings." The bishop did not specify whether he was speaking of Tornay, or Estermann, or both.

Such doubts failed to reach the third loggia of the Apostolic Palace. When the pope appeared at the window of his study for the Angelus, his noon greeting to the crowd in St. Peter's Square, on the Wednesday three days after the deaths, he had only a brief comment to make on Tornay: the lance corporal was now before the judgment of God, "to whose mercy I entrust him."

The pope was more loquacious in a telegram he sent to Estermann's parents. In it he spoke of a humanly incomprehensible situation, invoked God, Lord of life and death, and sent his apostolic blessing in the hope of the resurrection of the dead. The pope's verdict was final; since the collapse of the Soviet regimes and its allies, in virtually no other institution around the globe do the words and decisions of the leader reign as supreme as in the Catholic Church.

✦

FIVE HOURS AFTER the Angelus, it fell to the most powerful cardinal in the Vatican, the secretary of state Angelo Sodano, to sanctify the official verdict in God's name. Sodano, a rotund figure with owlish glasses who were it not for his imposing stature would look like a humble country priest, is so powerful a figure that he likes to think of himself as a possible successor to John Paul once the latter's death is verified, as tradition demands, by tapping him on the forehead with a silver hammer. Most odds, however, are on the seventy-year-old Sodano not as a successor, but as one of the "kingmakers" in the next conclave when it meets to elect a new pope.

With John Paul's blessing, Sodano was to conduct a funeral Mass for Estermann—who, were he still alive, would at that moment have been leading the swearing-in ceremony for the new recruits—and his wife, Meza Romero, in St. Peter's, a location that represented a rare honor for lay workers. The Basilica and the entire Vatican would be purified, cleansed of the outburst of violence that had stained its sacrosant territory. On the orders of Sodano, whose office shapes news from the Vatican, and to whom Navarro-Valls reports, journalists were banned from the apse where it was held. But no one stopped me from mixing with a group of tourists and getting close enough to see the ceremony and hear Sodano's homily.

The two coffins lay not far from the high altar of the Basilica. Estermann's sword and white-plumed silver helmet rested on his casket. Twenty-four soldiers in dress uniforms mounted a guard of honor, as rigid as the marble statues of popes and angels surrounding them, their halberds glinting in the sunlight that leaked through Michelangelo's giant dome. Around the base of the dome runs the inscription TU ES PETRUS . . . *Thou art Peter and upon this rock I will build my church. To you I will give the keys of the kingdom of heaven.* Below the coffins, in the crypt of the Basilica, lie the remains of nineteen pontiffs, including, the Church believes, the Prince of the Apostles.

As the bells of the Basilica began to ring out five o'clock, rows of arc lights illuminated the immense nave like frozen lightning, and Sodano led a parade of precedence and privilege—cardinals, bishops, and priests, a sluggish, unending stream of scarlet, purple, and white— toward the coffins. Among them were Dziwisz, the so-called Rasputin of the Apostolic Palace, and Jehle, the Guard's chaplain. Behind the prelates marched another forty-eight guards.

Dressed in bright turquoise robes and a tall miter, Sodano performed the service in Italian: "It is now Easter, a time which marks the victory of Jesus Christ over death," he intoned in a nasal voice as he stood in front of a giant coffin of veined marble adorned with figures three times his size. "And it is death that calls us here today. Faced by the mystery of death, of this sudden and violent death, we can only collect our thoughts in silence. In times like these we feel above all the need to be silent." But the pope, Sodano continued, had only words of praise for the members of the Swiss Guard: "Dear officers of the Holy See, the pope renews his trust and his gratitude. The black cloud of one day cannot obscure more than five hundred years of service."

If Sodano felt any tension, he did not show it. His homily over, he sprinkled the coffins with holy water, and as the pallbearers lifted them to their shoulders, the congregation began to sing the lament "In Paradise the Angels Will Lead You." As they passed by the altar, obeying orders that were scarcely more than a whisper, they paused for a moment as a guard lowered the gold-and-red flag of the corps, a black veil knotted round its tip, so that it lightly touched the caskets.

The prayers for Estermann's soul were still being said in the Basilica when two days later he was abruptly knocked off the pedestal that the Vatican had so carefully erected for him. The apparently shattering blow to his reputation originated in the former East Berlin, which until a decade earlier had been part of the Communist bloc so hated by John Paul.

A local newspaper, the *Berliner Kurier,* reported that he had been an agent for East Germany's secret police, the Ministry of State Security. Known, feared, and hated simply as the Stasi, it had penetrated the daily lives of East Germans to such a degree that it made even the KGB envious.

The newspaper claimed that as both a close associate of the pope and the owner of a Vatican passport that allowed him to pass through border controls unchecked, Estermann had become one of the Stasi's prized agents, operating under the code name "Werder." During his first four years with the Swiss Guard, the paper claimed, Estermann had sent at least seven files to his Stasi minders, depositing them in the Rome–Innsbruck night train.

The world's media seized on the story. No news editor could afford to miss the report that John Paul, a crusader against what President Reagan had branded "the evil empire," had been betrayed by his most trusted bodyguard. It was not until the day after the story had first broken that Navarro-Valls reacted, saying the Vatican "is not even taking it into consideration." A relative of Meza Romero called it "pure folly."

No honors similar to those accorded to the Estermanns accompanied Cédric Tornay on his last journey. His funeral was held not publically with the grandeur of St. Peter's as a stage, but privately in the small St. Anne's Church, which was originally built for the papal grooms and is tucked away on the very border of the city-state.

There was no helmet on Tornay's coffin, only white gladioli, and no black-tipped banner was lowered to touch his casket. His comrades-in-arms formed a row along a wall, leaving an empty space where Tornay had usually stood. His popularity was evident. There was no room for the numerous Roman friends Tornay had made, so many of them waited outside the church in silence, straining to hear what went on inside.

"God will forgive him for what he did because of the fragility of the human condition," Monsignor Amédée Grab, a Swiss bishop, said in his homily. "There is always progress to be made, perhaps even in the organization of the Swiss Guard, but you guardsmen are nonetheless an example of reliance, courage and responsibility." The remark, somewhat cryptic, was the first hint by a senior man of the cloth that there might be a link between the three deaths and unspecified failings in the Guard itself.

The next day, the contents of the letter left by Tornay, which

Navarro-Valls had apparently been at such pains not to disclose, were published in the Italian newspapers. Somehow a key piece of evidence, which should have been covered by the secrecy of a judicial investigation, had been leaked. There were only two possible sources: the Vatican, or Tornay's family, if it had already taken possession of the letter. The original text of Tornay's message, written in French, was littered with grammatical and spelling mistakes. In it, he referred to the so-called *benemerenti* medal, a medal that is routinely awarded to guards after three years' service:

> *Mummy,*
>
> *I hope you will forgive me because what I have done but they were the ones who drove me on. This year I was due to receive the benemerenti and the Lieutenant Colonel refused it to me. After three years six months and six days spent here putting up with all the injustices. The only thing I wanted they have refused it to me. I must do this service for all the guards remaining as well as to the catholic church. I have sworn to give my life for the pope and this is what I am doing. I apologize for leaving you all alone but my duty calls. Tell Sara, Melinda and Daddy that I love you all. Big Kisses to the Greatest Mother in the World.*
>
> *Your son who loves you.*

None of the newspapers ventured an explanation of the phrase "they were the ones who drove me on." The letter showed that Tornay had resented not only Estermann, but others, too. But who were they? What were "all the injustices" Tornay had suffered during his years of service? And why was Tornay so certain that he was giving his life "for the pope"?

His last words were echoed, only a few days later, by none other than Estermann's predecessor as commander of the Guard, Colonel

Roland Buchs. At the funeral service in the Swiss town of Saint-Maurice where Tornay grew up, Buchs sketched a portrait of the lance corporal that did not match the sad, paranoid figure that the Vatican had crafted.

The views of a former senior officer who had known Tornay well struck such a discordant note that Sodano's secretariat, to which Buchs had to show his planned speech, prevented him from delivering it at the funeral in the Vatican. Buchs allowed himself to be silenced only temporarily. He must have decided that the Vatican's influence did not extend across the Alps, and gave the speech in Saint-Maurice instead. I obtained a copy of it some time later.

"Cédric Tornay loved life," Buchs's speech began. "He was full of joy. His comrades appreciated his company. Wherever he was present, joy was there, too . . . Tornay had idealistic views. He wanted to commit himself for a better world. His first step as a young adult was to put himself at the service of the Church, and that way to make his contribution to the common good." It was the first public expression of gratitude for Tornay's decision to leave his homeland and put his life in the pope's hands—all for a wage of a little more than six hundred pounds a month.

There was more heresy to infuriate the Vatican censors: Buchs went so far as to pay tribute to Tornay's professionalism, saying that the lance corporal took his duty to protect the pope seriously, but that in common with many young men of his age, the daily restrictions imposed on him weighed heavily. He dreamed of a "wider freedom."

"He was sensitive to the way other people treated him, and their reactions affected him deeply. The tension was almost heartrending for him." Buchs did not specify the nature of either the reactions or the tensions he was referring to in such an oblique way. Nor did he name any names, but he seemed to be pointing a finger at a figure of authority within the Guard, perhaps Estermann, and hinting that he had in some way treated Tornay unfairly.

There was, however, no mistaking Colonel Buchs's rejection of the Vatican's reconstruction even if he kept it as implicit as he could: "His act remains mysterious. Who can understand his last gesture? At this tragic time, many 'whys' and 'wherefores' remain in suspense. Only God knows the answer to our questions."

In the cemetery off the road leading to the Grand-Saint-Bernard Pass, the questions must have hung in the chill mountain air, unanswered, as lumps of frozen earth were shoveled onto the mahogany of Tornay's coffin.

CHAPTER TWO

AFTER THE THREE VICTIMS were buried, silence engulfed the events surrounding their deaths. The muteness of the Vatican was so deep, the three might as well never have existed. The world's media soon lost interest in the case. But I remained fascinated by it. I had written two books on crime. The first was on the Sicilian Mafia, in which I had focused on how the local mentality had helped to shape the secret society. The other, a biography of Carlos the Jackal, was an attempt to understand how a Communist lawyer's son from Venezuela could turn into the world's most wanted terrorist.

Here in the Swiss Guard deaths, I thought, might be a chance not only to find out how such a crime could take place on holy territory, but also to probe the mind of the alleged killer. Was it all an act of folly, or had the rarefied atmosphere behind the Vatican's gates helped to shape that act in some way? And no less intriguing was the way the case had disappeared from public view.

I had no religious axe to grind: my French father had been brought up as a Catholic, receiving his first Communion at the age of eleven, but he had long stopped going to church. My English mother was given no religious guidance by her parents, but converted to Catholicism to please her fiancé's parents. She was rewarded with a wedding in the cathedral at Rouen in Normandy. It was a conversion only in name: she did not go to church either, and neither I nor my two sisters were baptized, let alone taught the Catholic faith, or any other faith.

The more I studied the way the Vatican had reacted to the deaths, the more I suspected that it was being economical with the truth. First, the Vatican had rushed to judgment only a few hours after the shots had been fired. Second, Navarro-Valls, the director of the Vatican's press office, had bizarrely predicted that the inquiry led by a Vatican investigating magistrate would confirm his verdict of "a fit of madness" on Tornay's part. Why such haste in releasing the "definitive" version? And how could Navarro-Valls be so certain that the inquiry would not stray from it?

Third, the official reconstruction was weak on Tornay's motives, looking no further back than Estermann's promotion and the refusal to award Tornay the medal, then maintaining that these two events had sparked what it described as the young guard's murderous folly—totally ignoring Tornay's mention in his letter of injustices suffered over the space of several years. Was there more to the clashes between Tornay and Estermann, I wondered, than insubordination by Tornay?

And fourth, the Vatican was from the very outset displaying an intriguing anxiety to keep the inquiry under its very tight control. When John Paul II was shot in St. Peter's Square, it was Italian police who arrested the Turkish gunman Mehmet Ali Agca and Italian public prosecutors who ensured his conviction. But from the moment the three bodies were discovered in the barracks of the Swiss Guard, the Vatican had refused all offers of help from Italian investigators.

When police patrol cars rushed to St. Anne's Gate as soon as the deaths became known that rainy night, they were barred entry. Three people had died violent deaths on Vatican soil, the pope's chief bodyguard had been shot, but no outsider was to be given a chance to probe behind the veil of prayers and incense. The Italian police were reduced to knocking on the doors of retired officers of the Guard in an attempt to find out at least who was leading the Vatican investigation.

The next day, the autopsies took place in complete secrecy, safely behind the Vatican's thick walls. Although the Vatican has its own health service and boasts a pharmacy that is so well stocked many Romans take their prescriptions there, it can hardly lay claim to an encyclopedic knowledge of forensic medicine. But Renato Buzzonetti, the pope's personal physician and the head of the Vatican health service, who was one of the first called to Estermann's apartment, helped to hide the bodies from prying eyes. The autopsies were carried out in the Vatican morgue by two forensic experts who were both long-standing consultants of the Vatican. Like others who took part in the Vatican's inquiry, they were made to swear never to speak of their work, and not to keep any copies of the reports they produced.

Officially, the Vatican's refusal to cooperate with outsiders—it even turned down a formal offer of help from Italy's interior ministry—was justified by the principle of territorial sovereignty. The city-state alone, it was explained, would deal with the aftermath of the crime, to safeguard the independence that had been granted to it in the Lateran Treaties of 1929, under which Mussolini recognized the pope as sovereign of the Vatican state. But the magistrates and judges who sit on its tribunals had no experience in investigating a murder. Their most demanding cases involved the death of an elderly cardinal, the suicide of a poor soul who had jumped into the void from the dome of St. Peter's, or the fall of a worker from scaffolding.

Responsibility for the inquiry was handed to a middle-aged Roman bureaucrat, Gianluigi Marrone, who almost fainted when he saw the damage to Tornay's head on the floor of the Estermann apartment. Marrone's main job is to head the personnel department at the Italian parliament. A few years earlier Marrone, who, although a qualified lawyer, has never practiced, published an essay on the intricacies of canon law that was noted with approval in the Vatican.

Since then, two or three days a month, the middle-aged Marrone awards himself a break from worrying about the amount of office space and perks allocated to ever-more-demanding members of parliament, in order to double up as a Vatican judge. A Catholic, he considers the appointment an honor, and readily agreed to swear, as required by his new office, "to be faithful and obedient to the Supreme Pontiff." It is not a taxing sideline. Judge Marrone has overseen and written up the sentences at the conclusion of no more than three trials in the last five years. The most serious involved theft.

Why such secrecy, and such insistence on conducting the inquiry without any outside help? Was this a cover-up? Was there something the Vatican was reluctant to confess?

It would not be the first time that the Vatican had published misleading information in the hours following a death on its soil. When John Paul I, whose first words to the cardinals after his election in 1978 were "God will forgive you for what you have done to me," died only thirty-three days later, the official version said that the pope's body was discovered by his secretary, the Irish priest John Magee. The death certificate was signed by Dr. Buzzonetti, who was already physician to the pope at the time. He attributed the death simply to "myocardial arrest," a form of heart failure.

In fact, as the Vatican confessed later, it was a nun, Sister Vincenza, who had discovered the body when, as every morning, she had entered the bedroom to bring the pope coffee. The secretary of state at that time, Cardinal Jean Villot, had lied because it was feared that Catholics would be shocked to learn that a woman was the first person to see their pope in the morning. The Vatican had also lied in reporting that the pope had the *Imitation of Christ,* a devotional work, in his hands when he died—a crude attempt to create an aura of sanctity around his passing. The lies spawned rumors that the pope had been murdered, but the most plausible explanation, as John Cornwell concluded in *A Thief in the Night,* was that the weight of his task combined with his suffering from abnormal coagulability of the blood, which no one attended to, conspired to kill him.

✦

OVER THE WEEKS that followed, I tried to reach Cédric Tornay's mother, Muguette Baudat. I knew very little about her. The only picture I had of her was in a Roman newspaper, and had been taken after the Vatican funeral service for her son by a paparazzo whose stock-in-trade was following film stars on a scooter. In the photograph, she held herself ramrod straight, her black hair tied in a bun, the skin on her face pale and taut. She wore a white sweater that contrasted with the dark clothes of the other mourners. When the bishop leading the service called on the mourners to exchange a sign of peace, Baudat turned and shook hands with Estermann's parents, who were sitting in the pew behind her. Her act of humility impressed many.

As far as I knew, this was her second visit to the Vatican. The first time was for her son's swearing-in ceremony in May 1995, when he was only twenty years old. A Protestant, she shook hands and exchanged a few shy words with John Paul, who blessed her in a hall of the Apostolic Palace when he received the parents of that year's crop of new recruits. The privilege of a papal audience was one that Baudat was unlikely ever to enjoy again.

I was anxious to speak to her because it was said in Rome that she had been shabbily treated by the Vatican after the loss of her son, that she was by no means convinced by the official version of events, and that she had hired lawyers and wanted to launch an investigation of her own into his death. I tried to check this. I left her messages on her answering machine at her home in a village at the foot of the Swiss Alps—the machine, which played a message from one of her two daughters, was on all the time. She did not call me back.

In June 1998, I wrote her a letter, which I tried to keep as brief and as neutral as possible. I told her I had seen her quoted in an Italian newspaper as saying that she wanted to contact journalists based in Rome to help her find out about her son's death. I told her that I thought any attempt to clarify what had happened to her son would require a lengthy investigation. I did not mention my doubts about the Vatican's efforts.

Still no reply. Sometime later I sent her another letter, this time with copies of the two books I had written. Again she did not reply. The weeks became months, but I heard nothing from her. To all appearances, since her brief public appearance at her son's funeral, Baudat had shut herself off from the rest of the world. I thought of traveling to Switzerland, finding her house, and knocking at her door, but I was reluctant to harass a mother who would be mourning the loss of her son.

In the absence of any communication from her, I decided to wait for the end of the Vatican's inquiry. I now realize this was a mistake and that my inaction amounted, in effect, to accepting as gospel truth the Vatican line that there was nothing more to the deaths at the Swiss Guard than it had claimed.

❖

ON FEBRUARY 8, 1999, ten months after the killings, press director Navarro-Valls's confidence that the inquiry would confirm his verdict became a self-fulfilling prophecy. The Vatican investigation ended just the way the pope's spokesman had predicted it would end, within hours of the killings: the conclusions reached were in line with his version of events.

Shortly after the Vatican's announcement that the case had been closed, I went to the press office to find out how much it had to say. The answer was very little. I was handed a statement released as part of the daily bulletin of papal activities and pronouncements, and described as "some extracts from the concluding pages" of the investigating magistrate's final report. When I asked for a copy of the complete final report, I was told that it would not be made available.

I sat down by the cell-like, narrow glass cubicles that Navarro-Valls had imposed on the *vaticanisti* journalists—an arrangement that they often complained killed the stimulating atmosphere of collegial discussion they were used to—and scanned the statement. I was immediately struck not by what was in the statement, but by what wasn't. The statement was full of nameless references to "Mr. . . . ," "Sergeant . . . ," "Sister . . . ," "Dr. . . ." The only names that were explicit were those of Estermann, his wife, Meza Romero, and Tornay.

This was, by any standard, an extraordinary document. All the names of the witnesses, none of whom had seen the killings take place, were omitted, an unusual precaution for an investigation that had formally been closed. Either the Vatican was eager to safeguard the privacy of these witnesses, whose accounts were frustratingly brief, or it wanted to make any independent verification of their testimony as difficult as possible.

Relying heavily on the findings of forensic experts, the statement did, however, review the events that occurred on the night of the deaths in much more detail than Navarro-Valls had done, starting with a telephone call that a friend—also unidentified—had made to the Estermanns' flat.

According to the statement, the friend was able to give the precise time of his call, since he glanced at his watch before dialing the number. It was 8:46 P.M. He wanted to offer his congratulations to Estermann. His wife, Meza Romero, answered the telephone, and the two chatted for a few minutes. She told him that Estermann was suffering from a bad cold, so the friend gave her the name of some pills she could get at the Vatican pharmacy.

Estermann then came on the line, and either immediately or at some later point in the conversation must have sat down in an armchair close to the telephone. The friend asked him about the annual swearing-in ceremony that was to take place in two days' time, because he wanted to bring along his wife and daughter, who was the Estermanns' godchild. Where would he be able to park within the Vatican? he asked. They started worrying about what the weather would be like that day.

It is then that the friend heard an interruption, an odd sound, as if Estermann had placed the mouthpiece against his chest or, as he was to say later, against "something soft." Puzzled, the friend was able to make out voices that sounded as if they came from some distance away. He recognized only one, that of Meza Romero. Then another buzzing or humming sound, followed by what he could only make out as two "sharp blows." More blows followed, but as far as he could tell, they sounded far away.

It did not occur to the friend that the noise could be gunfire. He thought some important guest had called on Estermann, and that the handset had been dropped to the ground by accident. So he simply hung up, thinking he would continue the conversation later.

According to the report, someone had indeed appeared at the Estermanns' front door—Cédric Tornay. As her husband was on the telephone, it was Meza Romero who opened the door. The lance corporal had changed his clothes after completing his afternoon tour of duty at the synod of bishops. He was dressed casually and wore a black leather jacket.

The corridor leading to the sitting room was so small that in no more than three steps Tornay was able to reach Estermann. His new commander was still on the telephone, holding in his right hand the remote control for the television set that he had apparently switched off moments earlier.

From where he was standing, slightly to Estermann's left, Tornay aimed his service weapon, a Swiss-made 9mm SIG pistol. He fired twice, hardly moving as he did so. Both bullets struck home. One penetrated Estermann's left cheek and hit his spinal cord. The other struck his left shoulder and also cut through the spinal cord. Estermann lost consciousness, his forehead striking the floor. The handset of the telephone dangled a few inches from the floor.

As Tornay turned to leave, he found his way blocked by Meza Romero. He fired again, but missed, and the bullet sped out through the open door of the flat and buried itself in the metal post of the elevator door outside. Tornay's fourth shot hit her in the left shoulder and reached the spinal cord. Meza Romero, paralyzed, slipped to the floor, her back sliding against the wall as her legs gave way.

Tornay had one last shot to fire. Turning his back to the window and to the Apostolic Palace beyond it, where at that moment the pope was praying in his chapel, he knelt down. Head bowed, he placed the barrel of his gun in his mouth. The speed of the bullet as it exited the barrel was supersonic, its force of impact equivalent to several tons of pressure per square inch. The barrel jumped as he fired, the light alloy chipping his two front teeth. The sound of the explosion, as loud as if he had been standing twenty yards away from a jet engine, shattered his eardrums. The bullet went through his skull, bounced off the ceiling, knocking plaster to the floor, and landed on Estermann's desk. The gun was later found under Tornay's body.

Only the final part of the statement attempted to explain the reasons for Tornay's actions. It ascribed them to the effects of a cyst, "the size of a pigeon's egg," which the autopsy had discovered in his brain. Located in what the experts labeled the "organ of civilization," in the left frontal lobe, it was the cause of Tornay's behavioral anomalies, which included, the report said, a series of arguments that he had had with Estermann and his failure to salute Estermann on one occasion. It also accounted for Tornay twice spending the night outside the Vatican without permission.

In addition to the cyst, the autopsy found traces of a derivative of cannabis in Tornay's urine, and the investigating magistrate speculated that if Tornay had been a chronic user—which, the magistrate admitted, was only a hypothesis—then he would have been subject to delusions and paranoia. The report quoted the letter that Tornay left for his mother as evidence that he was indeed suffering from both.

On top of all this, according to the autopsy, Tornay had bronchitis at the time, which left him in a particularly vulnerable condition. Thus it had taken just two items of bad news to exasperate Tornay to the point of committing a double murder followed by suicide: Estermann's promotion and the refusal to award him the medal that he coveted.

Case closed? Navarro-Valls had no doubts at all, and he explained that the Vatican had endorsed the conclusions of the investigating magistrate in their entirety. "When an investigation is carried out with such thoroughness, the results are to be accepted. And *basta* [enough]," he told a television interviewer. There was more than a touch of pique in the remark, a reaffirmation of the age-old principle of papal primacy—*Roma locuta, causa finita est* (Rome has spoken, the case is closed).

In fact the way the Vatican closed the case was a shocking travesty of justice. It amounted to a presiding judge accepting the findings of a public prosecutor without anyone—let alone lawyers for the accused (in this case, Tornay)—being granted a chance to challenge them.

The parallel between the Vatican's condemnation of the dead Tornay and the treatment meted out to dissident theologians who dare to contradict the pope's teachings is striking. A body that is now called the Sacred Congregation for the Doctrine of the Faith, but that is more notorious as the barbaric Holy Inquisition that condemned Galileo, even today gives dissident Catholics scant freedom to defend themselves. They are refused permission to see the files of the case against them, they are denied the right to the services of an advocate at their hearing, and they cannot appeal to an independent body.

And just as secrecy has always governed these proceedings, the files of what the Vatican must have prayed were the swan song to the case of the Swiss Guard were hidden away, as inaccessible as if they had been cloistered in the secret archives. They have taken their place alongside the thousands of other papers that this pope and his predecessors, who are accountable only to God and act for reasons known only to themselves, have decided to lock away forever.

CHAPTER THREE

"*BONJOUR,* DO YOU KNOW WHO THIS IS?" The voice of the woman who had telephoned me at my office was completely unfamiliar. I noticed that it sounded gritty, like the voice of a heavy smoker, and that the marked singsong accent was typical of French-speaking Switzerland.

"Who's speaking?" I asked.

"You wrote to me. This is Muguette Baudat." Cédric Tornay's mother. The woman I had first tried to contact eight months earlier paused as if this was all she wanted to say to me. I glanced at the date— it was a Friday, five days after the Vatican had closed the investigation into the deaths at the Swiss Guard. I was too taken aback to realize that the line was very clear, surprisingly clear for a long-distance call.

"I'm in Rome for a visit. I'm not staying long," she continued. "Could we meet tomorrow, if that's not too inconvenient for you?"

Saturday morning is rush-hour time around St. Peter's. Coaches with Eastern European license plates and cargoes of pilgrims to unload block the traffic, to the fury of the Eternal City's drivers, who sound their horns and make rude but expressive gestures while a handful of elegant policewomen try vainly to restore order. As if this were the road to the Tower of Babel, souvenir sellers brandish their rosaries, crucifixes, and statues of the Virgin, shouting greetings in a medley of languages to Polish nuns, African missionaries, and Peruvian pilgrims in traditional dress.

Oblivious to the chaos it left in its wake, that day the sea of pilgrims flowed toward the Paul VI Audience Hall, a vast auditorium and an eyesore built like a 1970s railway station where the pope would soon hold his general audience. Above the throng, banners and flags in the Vatican colors of white and gold swayed in the strong wind, just as they had done for centuries.

Battling the tide of chattering worshipers, I made my way to the St. Peter railway station, which is just south of the Vatican walls. From there, I could see the dome Michelangelo designed for the Basilica, sprouting incongruously between two modern apartment buildings on whose terraces clothes had been strung up to dry. The petticoats and sheets did nothing to diminish the dome's majesty.

I was stealing a glance at the photograph of Baudat taken at her son's funeral when I heard a voice speak in heavily accented French behind me. "*Bonjour,* it's easy to spot someone waiting for you in Rome. Everyone else is rushing around." Baudat introduced herself with a short handshake. She had brought along her oldest daughter, Mélinda, who was in her mid-twenties.

Dressed in a gray knee-length skirt and an orange wool jumper, she looked much older than the solemn woman in the photograph. The months since her bereavement had etched deep lines across her fore-head and stamped dark smudges under her eyes, but her manner was determined and she strode along as we made our way to a nearby café to have some breakfast.

As I went to the counter to order croissants and cappuccinos, join-ing the line of Romans fortifying themselves with a quick coffee before work, she and Mélinda settled in a back room, as far from any-one else as possible. When I returned, Baudat was adjusting her lipstick in a wall mirror. She snapped the lipstick tube shut, leaned back in her chair, and folded her arms. Then she gave me a long appraising stare. "I won't talk; I just want us to get to know each other," she said.

It was hardly a promising beginning, and for a while I had to do the talking. But eventually she began to relax, taking short sharp puffs from a thin white cigarette, a Vogue menthol. She told me that she had raised her son and two daughters in the Catholic faith of their father. She didn't have much choice; it was a promise she had been forced to make when she got married in the Valais, the strongly Catholic Swiss canton where they lived, and the region with the country's highest mountains. She was surprised, she said, when her son told her that he had decided to join the Swiss Guard, and worried that the Vatican would turn him into a priest.

Without any prompting from me, she began to talk about the eve-ning she had learned of his death. "My other daughter, Sara—she's seventeen—was alone at home. A guard telephoned from the barracks at nine-twenty P.M. He said he had to speak to me. I was at a friend's house for a dinner party. He said he would call back, but he never did. Then an hour later the parish priest arrived, also looking for me. He didn't want to tell Sara anything, but she's a tough nut: she forced him to say what was up."

Baudat's gaze turned to Mélinda, who remained silent, staring down at her cappuccino. "Sara didn't call me right away," Baudat continued. "She phoned Mélinda, who came around right away. When they got through to me to say something serious had happened, I thought Sara had been raped or something. Then I thought something had happened to Mélinda. I thought of everything except Tornay. I drove back as fast as I could, and the priest said to me: 'He died of a gunshot wound, he committed suicide.' I burst out laughing. I said it's not funny; think of something else. The priest said: 'It's worse than that. He killed two people.'"

Mélinda looked up and spoke for the first time, apparently making an effort to sound as matter-of-fact as possible: "We sat up all night after that. We didn't eat or drink anything. We watched the TV news every hour. They gave out my brother's name before we got a chance to start calling our relatives and friends. But it wasn't clear what had happened."

"It still isn't," Baudat said. She finished her coffee and briskly suggested we go for a walk. The streets leading to St. Peter's had emptied, save for long lines of parked coaches, as the papal audience was under way. As we passed the gate near the Sacred Congregation for the Doctrine of the Faith, the former Holy Inquisition, we had to walk past two fresh-faced Swiss guards standing immobile on sentry duty, resplendent in their striped uniforms. Both Baudat and her daughter looked away as we passed them.

The gate also led to the auditorium, which would now be packed with pilgrims. It was there that Tornay had worked his last shift. Mélinda then hung back as we passed under the colonnade that surrounds St. Peter's Square in a broad embrace. She stood still, dwarfed by the columns. Tears ran down her cheeks.

I stopped to wait for her, but Baudat tugged at my sleeve. "It's best to leave her alone. She didn't come to Rome with me to fetch Tornay; this is her first time here since he died. She hasn't come to terms with it yet. It's still torture for her to even walk into a church."

Baudat herself remained dry-eyed. She guessed what I was thinking. "I haven't cried since Tornay's death. I'm still holding it all in."

I asked her why she called her son Tornay, and not by his first name. "It's my way of coping. I prefer to talk of Tornay, not of my son, Cédric. Otherwise I take it too much to heart. My friends tell me that I haven't yet realized that my son is dead."

I was uncertain why she had agreed to see me. The answer came as we crossed the square. Apart from us and a trio of nuns who were rushing because they were late for the pope's audience, St. Peter's Square was deserted, which made it seem more immense than usual. Buildings occupy only a third of the Holy City's territory, which spreads over only 108 acres; the rest is taken up by the Vatican gardens and a mosaic of squares and courtyards, of which St. Peter's Square is by far the biggest.

The grandeur of the square was of no interest to Baudat, whose eyes were fixed on the cobblestones. She motioned to me to stop walking. She stared at me, wanting my full attention. I realized there was no one to overhear us.

"I think you should try to investigate what happened to my son," she said. "Independently of the Vatican. There's not much I can do from Switzerland. I'm on my own. I've tried to talk to my son's friends in the Guard. But they won't talk, they've been ordered not to. The Vatican is so secretive. I thought you might stand a chance."

She must have sensed my hesitation because she added quickly: "Don't worry, you won't be working for me. I've hired lawyers, who represent me. I haven't lost faith in Vatican justice, or in the pope. And I'm not trying to wash Tornay clean. I don't believe that the Vatican has proved that he's guilty. And if he did do it, I want to know why. Now is the time to start, now that the Vatican has closed its inquiry, and has said everything it's ever going to say."

"Have you got any reason to doubt the Vatican's explanation for what happened?" I asked.

"Plenty of reasons," she shot back. "There's the way I was treated when I came to fetch my son's body. They didn't even want me to come. There's the fact that the Vatican refused to work with the Italian police and kept everything under wraps. And for months now I've been waiting to see the complete files of the Vatican's investigation. Why have all my requests been ignored? The Italian courts have no jurisdiction over the Vatican, so what do I have to do, go to the European Court of Human Rights to demand to see the files?"

"Maybe the Vatican is just being as secretive as it has always been."

"It's more than that. I think that they're hiding something. Either about the night my son died or about the events that led up to his death. Take a look at what has come out since. He's been more vilified than the dictators who carry out genocides. They make my son sound like a drug dealer. My son wouldn't have killed someone just because of a medal. And if he was as bad as the Vatican says he was, why was he ever recruited in the first place? Why was he promoted to the rank of lance corporal?

"And then there's that letter he sent me," she continued. "Several things about it are odd. There's the paper he uses; it's not the usual kind. He writes that he's been in the Guard three years six months and six days, but that's wrong. There's one month too many. He was usually very precise. And the name on the envelope—it's addressed to me as 'Madame Muguette Chamorel.' That's the name of my second husband. But in all the letters he'd sent me from Rome, he always used my maiden name, Muguette Baudat. And he put my phone number on the envelope, which he'd never done before. Why? Perhaps he wasn't alone when he wrote the letter."

Baudat had more questions for me than answers, but her suggestion was tantalizing. Across the square the Basilica, monumental tomb of popes and backdrop to myriad pageants, stood cloaked in scaffolding in preparation for the Holy Year that would coincide with the millennium. It struck me that the square was shaped like a giant keyhole with the Basilica as the lower part. I wondered how difficult it would be to unlock the City of God.

To penetrate not only the closed world of the oldest institution in the West—the Roman Catholic Church—but also another, just-as-secretive institution at its very heart—the Swiss Guard, a military unit to boot—would be extremely difficult. Let alone the effort to reconstruct the events that had led to a crime committed in its barracks. As Baudat set off again with her decisive stride toward the northern edge of the square, her daughter still following at a distance, I asked her how much resistance she had encountered in trying to find out the facts behind the death of her son.

"I sent a letter to people who might be able to help, asking for some information about his time in Rome. I wrote that the truth had probably been hidden, and that no one wanted to admit it. But nobody would talk to me."

"Did you ever hear anything from the Swiss Guard?"

"Just once, immediately after Tornay's death. They tried to stop me coming to Rome. Monsignor Alois Jehle, the chaplain of the Guard, told me it was hot in Rome and the body was in a state of putrefaction. I asked him: 'Don't you have cold storage in your morgue?' I said that I had seen Tornay naked enough times before; I had given birth to him. Then I was told that Tornay's head had been ripped off. I said that even if there was only my boy's left big toe, I would go to Rome to fetch it. So they tried telling me that all the hotels were full. All they wanted was for me to stay where I was and wait for the little chalet without windows—that's what we call coffins back home in Switzerland. But I flew to Rome all the same."

"Did you get to see the body in Rome?"

"Yes. They'd put him in Saint Martin's, the Guard's chapel just behind the barracks, right under the pope's windows. Tornay was lying in an open coffin. They'd dressed him in his gala uniform. He looked completely relaxed; he was smiling with his eyes closed. He was so handsome, just like when he slept in his bed at home. I remember stroking his uniform. Only his two front teeth had been chipped; a prelate said my son's teeth were fragile. Can you imagine? He'd been shot in the mouth, the gun barrel knocked into his teeth, and this prelate says they're fragile! When I took him in my arms, there was a hole in the back of his head so big that I could have put my fist in it. For me, it was impossible that someone could have done something so awful and look so blissful, so at peace."

She threaded her way through the colonnade that surrounds the square. I realized we were heading for the Guard's barracks.

"And then suddenly there was this strange scene," she continued. "A thin young man who was sitting on a bench started crying and shouting. Nobody went up to him, so I felt obliged to go to him and console him. He told me his name was Yvon Bertorello, that he was a priest, and that it was all his fault. That he should have been there to stop Tornay from doing what he did. He even said that my son had been murdered."

"You believed what he told you?"

"I don't know what to think—perhaps there was another man present, perhaps he murdered all three of them. A military officer like Tornay doesn't shoot himself in the mouth; he would shoot himself in the temple, that's the key point. Bertorello told me he had the proof in his briefcase that my son had been murdered. I asked him why he was carrying it around with him. I told him someone could come up and shoot him. But he wouldn't tell me any more than that, not even when we had dinner together later.

"The Vatican people told me he was Tornay's spiritual father," she continued, "and no other churchman looked as saddened as Bertorello. The funeral service was the next morning, and after it I was told to stay in my hotel and wait for a call because the pope might find time to see me."

"And did he?"

"I never got a call. Then I had to catch the plane back to Switzerland that evening because Tornay's body was on its way home. So I've only ever met the pope once, with Tornay when he first joined the Guard. Tornay had told me to hold the pope's hand tightly so that he would not go away but stay and talk with us. I'd brought a couple of rings for him to bless. He patted me on the shoulder and he said: 'You have a wonderful family.' But he didn't know Tornay from Adam, or my daughters, for that matter. I suppose he was just making small talk."

"Did you find out anything more about this Bertorello?"

"Only that he had both French and Italian nationality, and that he had studied at Econe, a seminary for Catholic fundamentalists in Lausanne. Then he got to the Vatican, and they sent him on all sorts of sensitive missions in Bosnia, Turkey, all over the place. I think he's some kind of spy for the Vatican. I've done all I could to find him, but the magistrates who led the inquiry into Tornay's death said they had no idea who he was."

His Holiness's secret service. During the cold war, there were plenty of known cases of foreign spies trying to infiltrate the Vatican, especially when a pope like John Paul, from Poland, from behind the Iron Curtain, struck fear into the Communist regimes of Eastern Europe with his appeals for freedom and democracy. But what need would there be for the existence of a Vatican intelligence service today? I wondered. Rumors about Vatican spies often made the rounds in Rome diplomatic circles, without ever being substantiated.

We stopped outside the barracks, staring in silence at the maroon facade, the grimness of its thickly barred windows only partly alleviated by the flags of the Swiss cantons tacked up by a few of its residents. It was in this building that Tornay lived when he first arrived in Rome. I asked Baudat when she had last spoken to her son.

"At lunchtime on the day he died. He'd been on duty from seven to eleven o'clock that morning at the Audience Hall, and he was due to work again from three to seven in the evening. He'd booked a ticket for me to attend the swearing-in ceremony; he was hoping that I would come and see him get the medal. But I wasn't sure I could get away. I called him on his mobile phone; we spoke for half an hour. We hadn't spoken for some time. Then he told me he had to hurry to get lunch in the canteen. He asked me how the girls were; we spoke about his shifts."

"Anything about Estermann, the new commander?" I asked.

"Yes. He asked me whether I'd heard what he called 'the bad news': Estermann's promotion. I told him it wasn't a huge surprise. He replied: 'Yes, but we were still hoping it wouldn't be him.' I told him I'd definitely come to see him the following month, in June. Then that night we were told that he was dead."

She paused and turned to look straight at me. "It was only a few days afterward that I remembered that Tornay had told me he had been investigating Opus Dei, which Estermann was close to."

I knew that Opus Dei was the strongest, most mysterious, and most controversial movement within the Catholic Church. *Opus Dei* translates as "God's work," but the movement's critics, of which there are many both inside and outside the Vatican, prefer to call it by less flattering names—the Holy Mafia, God's Octopus, or God's Fifth Column. Unified by an ultraconservative agenda, it kept the identities of its members secret and demanded that they practice self-flagellation. Although often denounced as a sect, it had flourished during John Paul's papacy, infiltrating the heart of the Curia to the dismay of more liberal-minded prelates.

Perhaps Estermann's ties to Opus Dei could explain why his bid for promotion to the rank of commander had been mysteriously blocked for seven months. It was rumored that his severity made him unpopular with the men. But he was so determined to succeed that he had already had his portrait painted, ready to hang in the barracks alongside that of previous commanders.

As we walked on around the Vatican walls—it was as if Baudat, who, like any other outsider, was unable to enter the city-state without permission, could not tear herself away from them—I asked her what Tornay had said about Opus Dei.

"In the autumn of the year before he died, he told me that he was looking into the affairs of the movement. He said he was investigating it with two other guards. I had no idea what it was at the time. He told me it was secretive and dangerous. I'd always taught my children that anything hidden was bad, so I can understand how Opus Dei would have worried him. When I asked him about it some time later, he said the less I knew about what he was up to the better. But later I found out from some friends of Tornay that Estermann was close to Opus Dei and had tried to recruit guards into it."

"Did these friends tell you what Tornay had found out?"

She shook her head. "The guards have all been sworn to secrecy by Monsignor Jehle. You have no idea how uncooperative the Vatican has been."

"So after all your efforts, have you got an explanation for his death that is different from the Vatican version?"

She pulled a long face. "I have no explanation. That's the problem. All I know is that from the start I was the victim of pressures, manipulation, dissimulation, and lies. And I still haven't been shown the files of the Vatican inquiry. I'll tell you something else: when I was driven through Saint Anne's Gate to the chapel where my son was lying, it struck me that the Vatican smelled of death. I was scared, very scared. I'd never thought that of the Vatican before."

She signaled to her daughter that it was time for them to go, then turned back to me to say good-bye: "I hope you decide to go ahead. If you do, good luck." I watched the pair disappear amid the crowd of Saturday shoppers, heads bowed so close together they were almost touching.

My mind was already made up.

CHAPTER FOUR

AT NO TIME had the Vatican given any importance to, let alone mentioned, the facts Baudat had told me about—including Estermann's close association with Opus Dei and Tornay's investigation of the movement. Neither was there any mention of the mysterious Father Yvon Bertorello and his claim that Tornay was murdered.

I tried to find him. When asked, Navarro-Valls stated that he knew nothing about Bertorello and denied that he had any relations with the Vatican. I consulted the red-bound *Annuario Pontificio,* the yearly directory that is the "bible" for anyone seeking to make sense of the Church's Byzantine bureaucracy of congregations, commissions, secretariats, tribunals, and nunciatures, or embassies not only in the Vatican but throughout the world. Bertorello was not in it. No one I contacted in the Vatican village knew anything about him.

Stalled—but only temporarily, I hoped—I decided to try a different track. Any attempt to shed more light on the deaths should begin where they took place—in the barracks of the *Cohors Pedestris Helvetiorum*, as the Swiss Guard was officially known. Easier said than done, I soon realized. A couple of colleagues whom I consulted, old Vatican hands who could remember the days when John Paul was still only a cardinal, told me my timing could not have been worse. Since the deaths, no journalists had been allowed to visit the barracks or observe the Swiss Guard at work from behind the scenes. Morale was still poor, and snooping outsiders were less welcome than ever.

Even more discouraging was the fact that all the guards, down to the latest recruit, had been sworn to silence about the murders. Any who disobeyed would be severely punished. So much for Navarro-Valls's assurance that the guards had chosen silence of their own free will to show their respect for the dead. It was obvious that in such a climate, any open request to investigate the events of May 1998 would be rebuffed.

As I hunted for some inspiration, I came across a reference to an outsider who had managed not only to penetrate the Guard's defenses, but also to document his feat. In the mid-1980s, Hugues de Wurstemberger, a young Swiss photographer, had signed on for three four-month terms as an auxiliary. He took as many pictures as he could of daily life in the barracks, telling any inquisitive officers that they were for his personal album. But he also took off-parade photographs with a miniature camera hidden in a pack of cigarettes.

When the result was displayed in the guards' Swiss homeland, in the city of Lausanne on Lake Geneva, most of the pictures were hardly provocative—guards laughing as they wrestled with one another to let off steam, friends gathered around a typically Swiss cheese fondue. But the Vatican became irate over a photograph of some guards sunbathing, crucifixes nestling on their hairy chests, on a terrace by some battlements above the barracks. It also objected to a picture of a guard lying naked on his bed, facedown, under the teasing gaze of *Playboy* magazine's Miss August.

The commander, Colonel Buchs, wrote a letter of protest to a Swiss Catholic newspaper, and pressure from the Church prevented De Wurstemberger from publishing his work in a book. Not since the last days of Pius XII in 1958, when his physician, Dr. Galeazzi Lisi, had surreptitiously taken pictures of the pope's deathbed agonies and tried to sell them to the newspapers, earning himself the nickname "the Leica Crow," had photographs caused so much outrage in the Vatican. De Wurstemberger was worth seeking out. I flew to Brussels, where he now works as an independent photographer. We met for lunch at an Italian restaurant near his home.

Plump and tousle-haired—hardly traits that would have passed muster with the Swiss Guard—he was still chuckling at his exploit more than a decade later. "Do you know the commander ordered an inspection of all the living quarters and censored the posters the boys had stuck on the walls? He even drew up new rules to cut down the quantity of beer and wine bottles each guard could keep in his room. The alcohol was real cheap, there was a big discount at the Vatican supermarket, so we'd buy whole crates of the stuff.

"The Guard was an amazing place," he continued. "Practically the only weapons available were machine guns, made mostly of wood, which dated from before the Second World War. We'd practice with them in a cellar under the barracks only once a year; that's how seriously they took our training. The cellars had these windows that looked out on the street above us, so we had to cover them with sacks because otherwise we'd scare the living daylights out of the tourists outside. Once, we had to test some gas masks in a tower next to the

Apostolic Palace. We used a smoke device for the test, and the rubber straps were so rotten that we all got intoxicated from the fumes."

"Doesn't sound like a very professional outfit," I said.

De Wurstemberger nodded. "Not in my time. Morale was bad. There was even a big rebellion by the men during the May 1968 student riots; they wanted to go to the press, but the officers managed to stifle it by hiking up their pensions. There's been a recruitment crisis ever since the 1970s. The Guard was down to forty men, less than half its normal strength. They had to close down a security post, and they even thought about signing up seminarians. Not that suprising, really. Some of the guards were real religious types who said their rosary on the night shift.

"Basically the Guard was divided between the 'saints' and the 'killers.' The killers come to Rome thinking they're going to be Rambos, with dark glasses and earpieces like the G-men at the White House. They're xenophobic; they moan about Rome being dirty and how it would be much cleaner if the Swiss lived there. They're a minority; I'd say ten percent. Then there's the bigger group, the saints; they go to Mass every morning at seven, they buy the pope's writings and study them in their spare time. No girlfriends, of course. But lots of chaps who did go to Rome were just out to have some fun.

"We were allowed to show friends around the Vatican gardens, which was quite a useful privilege since it allowed us to pick up girls, but then one day a cardinal found a guard busy with his fiancée behind a pink oleander. The cardinal was so enraged he decreed that only groups of more than three guards could be allowed into the gardens. One day a prostitute came to the barracks asking to be paid for the time she'd spent with a guard. She got kicked out, and so did the guard."

"What do you remember about Estermann?" I asked.

"He hadn't been there long; he'd joined as a captain in 1980, but already you could tell that he was going places, or at least that's what he'd decided. He was the youngest officer, always impeccable, closely shaven, and smooth all over. He was a practicing Catholic and he made no bones about it; for him it was an honor to be a Catholic soldier. He was very, very strict—the smallest mistake, and *bang,* he'd stick a report on you and you'd have to spend a day scrubbing the rust off the breastplates."

He paused. "There is one thing I find fishy, though, about these deaths. This Tornay, he was promoted to the rank of lance corporal, right? Well, he can't have been as bad as the Vatican made out after his death. I mean, the commanding officers must have seen him as promising material, because the job of lance corporal isn't child's play: you can be in charge of all the guards deployed in the Apostolic Palace, or responsible for Saint Anne's Gate, which is the key entry point into Vatican territory."

"Any ideas on how I could get in to see the Guard from close up?"

"Here's my advice to you. First, seek official permission. Don't mention the shootings. See if that gets you anywhere. Then do your own thing. Good luck."

✦

BACK IN ROME, I puzzled over de Wurstemberger's description of the Swiss Guard as he knew it in the first decade of John Paul's papacy. The corps prided itself on its historic duty of protecting the pope, and yet he had derided it as ill equipped.

To find out what the Swiss Guard was up against, I looked into the history of plots to assassinate John Paul. The one that had come closest to achieving its objective was the May 1981 shooting in St. Peter's Square, but Italian and foreign security and intelligence services had discovered a string of others.

In February of that year, a hand grenade exploded close to the altar that had been set up in the stadium of Karachi in Pakistan, twenty minutes before the pope was due to arrive. The attacker had been carrying the hand grenade in his pocket and was killed instantly. The following year, 1982, a Spanish priest shouting "Down with the pope! Down with communism!" tried to run the pope through with a bayonet at the shrine of Fatima in Portugal. The priest belonged to a conservative order led by Archbishop Marcel Lefebvre, a Frenchman who rejected John Paul's authority and who believed a "Marxist movement" inside the Vatican was wrecking the Church. In 1984, during a gathering held in John Paul's honor in Toronto, Canada, police arrested a man who had been carrying a stolen invitation and a knife, and who was waiting for the arrival of the pope.

In 1995, the CIA foiled an attempt to kill the pope during a visit to the Philippines. The plan was either to use a small plane with a kamikaze pilot or to disguise a group of Islamic fundamentalists as priests so that they could get close to the pope. Bibles, Roman dog collars, and a map showing the pope's route were found at the attackers' safe house. The plot was the brainchild of Ramzi Ahmed Yousef, a terrorist linked to Osama bin Laden, who only two years ealier had organized the bomb attack on the twin towers of the World Trade Center, leaving six people dead and a thousand wounded.

Two years later, in 1997, an Iranian-controlled network concealed a bomb under a bridge that the pope was scheduled to pass over during a visit to Bosnia-Herzegovina. The device contained more than fifty pounds of plastic explosives wrapped around twenty antitank mines. Police discovered the bomb in time. That same year, terrorists close to Hizbollah plotted to set off a bomb in the colonnade of St. Peter's Square, thirty feet from where the pope's car regularly passed when he greeted pilgrims in the piazza.

John Paul himself has never betrayed any concern about such

threats. "I feel a great peace when I think of the time when the Lord will call me," he has said. "At the time of my death, call me and order me to come to You." To Dziwisz, his secretary, the pope has reportedly confided his belief that "when death comes, life is not destroyed, it is transformed."

CHAPTER FIVE

I WAS RELUCTANT to approach any figure of authority in the Vatican without a personal recommendation from an intermediary—a system that could open doors in the heart of the Catholic Church that would otherwise remain closed. After weeks of probing, during which my sense of frustration intensified with each door that closed in my face, I found a sponsor: an American documentary-film maker who, some years earlier, had been commissioned by the Vatican to film the Swiss Guard. The film contained brief glimpses of Estermann and a single shot of Tornay marching, as well as a curious scene of guards relaxing one evening with some traditional Alpine yodeling.

Although the filmmaker was no longer based in Rome, he had remained in touch with the Guard, and attended the annual swearing-in ceremony as regularly as he could. But despite his connections, weeks passed before he managed to help me obtain an appointment with Colonel Pius Segmuller, the army officer who had succeeded Estermann as commander of the Guard. The reason I gave for wanting to see Segmuller was that I planned to write a book about the Vatican, and the Swiss Guard would be part of the book.

When I arrived at St. Anne's Gate on a sunny but crisp morning, I had not yet made up my mind how much to tell Segmuller about my quest. I stopped outside the gate, one of the five entrances into the forbidden city, trying to think it out. Three guards in dark blue fatigues and berets were stationed just inside Vatican territory. The rusty gray wrought-iron gate was hardly impressive. It was badly in need of a new coat of paint, and with its two stone eagles, it could have stood outside a ramshackle villa in the Tuscan hills had it not been for the papal coat of arms surmounting it.

One guard stood in the middle of the Via di Belvedere, the street leading into the Vatican, asking the driver of an antiquated Fiat van to show him his papers before waving him in. His companions were busy with three elderly nuns who clutched empty plastic bags. "Annona," the nuns said in unison in Latin as if they were singing a religious chant; Annona (yearly produce) is the name of the Vatican supermarket, which, because of its duty-free status, is 30 to 50 percent cheaper than its Roman competitors across the border.

To my right stood St. Anne's Church, where Tornay's funeral was held. A hearse was parked at a twisted angle outside it. The undertakers, as I guessed they must be from the practiced expressions on their solemn faces, chatted on the steps, hands shoved into the pockets of ill-fitting dark suits and hunching their shoulders against the cold.

I decided that I would try to mention the deaths to Segmuller as casually as possible, gauge his reaction, and take it from there. I went up to the guards, and they directed me to a reception room across the street from the church. There, another guard, his beret at his elbow, sat behind a curved wooden counter. Hanging on the wall above him was a crucifix, a photograph of the pope so faded it gave him a complexion as pale as the parchment of a medieval Bible, and an old-fashioned clock, the name of its manufacturer—Swiss, how could it be otherwise?—still visible on the yellowing dial. The only touch of color was a row of pocket-size flags of the Swiss cantons, the bases marked, in Gothic lettering, with the number of guards each had contributed to the corps.

As I waited, I glanced through a recruitment leaflet printed in four languages. The Guard was certainly eager to get in touch with any candidates: the form on which they were supposed to print their name and phone numbers even asked them to specify at precisely what time they could best be reached.

"Dear friend," the leaflet said. "You are young, modern, lively and dynamic, athletic. Your ideal is a fascinating life and your dream is an existence useful to the human community. You value order and respect, you want to exercise responsibility, and you are attracted by courageous acts . . ."

I was interrupted by the sound of heels clicking to attention. Thin-faced and clutching a battered briefcase marked SWISS ARMY in worn gold letters, Segmuller bowed his tall frame and stiffly unfolded his long right arm as if it was an attachment on a Swiss pocketknife. He gave me a short, tight handshake.

"Pius Segmuller," he said with an emphasis on the "Pius," which sounded so much like "pious" it was only then that it struck me as a particularly suitable first name, and quite a demanding one to live up to, given his surroundings. Poker-faced, and walking as rigidly as if he had swallowed a halberd, he ushered me through the empty barracks on the way to his office.

"Halebardiers' lodgings," he said as we passed down a dark passageway so narrow that I felt a jab of claustrophobia. To our left was the home of the lowest-ranking soldiers, which squatted on the Vatican's border with Italy. A set of children's swings stood forlornly in one corner, and behind a turreted wall I could glimpse the back of Bernini's colonnade on St. Peter's Square, which I had walked through with Tornay's mother.

We went through an archway and came out in the main courtyard, a narrow rectangle that also served as the drill yard. The cobblestones had been picked as clean as a village scene on a Swiss chocolate box, and there were no cigarette butts wedged into the cracks. Flags with the colors of the Swiss regions, larger versions of the ones I had seen in the reception room, hung limply from the sides of the courtyard in the still air, the only attempt to soften the edges of two severe buildings whose gray-and-brown facades must have recently been washed down, as they were uncontaminated by Rome's grime. It was so quiet that the only noise was that of a plane flying high overhead. After the dirt and noise of the city, it felt like another country. Which, of course, it was.

"Junior officers, officers' mess, armory," Segmuller barked as if pointing out his unit's positions on the front line. At the last word he jerked his head toward four prisonlike windows that had been sealed off not only by heavy iron bars but also by thick wire mesh. I silently hoped that I would one day be allowed to take a closer look than this.

He stopped suddenly and pointed to a fountain of porous travertine stone, bearing the papal coat of arms, that stood at the end of the drill yard. Above the basin, a bearded soldier in a suit of armor, sword in hand, stood with a grim expression above two agonizing figures and the words PATRIA MEMOR.

"That's what we're about," Segmuller said. "You know why the swearing-in ceremony is always in May? Because we commemorate the deaths of one hundred and forty-seven guards during the Sack of Rome. They were all slaughtered in 1527 when they defended the

Medici pope, Clement the Seventh, against the German and Spanish troops of the Holy Roman Emperor, Charles the Fifth. The Holy Father managed to escape alive."

The bravery of the guards, who fought with their backs to St. Peter's as the invaders slaughtered their way to the high altar, allowed the pope, his white robes hurriedly hidden below a scarlet cloak, to flee down a secret corridor in a high wall, the Passetto, that connects the Vatican with the fortress of Castel Sant'Angelo and still stands today. When Spanish mercenaries discovered the Guard's wounded commander, they hacked him to pieces. His wife tried to embrace the body, so they chopped off her fingers.

Segmuller led me to a three-story building that was the part of the barracks deepest in Vatican territory. It was not ocher-colored, like so many of the palazzi of central Rome, but a drab brown. When he entered his office on the ground floor, he started adjusting the neat thin piles of papers on his desk and did not look up. Above him was a portrait of a stone-faced Estermann, which hung along with those of his predecessors in a long series that formed an uneven frieze just under the ceiling. The painting of Estermann, prominent chin jutting out over a spotless pleated collar, was a blaze of red and yellow, in gaudy contrast to the darker tones of ancient commanders with flowing whiskers. Only a few yards away, a couple of floors above us, was the apartment where he died.

Segmuller stiffly leaned back in his black leather chair, the coat of arms of his family and that of the pope stamped on a large banner behind him. Unlike many of his predecessors, he told me, he did not have a purely military background. He had studied both philosophy and pedagogy in college before giving up on schoolteaching to join the Swiss army and a special humanitarian contingent that flew out to disaster areas at a moment's notice.

"What made you decide to become the thirty-third commander

of the Guards, and bring your wife and two young children to Rome?" I asked.

"I am very religious; that for me is the base of everything. And I thought this would be a unique experience. Something interesting," he replied.

It soon became apparent that Segmuller had his own checklist of questions that he wanted me to answer. What languages did I speak? he wanted to know. How long had I been in Rome, was I accredited to the Vatican press office, what did my job involve, where did I live? It was only after he had run out of such questions, and others about my family, that he pulled out of his briefcase an official history of the Guard written by a priest and handed it to me.

Segmuller pointed to three photographs on the wall. "You see these snapshots?" he said. "They're important to me. One is a guard praying, the second is a guard on security duty, and the third is a guard on parade. We are at the service of a religious institution; religion is our foundation. Our structure is military, and our duties are those of a police force at the service of the Holy Father.

"The Holy Father is not an easy man to protect; he wants to be close to the faithful all the time," he continued. "And the last thing he wants is police officers waving machine guns around him. So we have to be discreet and do things that he doesn't see. When he's in Saint Peter's Square, we have men in plain clothes who are very close to him, and they are ready to intervene. They're armed, but I can't say anything more than that. We man all the entrances to the Vatican. And we're the only security in the Apostolic Palace. The Guard can't be relegated to just a military parade role. It is something I have insisted on since my arrival."

His remark reminded me of rumors that the Guard's duties might be reduced in the wake of the murders. "What would be the problem with replacing the Guard with a normal police force?" I asked.

Segmuller's thin face tightened. "But we are wanted here. We were called here. In 1505, Pope Julius II saw how well the Swiss mercenaries fought against the French, against the Habsburgs, against the Venetians, and he called us and created the Swiss Guard. And after the death of Estermann it was said that the events of a single day could not obscure the services of five hundred years. The cardinal secretary of state said it in Saint Peter's, but it was a message from the Holy Father himself.

"After I was appointed," he went on, "I met the Holy Father for the first time. He said to me: 'You are young.' I said that I was forty-seven years old. The Holy Father repeated that I was young. I took him to mean that there was much work in store for us."

Segmuller had been the first to mention Estermann's name, and this encouraged me to press him on what was undoubtedly a sensitive subject for him. "What led to the death of—"

He broke in smartly, his knuckles rapping against the desk twice. "I arrived here after it all happened. I didn't know Estermann or Tornay. I don't want to get involved."

"But don't the guards talk to you about it?"

I felt, even more than I saw, his eyes bore into mine. "Some people are for Estermann; some are for Tornay. It's part of the historical Swiss animosity between German speakers and French speakers, which also exists in the Guard because we have recruits from all over Switzerland. The guards are worried about those deaths, but they are trying to forget them now. Every time those events are talked about, the old wounds are reopened. But you are not interested in those events, are you?"

It was more a statement than a question. If I confessed, the walls of the Vatican would become as impenetrable to me as the pope's bedchamber. "No," I said.

I would have to look to others for information about the three deaths and the events that had led up to them. In any case, Segmuller had joined the Guard four months after they had happened. But I still wanted to find out how much other help, if any, he would consider giving me.

"What are the chances of an outsider finding out how the Guard works?" I asked. "Would you give me permission to tour not only the barracks but also the various areas of the Vatican and the Apostolic Palace where the guards are stationed?"

"Well, first we need to understand someone before we can think of allowing them to do such things," he answered.

I was tempted to remind him of the personal questions he had asked me at the start of our talk, and tried to pin him down. "You think I'm a security risk?"

"No, it's not that. It is a question of opportunity. And there are many different offices that I have to consult. To show you the barracks, I need the permission of Cardinal Sodano, the secretary of state. To get you into the Apostolic Palace, I need the permission not only of the prefecture, but also of the Pontifical Commission for Social Communications. And all the authorizations have to be in writing."

My heart sank. I had a vision of my request being passed in triplicate around a labyrinth of ecclesiastical offices for eternity.

✦

AS I WAITED to hear from Segmuller, I tried to lobby for my cause directly at the Secretariat of State, which has authority over the Guard. A Roman friend gave me the name of an Italian monsignor whom he had known since they went to seminary together, but warned me: "He'll be a bit short with you on the telephone. Many of those who work at the Secretariat think their phones are tapped. But if you manage to get him out of the Vatican, he may let you in on a thing or two. He doesn't like the Vatican's habit of burying its head in the sand. Just make sure his name never comes out, or he'll damn you forever."

Sure enough, there was a harassed edge to the monsignor's voice when I phoned him. But he agreed to meet on the Gianicolo Hill above the Vatican—"at the worst I'll see a bit more of Rome than I see from this place," he said before hanging up.

The appointment was outside the Finnish embassy to the Holy See. I had no idea such an institution existed, but it turned out to be an attractive pink villa with a view that swept from the Villa Borghese park in the north to the Colosseum, and even beyond, as far as the town of Tivoli, where a pleasure-loving cardinal in the sixteenth century had erected an orgy of fountains and terraces to which Romans now flocked for refuge from the suffocating summer heat. Only St. Peter's and the Vatican were hidden from view, tucked behind the hill. Perhaps that was why the monsignor had chosen it.

He turned out to be a well-built man with a heavily lined, weary face. I guessed he was in his late fifties or early sixties, but although he had walked here uphill from his office, he wasn't out of breath. Like many clerics in Rome, the sacred center of Christendom, he was dressed in an anonymous gray suit that did not betray his vocation.

The first thing I learned about him was that he had a weakness for ice cream. So a swift purchase later, clutching our ice-cream cones, we picked our way under the umbrella pines along the gravel path that runs atop the hill, the view regularly obstructed by dozens of young couples—Latin lovers with a taste for a romantic setting, and with a highly developed sense of balance, since they managed to embrace despite being perched on the saddles of their *motorini,* the scooters that are as Roman as the Colosseum.

I took to him immediately and decided to risk a direct approach. I told him I was interested not only in the Guard but also in the three deaths, and asked him how he rated my chances of getting into the barracks.

"You may get in, but you'll be lucky to get them to talk. Any soldier who talks about it is given a punishment much worse than scrubbing floors. It's a one-way ticket on the first flight back to Zurich, and then onto the dole. They were all ordered to keep mum by Jehle, the chaplain. He pulled them out of bed at seven o'clock the morning after, lined them up in the courtyard, and ordered them to stay quiet. He said that in the name of unity they shouldn't accuse or blame anyone in the Guard for what happened. Other than Tornay, obviously. Some swearing-in ceremony."

Jehle is the chaplain who lied to Tornay's mother, telling her that her son's head had been ripped off his body, to try to stop her from coming to Rome. "Why did Jehle give that order?" I asked.

The monsignor eyed me shrewdly through black-rimmed glasses. "Because he was told to. In case you're wondering, by my boss."

The "boss" in question is Cardinal Sodano, sometimes referred to as the Vatican's viceroy. It came as little surprise to me that Sodano had stifled any voice other than that of Navarro-Valls, who is under his authority.

Sodano is one of the guardians of Vatican secretiveness, and has over the years written repeatedly to the heads of Curia departments commanding them not to talk to the press without his permission. He loves secrecy as much as he hates criticism. When bishops dared to criticize his way of governing at a synod, he burst out in a pained tone of voice: "He who loves does not criticize." He drew much angrier protests when, as papal nuncio, or envoy, to Chile, he prompted and organized John Paul's visit to Santiago in 1987, during which the pope appeared side by side with General Augusto Pinochet on the balcony of the dictator's Moneda palace. This, along with Sodano's refusal to confront the Pinochet regime, despite its jailing, torturing, and expulsion of priests, made the visit one of the darkest pages of John Paul's papacy. But it did no harm to Sodano's career, and he has headed the Curia's most important department for the past two decades.

"You remember what Sodano said at the funeral for the Estermanns in Saint Peter's?" the monsignor asked. "Something about feeling above all the need to be silent? That was the result of an emergency meeting held in the Apostolic Palace with Monsignor Gianbattista Re, the deputy at the Secretariat of State. Navarro-Valls and Judge Marrone were also there. It took them just half an hour to decide what to say about the deaths, and who should say it. By the way, Sodano and Re are also the ones who prevented Tornay's mother—and anyone else for that matter—from getting access to the files of the inquiry even after it ended."

Re's power is second only to that of Sodano. He is one of the few senior churchmen who gets to retain his office on the death of a pope—unlike Sodano. A workaholic capable of working fifteen-hour days, Re is a pure Curia bureaucrat, having risen through its ranks over two decades to a position of such influence that he enjoys the rare privilege of direct access to the pope, without needing to make an appointment.

I had watched Re at a Vatican ceremony sometime earlier. Smiling through rabbit teeth and narrow eyes, his skin pale, he had perfected a masterful technique for acknowledging the tributes paid to him by the long line of priests, nuns, monsignori, and diplomats attached to the Vatican. While extending his right hand for his gold ring to be kissed, he would clamp his left hand on the shoulder of the well-wisher to prevent any attempt at an embrace. It was Re who announced Estermann's appointment in the barracks at eleven o'clock on the morning of the killings. With Navarro-Valls, he was one of the first to reach the commander's apartment that evening.

"And the pope? Wasn't he the one who decided what should and shouldn't be said about the deaths?" I asked.

"You must be joking. His Holiness just went along with what Sodano cooked up. The Holy Father is so ill he's become a prisoner of the Curia. You realize, he's had five operations since the assassination attempt in 1981. Now he takes this drug against Parkinson's disease; it's called levodopa and the side effects make him feel good one minute and shattered the next. Oh, and add to that confusion, paranoia and hallucinations. But no one will ever admit it; the Holy Father has to appear in control, otherwise his courtiers go down with him. There's a Vatican saying: popes never fall ill, they just die. So Dziwisz, his secretary, does all he can to make John Paul appear in control, but at night he's woken up by his boss, struggling to get up and pray when he is in pain."

I could understand the Vatican's reluctance to discuss the pope's state of health. But what was shaping up as another apparent taboo puzzled me. "Why did the Vatican rush to put out its explanation for the Swiss Guard deaths? And why are people so reluctant to discuss the events that led up to them?" I asked.

I heard a sharp intake of breath at my side.

"I think you'll find there's too much at stake," he said. "We're talking about the security of the Holy Father. Don't forget he has already been the victim of one assassination attempt. Nobody wants to expose the failings of the organization in charge of his security, if that's got anything to do with what Tornay did. And especially less than two years before the Holy Year that coincides with the millennium. They expect thirty million pilgrims to flock to Rome, and the CIA warned that the event would make the Vatican an ideal platform for a terrorist attack. It's no coincidence that they put a chap like Raoul Bonarelli, who works for the Vigilanza police force, in charge of the inquiry into the three deaths. He's worth looking into, by the way."

I made a mental note to follow this up. But from his downcast eyes, I sensed the monsignor was holding something back. "Is the pope's security the only reason for the silence?" I insisted.

He stopped short and stared out at the Roman skyline, which offered up to heaven more TV aerials than cupolas or crucifixes. Without turning, he replied: "Well, there is something else which springs to mind. If you think about it, there's one common thread running through this, and it's the Opus Dei movement. The Estermanns were both close to it. Navarro-Valls is a member, and he was very fast in getting to the scene of the crime when he was alerted. And the Holy Father's shadow, Dziwisz, is said to be supportive of Opus Dei. Given the movement's taste for secrecy, all these people are going to follow the principle that the less said the better."

"Is that why Estermann's promotion was blocked for so long? Because of his links to Opus Dei?"

The monsignor flushed like a choirboy caught sipping at the altar wine. The familiar panorama seemed to acquire a sudden fascination for him, as if he were seeing it for the first time. "Some of us wanted to find a noble to lead the Guard, and we sent envoys to Switzerland to try to find someone else because Estermann was of peasant origin. I'm no snob myself. But it's true that many people in the Vatican feel that Opus Dei has got its finger in too many pies. There's so much intrigue in the Vatican, so many factions, sometimes I get the impression the Holy Spirit never got past Saint Anne's Gate. He was an odd guy, Estermann was. Did you know that he'd thought of joining the French Foreign Legion before coming to the Vatican? He was lucky he had Meza Romero for a wife—she worked hard for him. One of the last things she did was to translate the speech he was due to give at the swearing-in ceremony."

No amount of probing would persuade him to say more. Nor would he get involved in my application to visit the barracks. He refused my offer to escort him down the hill, and with a hurried apology set off at a brisk pace toward his office, weaving his way through the *motorini* and the amorous couples.

✦

OVER THE NEXT FEW DAYS I waited in vain for an answer from the Swiss Guard. I concentrated on Bonarelli, the investigator from the Vigilanza police force whom the monsignor had mentioned, and found out that he was indeed "worth looking into." On the very day that the Vatican closed its inquiry, Bonarelli had been promoted to deputy head of the Vigilanza—an unmistakable sign that his sleuthing had been looked upon with favor from on high.

This was surprising since his name had previously been dragged into one of the biggest scandals of recent Vatican history—the kidnapping of Emanuela Orlandi, the fifteen-year-old daughter of a messenger who worked in the Apostolic Palace. On the evening of June 22, 1983, she vanished after attending her weekly flute lesson. Her disappearance was believed to be part of an attempt to force the release of Mehmet Ali Agca, the Turkish gunman given a life sentence for his attempt to assassinate the pope.

When Italian investigating magistrates who wanted to question Bonarelli about the disappearance sent him an official summons, they also ordered that his home telephone be tapped. In the words of one of the investigators: "The interception brought to light a certain degree of concern on Bonarelli's part concerning the imminence of his testimony before this office."

From a contact in the Rome law courts, I obtained a transcript of the telephone conversation between Bonarelli and a superior, believed to be the secretary of state at the time, Cardinal Agostino Casaroli. Neither man knew that Bonarelli's telephone had been bugged. In the following conversation, they are discussing what Bonarelli should tell the magistrates about the case—or rather what he shouldn't tell them:

SUPERIOR: I've spoken to . . . and he says . . . Nothing, we know nothing . . . we find out things from the newspapers . . . it was outside the Vatican's responsibility . . . it's under Italian jurisdiction.

BONARELLI: Ah, is that what I should say?

SUPERIOR: Well, what do we know? You could say: I have never looked into it . . . the office passed it on and this is something which went . . . don't say it went to the Secretariat of State.

The latter statement is a lie. The kidnapping case certainly was passed on to the Secretariat of State since it was they who had masterminded the telephone contacts with Orlandi's presumed captors, but details of these conversations were never released to the Italian investigators. Bonarelli was formally notified that he had been placed under investigation on suspicion of misleading the magistrates.

To be fair to Bonarelli, his behavior was in line with that of the Holy City's most eminent authorities. Both Cardinal Sodano and Monsignor Re turned down a request to appear as witnesses before the Italian judge. Re did let it be known that he had spoken to the girl's captors on the telephone, but he added that no notes of these discussions were available, and that in any case the talks were of no interest.

Re's statement failed to convince the magistrates, who had found out about a special hotline set up by the Vatican for discussions with the kidnappers. Not for the first time, the Vatican's brazen refusal to cooperate infuriated the Italians, and they accused it of jeopardizing the girl's safety. Rosario Priore, the veteran antiterrorism magistrate who had led the investigation into the pope's shooting, has for his part bluntly denounced the Vatican as "intent on closing all inquiries into the crime, and on placing a tombstone on the search for truth."

Orlandi has never been found. Every day, her elderly parents walk into the Vatican Gardens and stop before a statue of the Virgin of Lourdes. There, they recite the rosary for their daughter and pray for a miracle.

CHAPTER SIX

IT WAS ONLY when I came face-to-face with the ghoulish sculptures by the altar that I realized that my tour of the Vatican was starting only a few yards from where Tornay had served on the last day of his life. Outside the church where we stood was the Audience Hall, the ugly papal auditorium where he had kept vigil at a synod of bishops.

Seven weeks had passed before Swiss military efficiency triumphed over a Vatican bureaucracy two millennia in the making and a non-commissioned officer, Lance Corporal Tiziano Guarneri, called to tell me that the commander and his ecclesiastical superiors had granted my request. But Guarneri also brought bad news. I had to agree to strict ground rules. He would act as my escort, and I had to stay with him at all times; I could not speak to guards without his permission; I would see the barracks, but I would not be allowed to visit the lodgings; nor could I attend any social gatherings.

Given such controls, Guarneri sounded more like a strict chaperone than a guide. Perhaps the Vatican authorities worried that, like the photographer De Wurstemberger had done, I would try to take pictures with a hidden miniature camera. Whatever the motive, I was in no mood to argue. I would try to bend the rule of silence at a later stage, with or without official approval.

With his morose countenance, gray suit, and gray overcoat, the bespectacled Guarneri seemed to blend in with the stones of the Vatican on the overcast morning when we met. He told me that he was the son of an electrician, but added quickly that he was also the descendant of an illustrious eighteenth-century lute maker, Giuseppe Guarneri del Gesù. He had come to Rome in July 1994, six months before Tornay's arrival. Both men had risen to the same rank. Tornay had been refused the *benemerenti* medal, while pinned to Guarneri's lapel was an even more coveted award, the *pro ecclesia pontificia,* which was awarded to a guard after five years.

The tour began at a Renaissance church, Saint Mary of Piety, a short walk up an alley called Sacristy Street that leads into the Vatican from the gates by the papal auditorium. Guarneri's choice made the morning seem all the more leaden. On either side of the altar were marble statues of skeletons, partly wrapped in shrouds. At their feet, human skulls with angels' wings leered horribly. It was difficult to tell in the dimness of the church, but despite our macabre surroundings I caught what looked like pride and pleasure on Guarneri's face. "The cemetery is very beautiful," he assured me. "As much as a cemetery can be beautiful. We of the Swiss Guard can ask to be buried there."

The burial ground was a damp oasis of frayed cypresses, palms, and orange trees heavy with fruit that apparently no one dared pick. Red candles burned on top of several tombstones, their smell mingling with that of pine needles. The wax congealed in the cracks of the stones like lumps of coagulated blood. One epitaph was dedicated to a member of the Pfyffer von Altishofen dynasty, Swiss nobles who since 1652, Guarneri told me, had supplied no fewer than eleven commanders of the Guard.

The past, and the ultimate sacrifice, were everything to a corps that had not fought for hundreds of years. From the official history that Segmuller had given me, I had learned that the Guard was the heir to a mercenary tradition that went back to the ancient Greeks, whose cities hired outsiders to fight for them when they did not have enough recruits of their own. In the Middle Ages, the Swiss dominated the battlefields, but their performance depended on whether their masters—including monarchs like Henry VIII and Louis II—paid up promptly.

A detachment of Swiss warriors could stand and fight to the last man and still win a battle. When, during the Renaissance, a few hundred of them crossed a river to surprise a French force that was fifteen times more numerous, they massacred three thousand of their adversaries before they were wiped out. The French fled.

The French became some of the keenest buyers of Swiss warrior know-how and hired up to 163,000 Swiss to fight their wars for them. An enthusiastic François I wished for more. He wrote to his mistress, Diane de Poitiers: "If my army was made up of Swiss, I would conquer the world in the twinkling of an eye."

Following the example set by the secular rulers, Pope Julius II, nicknamed Il Terribile for his irascible nature, and best known for browbeating Michelangelo into finishing the ceiling of the Sistine Chapel, hired his own men and founded the Swiss Guard in 1506. A warrior pope with a passion for leading his armies into battle clad in a brilliant silver suit of armor, he himself blessed the first Swiss contingent, a hundred and fifty strong, which he had summoned to Rome "to protect our palaces."

Over the centuries, the mercenaries paid for their fame in the number of casualties they suffered during such campaign as the Sack of Rome in the sixteenth century, during which St. Peter's and the Sistine Chapel were turned into stables for horses, and in other ways as well. In 1688, the word "nostalgia" was invented to describe their condition by a Swiss medical student, who ran together the words *nostos* (return) and *algos* (pain). The student described the sickness they were feeling, trapped far away from their mountain villages, as potentially fatal. Despite such obstacles their reputation survived untarnished, and their admirers included Napoléon, who observed, with no trace of French chauvinism: "The best troops—those in whom you can have the most confidence—are the Swiss."

During World War II, Joseph Stalin once asked sarcastically: "The pope? And how many divisions has the pope?" Today the answer to that question would be one, and that is the Swiss Guard. When Pope Paul VI launched a purge of Vatican pomp and circumstance in 1970, the Swiss Guard was the only armed corps to survive intact. Its two rivals, the Noble Guard and the Palatine Guard, were disbanded.

Compared with the size of the Vatican—eight Vatican cities can fit into New York's Central Park—the pope's private army is, at least on paper, an impressive force: all things being equal, the United States would need to have an army of 80 million men to be as "militarized" as the Vatican.

The Guard's official history makes no mention of Machiavelli's opinion of the mercenaries, the Swiss included, who turned his homeland into a battlefield. In *The Prince,* he described them as both useless and dangerous: "Mercenaries are disunited, thirsty for power, undisciplined and disloyal; they are brave among their friends and cowards before the enemy; they have no fear of God, they do not keep faith with their fellow men; they avoid defeat just so long as they avoid battle; in peacetime you are despoiled by them, and in wartime by the enemy. The reason for all this is that there is no loyalty or inducement to keep them on the field apart from the little they are paid, and this is not enough to make them want to die for you."

Nor does official history refer to the darker side of the Swiss Guard, which in the twentieth century saw episodes of mutiny and indiscipline that would not have surprised Machiavelli. From the yellowing newspapers of the period, I learned that in 1913 tension had run so high that some guards hid their weapons to have them ready for an insurrection.

The revolt was triggered by a particularly severe commander, Colonel Jules Repond, who sent his officers to drag a sick guard, one Giuseppe Pralong, out of his hospital bed and order him to return to duty. Pralong refused, and was dragged off to the barracks prison, but on the way he found the strength to draw his sword and threaten his escort. Guards came running, but instead of helping the officers who were escorting Pralong, they defended him and helped him escape.

The guards promptly drew up a list of demands—more recruits, a pay raise, and an end to a ban that prevented them spending their evenings in the local taverns, where prostitution was rife. Above all, they demanded an end to the military reforms instituted by Repond, which included such delights as constant bayonet charges and exercises during which they were required to inch along on their stomachs over the roofs of the Vatican, pointing their rifles at imaginary assailants. They also thought it demeaning to be required to shoot at puppets resembling geese and hares during target practice.

But when the protesters formally handed over their list of grievances in the courtyard, a senior officer lit a cigarette and burned the list under their noses. A few hours later Repond agreed to receive a delegation, but he lost his temper and waved his gun at its members. Infuriated, the guards threw their uniforms out of the windows and staged a protest march in St. Peter's Square, during which they sang "La Marseillaise," the French national anthem.

When he found out what was happening in the barracks under his windows, Pope Pius X threatened to disband the corps. The mutiny finally ended when the cardinal secretary of state intervened and dismissed Repond. The ringleaders were disarmed and expelled. Baron Pfyffer von Altishofen, who had resigned as commander a year earlier, commented that he had expected the men to mutiny, given their exhausting, forty-eight-hour tours of duty and the tension caused by the recruitment of French-speaking guards.

Until then, the overwhelming majority of the guards had been from German-speaking areas, men who, in the baron's words, were "uncouth but loyal, mountain-men with few ideas in their heads, but those few ideas are solid and honest. The French-speaking recruits come mainly from cities and towns, and they have brought with them ideas that are excessively advanced."

Tensions never quite abated; indeed, there was even an apparent precedent for Tornay's gesture. In 1959, Adolf Ruckert, a lance corporal, shot his commander, Robert Nunlist, in the barracks after being dismissed. Nunlist survived. In more recent years drunken brawls tarnished the corps' record: in the worst incident, guards from Tornay's region, the Valais, started smashing up cars outside the Vatican after the Sion Football Club won the Swiss League Championship. When police tried to calm them down, two guards had to be arrested and two police officers ended up in the hospital. Another time, a drunken guard dived naked into a fountain in the gardens of the pope's summer residence of Castel Gandolfo on Lake Albano, south of Rome, shouting insults in French and German at all those who approached him until two companions fished him out.

I thought it was unlikely that Guarneri, my guide for the morning, would be willing to tell me about current tensions in the Guard. As he led me out of the cemetery and across a small cobblestoned piazza, the Square of the First Roman Martyrs, I asked whether religious faith had been the main reason why he had signed up, given the modest monthly wage that guards were paid.

"I had no religious motive," he admitted. "I just wanted to leave Switzerland. And I liked the sound of 'Swiss Guard in Rome.'"

"Was it hard to be selected?"

"Not at all. There are only a few basic requirements—you have to be a Swiss Roman Catholic, obviously, aged between nineteen and thirty years old, at least one point seventy-four meters tall, and have a good reputation. And that's it. The Guard didn't bother to do interviews."

"Surely someone had to vouch for you before you joined?"

"All it took was a letter from my parish priest."

It seemed a rather casual procedure for selecting the men who would protect the pope.

Just then, an officer wearing what looked like a Victorian coachman's cape with red flashes on the shoulders greeted Guarneri, who responded tersely and pressed on. "The Vigilanza, the Vatican cops," Guarneri said. "We don't have much time for them; they're just in charge of the traffic and little else."

I followed him past the pair of Swiss Guard standing at the Arch of Bells, the entrance used by visitors with business in the Vatican law courts or in the governor's palace. Heads of state would sweep through here in their motorcades on their way to call on the pope.

Tornay had walked past here one last time when his tour of duty at the Audience Hall ended. Perhaps he had taken in the grandeur of the Basilica above his head, and of the broad sweep of St. Peter's Square stretching out before him. Or more likely, they had grown too familiar for him to take any notice of them, and he had instead been thinking about how he would celebrate receiving the medal that he already considered his by right.

The most impressive entrance to the Vatican, the papal "front door," was farther down the square, at the Bronze Doors tucked under a corner of the colonnade. Three guards were on duty, including one who stood unsmiling and as still as the columns, his feet at sixty-degree angles, his right hand turned at the regulation angle, and his halberd— all six kilograms and two meters of it—also tilted as tradition decreed. Pilgrims and tourists lined up to take his picture.

Guarneri sniffed. "The guy with the halberd is the most photographed, but he's the one who does the least. All he has to do is keep perfectly still and not smile. He's not allowed to talk to anyone; that's why there's always another guard next to him—to stop anyone coming up to him. We usually put someone who's pretty green there, like a new recruit. His job is simply to watch and learn. And to present arms to important people. That's cardinals, bishops, and ambassadors to the Holy See."

For centuries the guards had been expected to drop to one knee whenever they encountered the pope. It was a complicated operation, made even more difficult if the guard carried a halberd—the left knee was supposed to touch the ground while a military-style salute was given with the right hand, and the halberd leaned slightly forward with the left hand.

The "good pope" John XXIII, who replaced the guards' rifles with halberds, put an end to such genuflection in the early 1960s, ordering that it be reserved exclusively for God. Since then, guards get down on one knee only during Mass, when the host is consecrated. But cardinals are still entitled to the *Schultern,* a salute that involves a pair of guards tossing their halberds into the air, catching them with one hand, and making sure the metal clanks before they hit the ground, all in unison.

We went through the Bronze Doors and made our way up a sloping corridor, the flaking plaster on the vaulted ceiling highlighted by the naked lightbulbs affixed to the walls, toward a staircase as grandiose as the corridor was shabby. This was the ornate Scala Regia, the royal staircase. Guarneri paid no attention to a florid equestrian statue, with angels blowing trumpets, and nymphs whose breasts spilled out of clinging robes in pagan abandon. Despite their frolicking, the nymphs were granted the honour of displaying a papal coat of arms.

At the top of the staircase, we came across a guard who stood alone in a vast hall where the pope, sitting on his throne, used to receive monarchs. Pope Paul VI had called the Vatican itself "a throne of gold" in July 1978, a reference to its huge collection of valuable works of art. He came up with the idea of selling some of them so that more money could be spent on the world's poor, and even asked an art dealer to try to sell Michelangelo's *Pietà*. But the plan came to nothing.

Along practically the entire length of one wall, under gigantic frescoes of papal ceremonies, two red carpets lay rolled up on the marble floor, leftovers from some ceremony. One fresco showed ships of war lined up facing each other as they prepared to do battle. Death, a skeleton with scythe at the ready, gazed at the scene from empty orbits, a leer of expectation stamped on its skull. There was no doubting who had designed the hall: the signature PAULUS III PONT. MAX (for Pontifex Maximus, or supreme priest) appeared more than a dozen times across the gold-and-gray ceiling.

"We're practically below the Apostolic Palace," Guarneri said, gesturing limply toward the various doors that led off the hall. "The Sistine Chapel, which is part of the Apostolic Palace, is just behind that door. Tourists use another entrance to see it; they're not allowed in here. The pope's vestments are stored behind that other door, and the saints are behind there."

"What, there's a crypt or something?"

Guarneri corrected me. "All the relics are there. If a priest dedicates a new church to Saint Martin or whoever, then he comes here and asks for a relic. There's no doubt they're genuine. I mean, they come from the heart of the Vatican."

I thought of the relics I had seen venerated in churches in Rome and elsewhere in Italy—if they were any guide, behind the closed door lay what was no doubt a well-ordered assortment of bones, skulls, pieces of skin, even fingers and once-vital organs. An old monk shuffled past us, crossing the hall along a diagonal as precise as if he had mapped it out with a compass. "That's one of the Augustinian fathers," my guide explained. "They manage the relics."

A succession of halls and galleries—only a tiny portion of the 1,400 halls and galleries, as well as chapels and apartments, that make up the complex of the Apostolic Palace—brought us to the first loggia, the frescoed first floor that was overhauled in the sixteenth century after the Sack of Rome took its toll on the Basilica and other sacred areas. Guarneri ignored the Baroque splendor and stopped instead by a dingy-looking corridor. Sickly poinsettias, their leaves a faded scarlet, had been lined up like victims for execution along the wall. Their battle to survive in the electric light was doomed to failure.

"That's the home of the cardinal secretary of state. His Eminence Angelo Sodano," Guarneri said. "All those plants are presents he got for Christmas. We've got one guard outside the door to his home, and another one outside his office, which is on the same floor."

He showed me into an antiquated wooden elevator, manned by an attendant in a blue uniform and peaked cap. "Sodano has his own private staircase up to the pope's apartments, but we're going up the easy way," Guarneri said.

A saint was depicted on a small silver medallion fixed to one of the panels. The attendant caught me looking at it. "Saint Christopher, patron saint of travelers! Because I am a traveler, I go up and I go down!" he exclaimed in a thick Roman accent, with a lewd wink and the wry humor typical of the Eternal City. Guarneri did not bat an eyelid at the play on words.

Such bawdiness was out of place in the Apostolic Palace, but there was a time when it would have surprised no one. In June 1493, when the Borgia pope Alexander VI held a banquet to celebrate the marriage of his thirteen-year-old daughter, Lucrezia, the female guests competed to pick up, with their naked breasts, as much confetti as possible from silver vessels that liveried pages held up for them—the winner, a woman by the name of Giulia, managed to collect eighteen pieces.

On the third floor, we turned left out of the elevator, and an NCO greeted us stiffly. The third loggia smelled of beeswax. Guarneri spoke in a hushed voice, although there was no one within sight apart from the other guard. He seemed to shed his despondency, as if he had become intoxicated by the grandeur of his surroundings, a marbled L-shaped corridor lined on one side with what was virtually a wall of glass and on the other with ancient frescoes of maps of the world, the blue of the oceans suprisingly vivid for their age.

"This is it, the most important place in the entire Vatican. The pope's apartment is around the corner, a few yards down," Guarneri said, lifting his index finger only a little as if he were scared of pointing at the bend in the L. "We always have at least an NCO here, and there is another guard behind the pope's door. They do a total of nine hours a day here, but in shifts of three hours maximum. There's a spy hole in the pope's door, but guests are always announced so the butler and Dziwisz, the secretary, know who to expect."

Guards were stationed on every floor of the pope's palace, but they did not appear to be armed. They did not even carry pikes, and a couple of the ones I came across were chatting quietly on telephones. "What would the guards do if an assassin got as far as here?" I asked.

"He wouldn't get this far, because there are half a dozen checks between Saint Anne's Gate and here. Even if he did get here, we've got what we need. That's all I can say. Anyway, we're not worried; the last time something happened was when the pope was shot. That was twenty years ago, and in the square, not here."

Guarneri cast nervous glances up and down the corridor. "The thing is, we have to be discreet, because the Holy Father doesn't want to be protected. If it was up to him he'd wander around Rome on his own. In the square there's nothing we can do for him. He should be in the 'popemobile,' the bullet-proof Jeep which has a special cabin of reinforced glass. But he can't bear even glass separating him from people, so he stands in an open car instead. We've got our work cut out worrying about the pilgrims who try to jump over the barriers. They don't want to hurt the pope, but they get carried away and we have to stop them in time."

I was reminded of a remark that John Paul had made when he first inspected the newly arrived popemobile: "All these precautions are useless. As soon as I go out, dressed in white from head to foot, I'm a target they can't possibly miss."

I remembered that Tornay had been found lying on top of what the Vatican said was his ordnance weapon. "Surely guards from the rank of lance corporal on up have guns of their own?"

"Well, yes. They're Swiss-made—a Sig Sauer 225 pistol which shoots nine-millimeter-caliber bullets. It makes nice holes."

The choice of words made me wince. I thought of the "holes" such a gun had made in the Estermanns and Tornay. "Do you carry yours around all the time?" I asked.

"We're not obliged to. I'm not too keen on walking around with it, so I usually keep it in my flat. It's got the charger in and it's full of ammunition; it's not much use otherwise."

"You don't have to sign it into the armory whenever you go off duty?"

"No, I don't. And in any case, my flat is locked. No one can get in."

It seemed a casual way to assign guns in military barracks. But Guarneri's tone implied that the discussion was closed, and he led me back to the lift. We emerged into the St. Damasus inner courtyard. The sky was still overcast, but at first, after the cavernous fustiness of the Apostolic Palace, it felt like a bright summer's day.

The courtyard had once been the private garden of Renaissance popes. Now the only sign of green was the moss that grew between the cobblestones, which a man in blue overalls was spraying with weed killer. There was no one else on the square apart from four members of the Swiss Guard, who, apparently bored, watched him intently from afar. Every inch of the square was familiar to guards, as they spent days on end here rehearsing for the swearing-in ceremony.

"This is the closest a VIP's bodyguards can get to the pope's apartment," Guarneri said. "They're not allowed in the Apostolic Palace. We don't care who it is. If it's a head of state visiting the Holy Father, we greet them with a twelve-man guard of honor. Then we take the guest up with a five-man escort. Even when President Clinton came, his security people had to wait down here."

"They can't have been too pleased about that."

"Sometimes the security men complain; they want to take their guns in everywhere. But protocol says they can't, so that's that."

We walked through an archway into the Belvedere courtyard, where Vatican personnel were allowed to park their cars, which could be refueled at the city-state's own cut-rate gas pump, in the shadow of the Borgia Tower. I noticed a few Vatican workers had ignored the "No Parking" signs, just the way drivers behaved in Rome's chaotic streets.

Guarneri pulled a face. "The Vatican cops can't be bothered to give out parking tickets, so some people dump their cars all over the place."

His tone gave me a sense of how much he preferred the order of the Vatican City to the teeming life outside its walls.

CHAPTER SEVEN

WHEN GUARNERI LED ME into the barracks, a corporal was trying to teach six novices the rudiments of standing to attention and turning in the drill yard. The corporal had scrawled chalk marks on the cobblestones, but he was not making much progress. He barked out his orders in Swiss-German dialect.

"That's the only language we use," Guarneri explained. "The men from the French-speaking region are expected to understand it."

I thought it best not to point out that schoolchildren in the French-speaking region were taught German rather than the dialect used by the guards. Guarneri led me across the courtyard to what he called the Guard's arsenal. We went down a few steps and came across an empty suit of armor that stood silent vigil. "A present the pope passed on to us—he had no idea where to put it. No one can get into it; the legs are too small," Guarneri said.

The suit of armor set the right tone for the firing power of the men entrusted with the pope's safety. The place felt more like a war museum, or a props storeroom for a medieval battle epic, than a well-oiled arsenal. A German note in Gothic script hung from the ceiling: PLEASE DO NOT TOUCH ANYTHING. A musty smell hung in the air. The shelves were stacked with breastplates bearing the papal seal that were three hundred years old, and with iron helmets that each weighed two and a half kilos.

But the halberds were the most numerous: dozens leaned against the walls. In the Middle Ages, the halberd was the prized weapon of Swiss mercenaries. Because of its design, the Swiss footmen were the only soldiers who could withstand a cavalry attack—the equivalent of infantry standing up to tanks today. The top of the halberd combined a curved ax at the front to cut a horse's legs, a hook to grab a passing rider and pull him down, and an evil-looking long spike to run him through.

Upright on racks were daggers and broadswords, blunderbusses and muskets, lances, and a big black mace that looked so heavy it must have taken two men to lift, let alone swing at an enemy head. I came across a Spanish Hispano-Suiza pistol machine. I looked at the date on it: 1943. Nearby was another World War II relic, a German Sten gun. How, I wondered, could the Guard even pretend to protect the pope when these were the means at its disposal? The only weapons that would pass muster in any other modern security force were ten-year-old, Swiss-made Sig assault rifles, and there were only two of them. Until two years before Tornay's arrival, the weapons available to the guards had been archaic carbines.

Guarneri was running a finger along the metal studs on the mace. Each stud was as spotless as the lenses of his glasses. He seemed proud of the items on display. I asked him how much importance was given to target practice.

"We practice once a year with an assault rifle," he said. "It's compulsory under Swiss law, and there's no exception for us even though we live abroad. We have to get a certain number of points to remain qualified as army reservists."

I was unimpressed. Guarneri must have realized it, because he ushered me out, past the struggling recruits and into the only fashion atelier on Vatican territory—that of Ety Cicioni, tailor to the Guard. The son of a seamstress, he was thirty years old, tall and athletic, with thick black eyebrows. Dozens of dress uniforms, unfinished, hung from the ceiling. Cicioni told me it took him thirty hours to complete each uniform, and reached effortlessly to fetch one down. I asked him about the story, which I had read in several guidebooks, that the uniform had been designed by Michelangelo.

"Everyone asks me that." He sighed. "There's no evidence for it. All there is, in a hall close to the Sistine Chapel, is a self-portrait by Michelangelo. He's wearing a uniform that is pretty similar. He was working in the Vatican at the time, so people say he created the uniform."

"Actually it was a commander of the Guards, Jules Repond, who redesigned it just after World War One. He went through all the pictures he could get his hands on that showed guards over the centuries, and then he overhauled the uniform. He didn't do too badly." This was the same commander whose severity had sparked a mutiny.

With nimble, practiced gestures, Cicioni picked apart the uniform, explaining that it was made out of a total of 154 pieces. The gaiters have a strap that has to be passed under the shoe, and a cord to tie them just under the knee, but this must be so tight that it hinders the circulation in the legs, which could have serious effects on a guard standing immobile for hours on sentry duty. I was reminded of the luckless guard who had to stand vigil by the open coffin of Pope Pius XII in 1958 as the faithful paid their last respects to the pontiff in St. Peter's. The body had been so badly embalmed that a foul smell seeped from the papal presence. After resisting as long as he could, the guard fainted, his halberd clattering as he slumped to the marble floor.

The puffed-out trousers had tiny hooks that had to be painstakingly fitted into the top of the breeches, the trouser bottoms rolled up to hide the hooks from view. Both jacket and trouser were embellished with thick bands in the blue, red, and yellow of the Medici dynasty, which had produced four popes. The colors are bright because of the tradition that soldiers should be easily recognizable on the battlefield. Guards, according to Cicioni, are forever catching the loose bands on door handles. The French Revolution has also left its mark: a tricolor ribbon cockade adorns the trousers worn by corporals.

Guarneri, who had been oddly jumpy during my conversation with Cicioni, interrupted to say that the tailor's job was a very difficult one, and that we shouldn't steal any more of his time. Cicioni had been talking quite happily, so I decided to contact him again as soon as I could shake off my escort. Perhaps he would let slip something about Tornay.

◆

THE TOUR OVER, Guarneri and I sat in the officers' mess, which was furnished like a Swiss mountain tavern with wooden tables and benches, and sported a large mural of the Guard's short-tempered founder, Pope Julius II, imperious looking in a flowing scarlet cape that covered his horse's flanks as he rode along a rocky mountain path with an escort of guards, the dome of St. Peter's looming oddly in the distance.

Guarneri poured some white wine. The label on the bottle proclaimed it to be the official wine of the Swiss Guard, from vineyards on the Castelli Romani hills south of Rome.

Guarneri sipped appreciatively. *"Buono,"* he said. I asked him how he felt about his job.

"At the start, everything was new to me; it was thrilling," he said. "I knew what I was letting myself in for, so I accepted everything. Now there are times when I get heartily sick of it all and want to chuck it in. But if I do another three years and a half, I'll qualify for a pension. It won't be enough to live on, but it would come in rather handy."

I was surprised by the candor of his answer. I gambled that now was the time to ask him about Tornay. "Was that what Tornay felt, too? He wanted to give it all up?"

Guarneri set his glass down sharply. "Sorry, can't talk about all that. The incident is closed."

On the orders of Segmuller, the commander, I thought. I could either insist, and risk jeopardizing what little benevolence I enjoyed from Segmuller, or bide my time. I chose the latter, and asked Guarnieri whether the guards had a heavy workload.

"People think of us as a quaint little army, but the pace is actually very tough. Our shifts are so rigid that you could ask me about any day in two years' time and I would know whether I'll be working or not. On paper, we work for two days and we have the third day off."

"Doesn't sound that bad."

"I said on paper. The day off is often no such thing because any tour of duty involving a papal audience, whether he's in the auditorium or meeting a head of state, counts as overtime. We have to do it during our day off. We're paid peanuts for it."

"What about the normal shifts—how long do those last?"

"We're not supposed to be on duty at the same spot for more than three hours at a stretch; otherwise we get too tired to be any use if something goes wrong. Three hours is a long time, believe me. We've learned how to get rid of an itch simply through concentration. Some of us recite the rosary to pass the time. At least we get moved from one place to another during the day. I once worked for seventeen hours in a single day. It was hell."

"When you do get an evening off, can you stay out all night?" I asked.

"I wish. As a lance corporal, I'm privileged. I have to be back in barracks every night at one in the morning, except for three nights a month when I can stay out until two. The halberdiers have to be back at midnight. If you jump curfew, you risk missing a papal assignment that was posted up at the last minute."

"What's the punishment?"

"A day removing the rust from the breastplates or cleaning up the canteen. Or the *Scheitstock,* that's a wooden execution block on which you cut up old uniforms. You have to cut them into squares that are ten centimeters by ten centimeters, with a hatchet, to stop anyone else wearing them."

Guarneri got up and went off to the kitchens in search of salty biscuits—"because otherwise this wine will hit us hard." When he returned, I asked him why there was such pressure on the corps.

"We're not at our full complement. There should be a hundred and ten of us, but there's been a recruitment problem for some time now, partly because the pay isn't too good, although the rent is free. A halberdier gets only two million lire a month; that's much less than the going wage in a country as wealthy as Switzerland."

In an interview before his death, Estermann had said that the commander was paid only five million lire a month, the same as a cardinal in charge of a Vatican department, and half as much as what an officer of an identical rank would be paid in the Swiss army.

I hadn't expected Guarneri to be so forthright in his criticism. Perhaps the wine had helped him to unwind a little, although he had stayed mum about the deaths. In any case, he did not sound like someone motivated enough to respect the oath he had sworn several years earlier. "Are you still ready to sacrifice your life for the pope?" I asked.

He carefully pinched the stem of his glass between thumb and index finger and moved it just a fraction along the table. "At the time I understood completely what that oath meant. You don't feel complete until you have been through that ceremony."

"And now?"

"Here and now I would say yes, I would throw myself in front of the bullets. But you'd have to see what the situation was."

I noticed the "but." As slowly as he had done a few moments earlier, he again took hold of his glass and moved it with overwhelming precision back into position. He frowned. "I mean, it's not something you expect."

✦

I ARRANGED TO MEET CICIONI, the tailor, a few days later on "neutral territory," at a bar near the Vatican. I had told him I had a few more questions about his work, and he chatted easily for a while, telling me about his experiments with lighter cloths for the guards' summer uniforms and about the problems he had persuading Vatican officials to accept change. But he began to cast nervous glances around him when I told him I wanted to question him about Tornay. "Was it true that Tornay was highly undisciplined?" I asked.

Cicioni's long body gave a squirm. "Nobody talks about that anymore. You know, people forget everything in life."

I didn't want to be put off. "Yes, but what was he like?" I insisted.

"Well, let's just say that when I first took up the job in the Vatican, Tornay was the guard who was kindest to me. If he had been a young Italian man working in a normal Italian context, he would have been considered perfectly normal. But this is the Swiss Guard, and it's dominated by recruits from the German-speaking areas of Switzerland."

He got up to leave. I got up with him and tried again: "When was the last time you saw him? And what kind of mood was he in?"

"The last day. He came to see me just after lunch. There were some buttons missing on his gaiters, and he wanted to show off his haircut to my wife, who often helps me out. She used to work as a hairdresser. Tornay had cut his hair on his own and wanted her opinion."

We were already out in the street. Cicioni shook my hand and said good-bye. I held his hand long enough to ask one last question. "And his mood; was he upset?" I said.

"No, he was perfectly calm. Smiling. No rancor, nothing. He offered to show me around the Apostolic Palace one day. I still haven't been there."

I watched as Cicioni powered along with lengthy strides toward St. Anne's Gate. He was in such a hurry to reach that refuge that I asked myself, not for the first time, how an entire community could have been so cowed into silence about such a traumatic event.

CHAPTER EIGHT

"FOLLOW ME!" the doctor to the dead shouted against the wind and the rain before he hopped back into his silver Rover and swung out from the grassy verge. With wisps of hair sticking out at crazy angles after his tussle with the Welsh weather, Professor Bernard Knight, distinguished forensic pathologist and veteran of countless causes célèbres, sped off toward the country pub he had chosen as the setting for his dissection of the case of the Swiss Guard.

I had traveled to Cardiff to meet Knight in frustration at the wall of silence I had come up against in the Vatican. Even though it had declared the case closed, the Vatican was still refusing to release the files of its inquiry. They did not want to give anyone a chance to challenge the original findings, which were destined to yellow over the ages on a shelf of the Secret Archives.

But if the original reports by the forensic scientists whom the Vatican had hired, and sworn to secrecy, were not available for scrutiny, a summary of their findings certainly was. The summary had been published when the case was officially closed, as part of the final Vatican statement on its internal investigation. It included references to the autopsies as well as to the results of ballistics and toxicological tests. When I contacted him from Rome, Knight agreed to study the documents for me.

As we sat down to lunch at the Unicorn Inn, which smelled of pipe tobacco, beer, and roast meat, Knight told me about the first time that he had rubbed shoulders with the Vatican. Italian prosecutors had hired him for an exhumation and autopsy on the body of Roberto Calvi, the Italian financier known as "God's Banker" because of his links to the Vatican. Ever since Calvi was found hanging under Blackfriars Bridge in London in 1982, investigators have debated whether he was killed or commited suicide.

"I went to the Milan mortuary's Christmas party; it happened to be on the same day as Calvi's autopsy," Knight confided cheerily. "Had a good laugh. Of course the party wasn't held in the mortuary; it was in a hotel."

As we sat wedged between a drafty bay window and a corner table as far away as I could manage from the pub's regulars—sport jackets, twin sets, and pearls clustered around the shoulder-high fireplace—the bespectacled professor spoke in a voice barely above a whisper. There was a piece of sticky plaster wrapped around the tip of his ring finger.

No, he answered when I couldn't resist asking, he hadn't cut himself while cutting up a corpse, but on his farm. He hadn't done an autopsy for some time. Calvi's was only one of some thirty thousand bodies that Knight has dissected in his time. His most notorious case is the Fred and Rosemary West murders, when he personally dug up twelve bodies in what the tabloids christened "the House of Horrors."

"It wasn't anything to write home about, scientifically. Just put the bits together and wrote up the report," he said dismissively.

Despite an intensely busy career, Knight had found time to write not only authoritative textbooks on forensic pathology but also medieval thrillers. The novel he was working on now was a parody of the legend of King Arthur, set in an apocalyptic future, after 95 percent of the British population is killed by a pandemic.

Knight pulled out a copy of the Vatican report that I had sent him and laid it on the table. Then he stroked a paragraph in the text with the point of his knife. His voice rose slightly. "The sin of my profession—I've battled against it all my life—overinterpretation," he said. The object of his irritation was the attempt by the Vatican-appointed experts to describe how Estermann, Meza Romero, and Tornay had been hit by the bullets.

"Bunch of prima donnas. These people read too much into it. Angle of shot is a very delicate subject. Often, in trials, the lawyers especially will ask was the killer tall or was he short. But you can't say. The autopsy only shows you the direction of the wound related to the anatomical landmarks. It doesn't tell you where the landmarks were at the time. It's quite possible that Estermann was sitting down, watching TV or whatever, but you can't know for certain. If the bullet hit his left cheekbone and came out of his neck, that doesn't mean you can draw a straight line through the entry and exit points that goes back to the weapon. Bullets get deflected inside bodies, they turn at right angles. You see so many weird things."

Knight sliced into the breast of his roast chicken and skewered a couple of fries. "And they've got no evidence for the sequence of the shots, it's just guesswork. Reasonable, but just an assumption. All you can say with any certainty is that the last shot was the one Tornay fired at himself."

"So are the forensic experts writing this way because they want to wrap up everything neatly? Or because they were told to do so by the Vatican?" I asked.

"A lot of doctors think they're Sherlock Holmes. That's their ethos. These chaps here are building a scenario; it's almost like a novel. They're making it up as they go along. There's a hell of a difference between the standard of proof needed for a criminal conviction and an airy-fairy scenario construction like this. For a criminal case, the standard of proof is 'beyond reasonable doubt.' In a coroner's court, it's a balance of probabilities, but a coroner wouldn't be allowed to express an opinion on culpability. All he could say would be 'murder by persons unknown.' Sometimes you can tell the sequence of events by estimating the time of death, but you can never get to within four or five hours."

"But the Vatican said in Tornay's death certificate that he died between eight-thirty and nine P.M. That's much more precise," I objected.

"That's too close. You can't do that. Anybody who gives a time of death within a fraction of an hour establishes himself as an idiot," Knight said, his light green eyes smoldering through his bifocals.

"This isn't just any doctor," I said. "This is Dr. Renato Buzzonetti, the pope's personal physician." Director of the Vatican health services for the past two decades, Dr. Buzzonetti was a trusted servant, always in attendance on papal journeys, clutching the briefcase that contained the medicine for Parkison's disease and other ailments, as well as small pouches of blood, should the pope need an emergency transfusion.

But Knight was not the type to genuflect before the Vatican hierarchy. "It's impossible. Believe me, I wrote the only book in English on estimating the time of death. It's three hundred pages long, and more or less it says you can't do it. The bracket is never less than four hours. You can refine it by other methods a bit, like putting drops in the eyes or giving the muscles electric shocks, but that is not usually acceptable."

I glanced at a young couple who had sat down at the next table. But Knight spoke so softly there was little risk of our being overheard. He was completely concentrated on the case at hand, his right forearm resting on the table, one hand placed on top of the other, as if he were leaning on the edge of the witness stand as he addressed a courtroom.

It was Knight's turn to ask a question: "When did the first pathologists arrive on the scene?"

"The Vatican said four hours after the bodies were discovered," I said.

"That's a very long time by our standards. The best they could have done would have been to get the bodies to the mortuary and estimate the time of death there. Then, on a scientific basis, they could have said the time of death was between eight o'clock in the evening and midnight. You don't let witnesses or anything else influence you."

I asked him about the Vatican's report that the exit hole of the bullet that had gone through Tornay's head was smaller than the point of entry in his mouth. I told him that some Italian newspapers had speculated excitedly that perhaps Tornay had been shot in the back of the head by a mysterious killer.

"Exit wounds are usually bigger, but not necessarily. I saw a case once years ago of a man who had three bullet holes in him from just one bullet. He was shot in the front, the bullet came out the back, hit the wall, and went back in again. The exit hole was tiny because his body had been pressed against the wall. And I've seen women shot through the chest; the exit hole in the back is very small because the bra holds the tissues very tight. Skin is elastic: when a bullet goes through, the skin stretches and then its elasticity shuts down again. Like a diaphragm in the lens of a camera."

"What are you saying? That Tornay did shoot himself in the mouth even though the bullet hole in the back of the head was smaller than the bullet hole in the mouth?"

"That's right. It's perfectly possible that he had a seven-millimeter hole in the skin at the back of his head from a nine-millimeter bullet. I've never heard of a murder committed by shooting someone in the mouth. And if someone had tried to manhandle him to shoot him in the mouth, there would be bruises and signs of restraint. The only logical reason to say there was or was not another killer is concrete evidence. There is no concrete evidence that there was another killer, so that's the end of that one. I don't think much of the way the Vatican conducted its investigation, but the evidence we've got is that Tornay killed the Estermanns and then he killed himself."

Knight put down his knife and fork, cocked his right index finger and thumb in the shape of a gun, and placed the index finger in front of his mouth. Thankfully, the couple next to us was absorbed in its food.

Knight was following his own line of thought: "The way Tornay shot himself . . . Whether he died instantly or not depends on what you mean by death. He certainly becomes totally immobilized, but his heart might beat for another twenty minutes. Death is a process, not an event. Your skin, for example; it lives on for another two days. Death is what you make of it."

The draft from the bay window suddenly felt more chilly. But the professor had not quite finished: "There's one last thing I noticed. Something odd. They mention possible addiction to cannabis. But as far as I know, cannabis makes you more benign rather than more aggressive. But I'm not a toxicologist."

Throughout our talk, Knight had spoken with clinical detachment. He had betrayed no reluctance to discuss the impact of bullets on the victims' insides. Our meal over, I asked him if he ever got squeamish.

"It's a process of natural selection really. If you get squeamish you don't do this job in the first place. Or you commit suicide. Take your pick. Half a dozen of my British colleagues have commited suicide, including a couple who were friends."

Knight answered my question before I could phrase it: "No, I never thought of committing suicide. I had too many interests. The books, the farm, the tractor."

He rubbed at a few stains that lunch had left on the Vatican report and pocketed it as we got up to leave. I insisted: "It never got to you? No nightmares?"

"Too busy, I'm hyperactive." He checked himself: "All pathologists get nightmares. You get these strange dreams that you are doing a post-mortem on a member of your family. Except that they are still alive. And you've got a deadline, you've got only five minutes left to sew them up again."

✦

AS I DROVE BACK to London, I mulled over Knight's evaluation. "Bunch of prima donnas . . . an airy-fairy scenario construction." His commentary amounted to a devastating critique of the Vatican's inquiry by a respected authority, delivered with as much daintiness as if Knight had been on his tractor plowing a field. In its eagerness to "sanctify" the version of events that was released within hours of the deaths, the inquiry had constructed a scenario that, from a forensic point of view, would not pass muster in a court of law.

Spurred on by Knight's last piece of advice, I decided to look into the effects of cannabis. In the extracts from the final report by the investigating magistrate, the Vatican had reported that the autopsy found traces of a derivative of cannabis in Tornay's urine, but not in his blood. This, the Vatican explained, meant that he had not smoked cannabis in the three hours before his death, and therefore did not present acute symptoms linked to such a drug.

But a search of Tornay's flat, it was claimed, had found twenty-four cigarette butts in a drawer, and tests revealed clear traces of cannabis derivatives. For that reason, the inquiry refused to rule out his being a chronic user, in which case he would have been vulnerable to hallucinations, delusions, and paranoid feelings. He would have suffered from anxiety, panic, and loss of insight. All of which, for the Vatican, fit Tornay's behavior in the last hour of his life.

For an independent assessment of the Vatican's analysis, I contacted the Forensic Science Service in London, an executive agency of the Home Office that undertakes both defense and police work. The forensic toxicologist I was put in touch with, Andrew Clatworthy, was refreshingly blunt in his put-down.

"The Vatican's conclusions don't fit the data it supplies," he explained. "You can and should rule out Tornay being a chronic taker of cannabis because his blood didn't test positive. In chronic users, both the blood and the urine test positive, not just the urine, as in Tornay's case. The fact that the Vatican says he had not smoked cannabis in the last three hours is further evidence that he was an occasional user. The consensus is that with an occasional smoker, you can only detect a positive result for a three-hour period."

I put Knight's point to him. "Even if Tornay had been under the influence of cannabis, would that have made him more violent?"

"Cannabis gives you a sense of euphoria, of well-being. It relieves inhibitions; it can make you giggly and very talkative. The panic and paranoia which the Vatican mentions are rare, and for them to happen you'd have to smoke a lot of it. And how did they know the cigarettes were his? Did they do a DNA test? There's no mention of one."

So much for papal infallibility. Tornay had not been an addict—and even if he had been, this would have shed little light on his supposed "fit of madness." There was nothing crazy or homicidal about cannabis smokers, who were so well tolerated in Switzerland that the government decreed that the practice be legalized, as medical studies had shown that cannabis was no more damaging to health than alcohol or tobacco.

Which left one final piece to the puzzle assembled by the Vatican, the last element that it had put forward as an explanation for Tornay's act. This was the cyst "the size of a pigeon's egg," or more precisely four by two and a half centimeters, which had been found in the left frontal lobe of his brain.

To explain the cyst's effects on human behavior, the investigators had turned to an authoritative tome, *Principles of Neurology* by R.D. Adams and M. Victor. The inquiry report quoted it briefly as saying that the left frontal lobe was traditionally called the "organ of civilization." Tumors in this part of the brain caused "impairment of cognitive function" and "disinhibition of behavior." This, the inquiry said, had prompted Tornay to quarrel with Estermann, and to twice spend the night outside the Vatican without permission.

With the help of the publishers of the book, McGraw-Hill in New York, I obtained a copy of the passage that the Vatican had quoted, from the same edition it had used. I soon found that the Vatican had been so selective in its quotations as to be misleading. Small lesions, according to the volume's authors, had no detectable effect on behavior. Even large lesions could be so subtle as to escape detection unless the patient was studied at home or in the workplace—which had not been the case of Tornay. In those cases where an effect on behavior had been detected, the most common was lack of initiative. Patients displayed "an idleness of thought, speech and action," and their spirits rose "with increased talkativeness and a tendency to joke."

Hardly a condition that would prompt murderous behavior.

CHAPTER NINE

FROM THE START of my inquiries, I had tried to establish contact with Opus Dei. But the movement's headquarters in Rome, at the Villa Tevere, had rejected my repeated requests to discuss Estermann's involvement, or even the extent of its support within the Church in general and the Vatican in particular. The law of silence in an institution dubbed the "Holy Mafia" is as unbreakable as among the Cosa Nostra mobsters of Sicily.

The only confirmation of the Estermann couple's link to Opus Dei had come from Alberto Vollmer Herrera, who as the Venezuelan ambassador to the Holy See had been Meza Romero's employer. He told me, when I managed to ambush him at a conference at the papal auditorium, that the Estermanns were "friends" of Opus Dei, but refused to discuss this in any detail.

It was while I was still in London that I found a former member of Opus Dei willing to receive me, Monsignor Vladimir Felzmann. I had seen him quoted by one interviewer as saying that the group was the closest the Church had come to re-creating the military orders of the Middle Ages—a particularly appealing image for "God's Fifth Column," I imagined, to a man like Estermann. I wanted to learn from him what Opus Dei could have meant to both Estermann and Tornay. He readily agreed to meet me when I telephoned him.

When I arrived at Archbishop's House, near Victoria Station, on a rainy Sunday, Felzmann was despite the foul weather waiting for me under the porch. A long, lanky man with a rubberlike face and a bald head shaped like an egg, he cautioned me cheerfully as he showed me into a spacious office on the ground floor: "Don't think this is mine; I only have a hole in the cellar. But the financial secretary lets me use this place when he is not here."

Although it was mid-morning, it was so dark outside that he flicked a light switch. The neon lighting buzzed quietly into life. We settled into two high-backed striped armchairs by the empty fireplace, Felzmann sitting down promptly when he caught me staring at a cushion on his chair. The cushion was cardinal-red and featured a pair of golf clubs. Just before he sat down, I barely had time to make out the motto stitched in cream lettering: MY HEART IS WITH GOD BUT MY BODY IS ON THE GOLF COURSE.

Behind the desk hung a framed photograph of Cormac Murphy-O'Connor, the archbishop of Westminster who just that morning back in St. Peter's Square was being made a cardinal by the pope. Among those also given the silk biretta, or three-ridged cardinal's hat, was a member of Opus Dei, the Lima archbishop Juan Luis Cipriani

Thorne—the first member made into a prince of the Church, courtesy of John Paul II.

Felzmann told me he had been born into a privileged Czech family with a diplomatic tradition. His grandfather had served as ambassador to Brussels and his father as first secretary in London. But the family lost everything it owned when the Communists seized Prague in 1948, prompting his father to resign and turn overnight from promising diplomat to political refugee.

Felzmann was nine years old at the time, and his religious vocation combined with the tragedy of the Communist takeover made him easy prey for Opus Dei. It held him for twenty-two years, until he left in 1982 and joined the Westminster diocese, where he works as the chaplain for young people.

I asked Felzmann how he had been recruited.

"Dead easy. I was on a Holy Week students' walk, I was barely twenty, and a man sidled up to me and became friendly. He turned out to be a member of Opus Dei. They use friendship as a bait. For me that's a terrible thing, because friendship is one of the greatest gifts that God gives you. Josemaría Escrivá de Balaguer, the founder, always told us that you have to be like an underwater diver, get in close to the fish you want to catch, and then shoot your harpoon.

"My father died of a heart attack; he was on holiday in Cornwall. I was only twenty-one at the time. Escrivá became a father figure for me. In those days, he was known as the Father to members, now he's Our Father in Heaven. He came often to London, and he was very affectionate toward me. I was director of Netherhall House, the main Opus Dei residence in Britain. I think Escrivá took pity on me. He saw I was in need of affection. He liked the fact that I was from a good family; that was important for him."

"Why did he call you to Rome?"

"He asked me to come to Villa Tevere, the Opus Dei headquarters in Rome, to study for the priesthood. I was useful to him in all sorts of ways. I was considered to be his right-hand man. I'd studied civil engineering at Imperial College, so he asked me to put in microphones behind the pictures hanging on the walls so that everything could be taped."

Felzmann sat back to enjoy my look of astonishment and pointed at a landscape painting above the fireplace. "Don't worry, I've switched that one off." He grinned.

It was the first I'd heard of Escrivá's interest in bugging devices. "He put bugs in his own office?" I asked, wondering to myself whether the fortress-like Villa Tevere was still as wired up as the Watergate building had once been.

"No, no, in the interview room where he would meet people. The reason he gave was that all records had to be completely accurate, and he didn't want to be accused of saying anything he hadn't said."

"But his guests had no idea they were being recorded?"

"Of course not."

We sat in silence for a short while, the only noise the engine of a taxi, the wheels swishing through the puddles. Glancing through the tall windows, I noticed the pub across the street was called the Cardinal.

I wanted to find out more about Escrivá. His beatification, the last step before sainthood, had been bitterly disputed, and Felzmann was among those who had tried to submit critical evidence to the Vatican. The attempt failed. "You said Escrivá was a father figure for you. Was he very charismatic?" I asked.

"He had a mixture of qualities which were almost contradictory, but taken together, they added up to leadership quality. He could be very affectionate, very gentle, but on the other hand he could be extremely hard. If anyone disobeyed him in the slightest, they were kicked out of Rome. He could shout like anything. If he found a door that was locked when it shouldn't be, he would kick and bang on the damn thing until someone opened it. Once he said to me, 'Vlad'—he always called me Vlad—'when I'm dead and people ask you how the Father was, tell them that he knew how to laugh, but he also knew how to shout.' After his death, Opus Dei said that he was always patient and always smiling."

He had held his palms upward as he made this last remark, rolling his eyes to the strip of neon with mock piety.

"Doesn't sound like a very charismatic character," I said.

His palms slapped down onto his thighs. "Oh, but he was. Escrivá was totally focused on building a sense of family in the people around him. He was totally committed to the growth of Opus Dei because he was convinced that it represented the salvation of the Church. It was the most crystalline, the purest form of Christianity, and he had received it as a direct inspiration from God. There's no doubt about it: he saw himself as the twentieth-century reincarnation of the word 'God.' A messiah, sent by God. You did what he said, you were guaranteed heaven. It was that absolute. As the father said in Spanish, *todo o nada*—all or nothing."

"You must have had your doubts."

"The thing that most stuck in my mind was a remark he made about Adolf Hitler. We were watching a film about the war and the gas chambers once, we were checking whether it was suitable for members to see it, and during the intermission he turned to me."

Felzmann leaned forward conspiratorially and dropped his voice. "The founder said to me: 'Vlad, Hitler couldn't have been such a bad person. He couldn't have killed six million. It couldn't have been more than four million.'"

Felzmann arched his eyebrows and sat up straight again. "Mad. I didn't say anything at the time, of course. The founder wasn't the kind of chap you contradict. But I could just feel that Hitler was one of his heroes, and he couldn't believe that Hitler had really done that. He just couldn't be anti-Hitler."

"Surely you told the Vatican about this when it was preparing to beatify Escrivá? What did the—"

Felzmann interrupted with a shout: "Of course I did! I told them, but they wouldn't listen. It's a perfect catch-22. As they see it, anyone who leaves Opus Dei is tainted and biased by antagonism toward the movement. Therefore, everything that person says has no value. The only evidence that was allowed was all in the founder's favor."

As I listened to Felzmann, the image of Opus Dei that stuck in my mind was of a legion of holy warriors, knights of the faith fighting a modern crusade. Perhaps a corps like the Swiss Guard, a military body at the heart of the Vatican, could be made part of such a grand design.

I told him what Tornay's mother had said to me about Estermann's links to Opus Dei and his attempts to recruit guards into the movement.

Felzmann nodded. "Estermann would be of great interest to Opus Dei. Escrivá's view was that if you had the head of an organization, you had everything. It was part of his notion of control. With Estermann in its grip, Opus Dei would be able to find out how the pope was, and who he saw from day to day. It would be privy to quite a few secrets about the cardinals, their health, that kind of thing. And among the cardinals is John Paul's successor. Never forget that for Opus Dei, knowledge is power. It would be able to get anyone into the Vatican; the guards wouldn't breathe a word. You have access, you have freedom.

"It's also a question of status. Estermann would have appealed because of his rank. Opus Dei likes titles. The founder fought a long battle to get a title for himself, that of marquis of Peralta. That was very important to him. He was after the aristocracy of blood, intellect, and money."

"Apart from Estermann, why would the other guards be of interest to Opus Dei?" I asked.

"They fit in absolutely, they would be ideal fodder. They're all young, and they're all supposed to have a strong religious commitment. The way Opus Dei would handle it would be to come in offering spiritual guidance, to help the young men be closer to God. It would teach them that the world would be a better place if they said their rosaries rather than going into the Eternal City and watching large-buttocked women and dreaming about them."

"Aren't the guards a bit too young to be recruited?"

"Quite the contrary. When I was a member, Opus Dei would take teenagers as young as fourteen, and they had to make a lifelong commitment to the movement. Minors are still instructed not to tell their parents about Opus Dei because they wouldn't understand. I get worried when parents come to me, saying something strange is happening to their son, he's left home and he won't speak to them. The founder used to say that a vocation was like an embryo, you had to protect it in the womb until it was strong enough to be born. At twenty-one you're ready to make your final vows."

The more Felzmann described the workings of Opus Dei, the clearer it became to me why Tornay would have found so much to dislike in it. Tornay's religious commitment was not the kind that could be exploited by Opus Dei. The fact that he "loved life" and was "full of joy"—as the former commander Buchs had said—was at odds with its shady practices. If Tornay's first loyalty was to the Swiss Guard and to the pope, he would not have accepted Estermann's attempts to recruit new members in the barracks.

"Tornay was twenty-three when he died, and he'd tried to find out about Opus Dei's real activities. What chances did he have?" I asked.

"Opus Dei is like a fire. If you get close you can get warm; if you get inside you can get burned. Tornay didn't stand a chance."

"Why not?"

Felzmann brought his hands up to his chin, the tips of his index fingers pressing against the corners of his mouth. "Because Opus Dei is a culture built on a foundation of fear, deceit, and paranoia. It was born under the terrible threat from communism. To survive, it had to hide, to pretend, to lie. Outsiders have no right to know anything about it. It's Orwellian, it rewrites history: pages are torn out of old internal pamphlets and new pages are stuck in to fit the current think-ing. Its members go to confession only with priests who are also mem-bers of Opus Dei. They believe that any means more or less justifies the end. And now it is one of the strongest powers in the Vatican, thanks in no small degree to the pope himself."

When the future pope was still a cardinal, and only days before the conclave from which he emerged pope, he visited the Villa Tevere headquarters to pray before the tomb of Escrivá. After his election, he granted Opus Dei the unique status of personal prelature, putting the head of the movement on a par with bishops, effectively answerable only to Rome. John Paul then pushed through the beatification of Escrivá, which took place only seventeen years after his death, a record for modern times. Cardinal Sodano, the secretary of state, showed equal enthusiasm for the cause, sending a circular to hundreds of bish-ops urging them to write to Rome to lobby for the ceremony. It was also John Paul who, as I talked with Felzmann in London, was giving one of its members a seat in the next conclave. It was hard to imagine what more John Paul II could have done for Opus Dei.

John Paul's benevolence contrasted with the wariness of his prede-cessors. Paul VI had seen Opus Dei as suspect, and feared that its priests within the Vatican were leaking confidential decisions to Escrivá, who, aware of the pope's hostility, had raged at what he branded "the rotting, something evil, coming from within the Church and from high up." The mystical body of Christ, he thundered, "is like a cadaver in malodorous putrefaction."

"What is it about Opus Dei that attracts John Paul?" I asked.

"The pope isn't a member, but they have a a lot in common, starting with the cult of the Virgin Mary. And the values of discipline, hierarchy, orthodoxy—all of which, by the way, would have also appealed to someone like Estermann. The pope is convinced that God has chosen him to lead the Church into the millennium, and Opus Dei believes the same thing about itself. Both are right-wing; they hate communism. Which explains why the pope turned to Opus Dei rather than the Jesuits. The Jesuits were too left-wing and too much into liberation theology."

"What do you mean, 'turned to Opus Dei'? The pope is actively involved with it?"

"Of course he is. In all sorts of ways. He wanted to learn Spanish before his first trip to Mexico. So a Spanish priest from Opus Dei had breakfast with him every morning. Money? We used to bank with Banco Ambrosiano; I used to deposit money in our account there. When the pope had to find two hundred million dollars that Calvi, 'God's Banker,' owed the Vatican in 1982, Opus Dei came up with it. And at that time Opus Dei was made a personal prelature. When the pope wanted a new spokesman, Opus Dei gave him Navarro-Valls. And all the time there is Opus Dei's hidden agenda, to grow and grow and grow. There are people in the Vatican who can't stand it, but that hasn't stopped Opus Dei from getting more and more powerful. Of course it would love an Opus Dei pope."

Navarro-Valls was the most visible manifestation of Opus Dei's power in the Vatican. "How can someone like Navarro-Valls be loyal to both the pope and Opus Dei? Isn't he serving two masters, even if the pope likes Opus Dei?" I asked.

Felzmann frowned, the wrinkles etching across his forehead in deep uneven lines. "Navarro-Valls has two masks. He lives in Villa Tevere, and every so often he has to meet his director there. That's an obligation for all members of Opus Dei. Navarro-Valls has to tell him about his job, about his concerns. Something like: 'The pope is not as well as he should be, but I am telling the world that he is healthy. Should I worry about this?' The director will absolve him, tell him that he's doing the right thing, for the good of the Church."

Felzmann continued. "I knew Navarro-Valls more than thirty years ago, when he was a journalist in Barcelona. Arrogant chap. He was so arrogant he was totally relaxed. I taught him English and he taught me tennis. I remember what he told me about serving. He told me to place the ball and throw the racket at it. And it worked."

He jumped up to demonstrate, his long arms swinging through the air and knocking against the armchair. Then he flopped down again.

"Of course Navarro-Valls was awfully committed to Opus Dei. He was very fond of the founder; he was a figure of authority for him. Psychologically, Opus Dei creates a childlike dependence. When we went to have a shower after a game, I saw that Navarro-Valls had a brown mark around his thigh. It was the mark of the *cilicio,* the chain-mail band that he wore for up to two hours a day. That's a requirement for members. It's got pointed metal spikes fixed to it; they scratch the skin and make you bleed. It's supposed to be worn tight during Lent. Members also whip themselves; it's up to you how much. Christ on the Cross showed his love by suffering, so you should do the same thing. At least, that's the argument. But the truth is, creating suffering for yourself artificially is pointless. It doesn't achieve spirituality; it's a form of arrogance."

The gruesome practices had been pioneered by Escrivá. The walls of his bathroom were said to have been constantly bloodstained because of his feverish self-flagellations with a meter-long whip, similar to a cat-o'-nine-tails to which fragments of razor blades had been attached.

Felzmann smiled apologetically and pointed to his watch. As we stood up, I asked him to sum up for me what had persuaded him to leave the movement.

"I came to realize that in Opus Dei there are lies, there is fear, and there is control. It's a sect; you're told that your director is your line of communication from the founder, and therefore from God. You're taught to accept what you are told. To criticize is to show pride, and that is a sin. Looking back, that was my weakness—not understanding early enough that God wants us to say things as they are."

"How difficult was it to get out?"

"Very. Opus Dei and God were identical in my mind. I was pretty screwed up inside. I was hurting. When I first said I wanted to leave, I was put under huge pressure. I was told that I was being tempted by the Devil. They took me to see the grave of a former member who was so depressed after he'd left that he stopped taking the medicine he was supposed to take for his heart condition. It was a passive suicide. I was told that I should pray for his soul. That was their way of warning me. Rule by fear."

Felzmann strode ahead of me down the hallway, down the staircase flanked with green stone columns, and past a nun who sat by the door in a wooden reception booth so dark I had not noticed it on my way in. As I walked out into the rain, he popped his head around the door. "God bless!" he shouted after me.

The next day I bought an Italian newspaper to find out what the pope had said in St. Peter's Square to his partners in crimson, the first cardinals of the new millennium who would join the world's most exclusive club, from which his successor would be chosen. The pope, whose white robes symbolize innocence and charity, exhorted his "venerated brothers" never to forget that the color of their new gowns was the color of martyrdom—"a symbol of the ardent fire of love for the Church which must feed in you the readiness, if necessary, to bear supreme witness to it with your blood."

The pope's remark reminded me not only of Felzmann's comments on the physical tortures imposed on Opus Dei members, but also of the Swiss Guard's oath to sacrifice themselves for the pope if necessary.

CHAPTER TEN

FROM LONDON, I traveled to Paris to meet a French author, Gérard de Villiers, who had spent some time researching the Swiss Guard deaths to draw inspiration for the latest installment in his best-selling series of thrillers, featuring a CIA spy with the code name SAS. There are enough erotic embraces in the book, *SAS: L'Espion du Vatican* (The Vatican Spy) to ensure it is read inside the Vatican with as much stealth as a heretic tract. But even more immoral for the men of the cloth is De Villiers's plot, which features a fanatical and homicidal priest called Father Hubertus Ramstein.

The thriller opens with Father Hubertus shooting Stephan Martigny, a young member of the Swiss Guard, then the corps' commander and his wife. Martigny's death is staged to make it appear a suicide, and Martigny is blamed for the murders of the commander and his wife. Hubertus is "a zealot, an apprentice martyr who literally burns with exaltation," and he "travels the world like a secret Crusader." Sensitive missions are his province, including monitoring the spread of Opus Dei within the Vatican, a task for which he has recruited Martigny.

Gradually the truth emerges: Martigny was sacrificed on the orders of a Spanish monsignor who wanted the commander dead. The monsignor had feared that the commander would expose his bartering of Vatican secrets for amorous favors from a blond employee of Vatican Radio's Bulgarian service.

De Villiers has taken more than a few liberties with the Swiss Guard deaths, but the similarities are umistakable. He names the young guard Stephan Martigny (Martigny is the name of the Swiss town where Tornay is buried) and leaves readers in little doubt as to who is the inspiration for Father Hubertus. The middle letters of the latter's name—HuBERtus—echo the name of Father BERtorello, who told Tornay's mother that her son was murdered. And Hubertus is Martigny's father confessor—Bertorello was Tornay's spiritual adviser. I wondered how much the unflattering portrayal of Hubertus mirrored Bertorello's real nature, and whether De Villiers could, and would, lead me to him.

When I called De Villiers, I suggested we meet for lunch near the former wholesale market of Les Halles. He didn't like that idea. "Yuck. That area gives me the creeps; I prefer the eighth or the sixteenth arrondissements," he replied, choosing two of the most chic districts in Paris. He named a place near the Arc de Triomphe.

Although I turned up early, there was already a sign on the door of Le Gourmet des Ternes: COMPLET. But when I looked inside, only a couple of tables were taken. I mentioned De Villiers's name to the waiter and was promptly given a table. "We only take regulars at lunchtime, and Gérard is a regular," the waiter explained. By the time an S-type black Jaguar drew up and a chauffeur jumped out to open the car door for De Villiers, the restaurant was indeed *complet*.

Friendly and talkative, the silver-haired De Villiers is a former journalist who covered Vietnam and the war of independence in Algeria. He told me he turned to writing thrillers when a publisher asked him to create a new spy to "replace" James Bond after the death of 007's creator, Ian Fleming. Over the past three decades, De Villiers has churned out more than four SAS books a year, selling 1.5 million copies annually. *SAS: L'Espion du Vatican* was his 132nd.

"There are several strands to this story," he announced out of the blue after chatting with the waiter and the owner of the restaurant. "First things first. Estermann was recruited by the Stasi, the secret police of East Germany. When a Polish pope was elected, the Soviets got really angry; the KGB was ticked off for failing to prevent it. As if they could. Anyway, the gentlemen of the KGB were told to get into the Vatican pretty damn quick and recruit agents. Estermann was picked up by the Stasi when he was still in Switzerland, but when he moved to the Vatican a couple of years later, the Communists couldn't believe their luck.

"Second, Bertorello had taken Tornay under his wing. Bertorello is the most interesting character in this affair. He's from a rich family; to my knowledge he's a priest. He certainly dresses like a priest. He's only thirty-five, but the Vatican hires him for secretive diplomatic missions. It sent him to Armenia, Bosnia, Africa, even South Korea. He's a member of the Fir Forest, that's the name Pope Pius X gave to the Vatican's intelligence service. Like a fir, because the branches stretch out horizontally in all directions. He was also charged by some bishop or other to spy on the Swiss Guard and find out how, and how much, Opus Dei was penetrating it. He was paid to draw up files on all the guards and ferret out their sympathy with Opus Dei. Bertorello used Tornay to find out which guards were close to Opus Dei. Tornay was glad to help—he was in a minority as a French speaker, and he was hated by Estermann."

De Villiers appeared to know more about Bertorello than anyone I had come across. I could guess at the answer, but I asked anyway: "How do you know all this?"

"Bertorello told me, I met him several times. It was hard work pulling him in; I checked him out first. He told me some very detailed stuff about the clans in Armenia, about the rivalries there. My mates in French intelligence told me it was all true. Bertorello taught me a lot about the Vatican. It's a closed world, full of intrigue and ferocious power struggles. They bury secrets like they bury the dead. They could massacre each other to the last priest in there, but for the Italian cops outside, it would still be on another planet. I made Bertorello into a murderer in my book, a particularly twisted one. He wasn't too pleased about it, which is hardly surprising."

"Why did Bertorello tell Tornay's mother that her son had been murdered?"

De Villiers paused only long enough to flick a crumb off his blue and gold Hermès tie. There was a hint of caginess in his eyes when he looked up. "I think you'll find he didn't say exactly that. He's a spy; he was ambiguous in what he told the mother. He said nothing that could prompt the mother to suspect something. The best thing would be for you to try to talk to Bertorello."

I wondered what kind of priest, and envoy to the ends of Christendom, could inspire such strong feelings in two people he had met— a mother convinced he had the key to her son's murder, and an author who fictionalized him as a multiple murderer. I was unsure about asking De Villiers to contact Bertorello on my behalf. Perhaps Bertorello was angry with him about the book and would not welcome a request from him. But I did not have any other way of reaching Bertorello. "Could you put me in touch with him?" I asked.

"Sure, after lunch," he said. It sounded so easy.

When the waiter brought us coffee, De Villiers surprised me by saying that he had worked for the French secret service in North Africa after his national military service. We were among the last to leave the restaurant. I followed him out and stood waiting as he eased himself into his car. He saw me standing there, motioned that I should get in, too, and told the driver to take us to his home.

In the wood-paneled study of his duplex apartment on the classy Avenue Foch, a short drive away on the other side of the Arc de Triomphe, De Villiers sat down at his desk and searched for his address book. While he rummaged in the drawers, one hand stroking his Siamese cat, I looked around the room. Official proclamations from World War II and from the Algerian war of independence hung on the walls alongside erotic Japanese prints. But the most arresting object on display was a stylized gold statue of a woman sitting on a small rock. What was unusual about her was that she had conical breasts and that she cradled a machine gun that pointed upward from her crotch.

"German MP44," De Villiers explained. "The statue expresses my universe, pretty much."

He found the number for Bertorello's mobile telephone and dialed it, his other hand still stroking the Siamese cat, who purred elegantly. Then De Villiers grimaced. "Damn. Answering service. I'll leave a message." His message was brief and tongue-in-cheek: "It is possible that an individual will call you in my name. Give him the warmest welcome in the name of God, all-powerful and merciful."

❖

THE WELCOME WAS A LONG TIME COMING. Back in Rome, I waited a few days for Bertorello to call me back. He didn't. I kicked myself for not getting his number from De Villiers in Paris and telephoned him to ask him for it. Then I tried the number myself, but infuriatingly, Bertorello either kept his mobile telephone switched off or he was always somewhere where he could not be reached.

I had more success tracking down a retired head of the Italian secret service, whose name, surprisingly, was in the phone book, to his apartment in a Rome suburb. Over a generous tumbler of Croft port, he told me that he knew nothing about Bertorello. But he did know about the Vatican's intelligence activities, as he had worked closely with his counterparts in the Church.

It was possible, he told me, that Bertorello was one of the eager young clergymen who traveled the world on supposedly diplomatic missions. The Vatican had no secret service as such, but its network of sources—from priests to papal envoys with diplomatic passports, from monks to monsignori—reaching deep into any country where the Church had interests, was the envy of the CIA and MI6. "But let me tell you one thing," he said, "the Vatican itself is impenetrable. *Im-pene-trable.*" I left him feeling more dispirited than before, and hoped he was mistaken.

Several days passed before I finally heard Bertorello's voice. By then I knew his telephone number by heart. I introduced myself, and told him that I was writing a book about the Vatican—given Bertorello's fondness for the shadows, it was best to remain vague for the time being. I mentioned that De Villiers had given me the number, but added that unlike him I was not planning to do a work of fiction. Could we meet?

Bertorello was silent for a few moments. It was obvious that I would be doing most of the talking for some time to come.

"How did you know I was in Rome?" he asked. His voice sounded wary.

"I didn't. I just dialed your mobile phone number."

"Did you travel recently to a French province?"

I was baffled by his bizarre questioning. "Only to Paris," I replied.

"Good. You see, I know that some scandal-seeking journalists have been looking for me, including one who bothered my parents in the south of France. Call me back in ten days' time."

He hung up before I could reply. Perhaps he needed time to check my background.

But the next time we spoke, he asked me whether I was accredited with the Vatican's press office, a question which implied that he hadn't done much research. I told him that I was accredited, but that I was interested in writing a book, not a newspaper article. I told him that De Villiers had told me of his—Bertorello's—"sensitive" foreign missions.

"So you are also interested in the secret services?" he asked.

"Of course," I said. It was the first sign that he thought we might have something to talk about.

"Ah. But we won't talk about that on the telephone," he said, ignoring the fact that he had just done precisely that. He told me he was off to New York and asked me to call again in another two weeks.

Bertorello was indeed, as De Villiers had written of Father Hubertus in his book, "as slippery as an eel."

CHAPTER ELEVEN

WHEN I REACHED the immense Alexanderplatz in the former East Berlin, a bespectacled punk with a fluorescent-orange Mohican haircut and a studded collar sat on a low concrete wall on the edge of the square, nursing a can of beer. Although it was early June, it was cold and wet, and the low clouds made the square, with its Stalinesque architecture and grayness, all the uglier. A couple of streets away, billboards proclaimed the *Berliner Kurier* BERLIN'S BIGGEST NEWSPAPER and FULL OF LIFE! The posters were close to the newspaper's offices, a soulless high-rise building on an avenue broad enough for tanks to roll down several abreast.

I had flown to Berlin to talk to Peter Brinkmann, a senior journalist on the *Kurier*. Before Estermann was even buried, Brinkmann had written an article headlined POPE'S DEAD BODYGUARD WAS A STASI SPY, branding Estermann an agent of the East German secret police, or Stasi for short—one of some four hundred thousand informers who, at home and abroad, had spied on their colleagues, neighbors, friends, and even relatives.

According to the article, Estermann first approached the East German commercial affairs bureau in Switzerland in October 1979, when he was a twenty-five-year-old officer in an armored troops battalion of the Swiss army. Eight months later he signed a contract with the Stasi and was given the code name "Werder." Money was the reason behind his betrayal—a credible enough motive given the low wage that he earned after he joined the Swiss Guard in 1980.

The article was based on an anonymous letter, and was short on evidence. The only source was a former Stasi major identified only as "H. Sch. (age 57)," said to be the officer in charge of Werder. The newspaper had approached this mysterious figure, but he was quoted only as saying: "I had nothing to do with it." Apart from the lack of sources, there was plenty about the article that was puzzling. Why should Estermann, with his military background, have approached the commercial affairs bureau and not the East German embassy? There was no indication as to how much he had been paid or what information he was supposed to have supplied, and nothing on why he had stopped spying shortly after being promoted to the rank of major three years after joining the Guard.

From Brinkmann's office on the eighteenth floor, the view stretched over much of the city, from the flags over the Reichstag by the gaping wound of building sites left by the vanished Berlin Wall to the planes landing at Tegel Airport on the horizon. His wispy gray hair combed neatly over his bald pate, shirt straining across his belly, Brinkmann sat back and stuck his feet up on a bookshelf. I asked him whether I could take a look at the letter that had prompted his article.

"I threw it away," he replied with a smile, in slightly accented English.

I could not have thought of a worse start. The surprise must have shown on my face because he added hurriedly, his smile vanishing: "It was an anonymous letter, I was sure I wouldn't get anything more out of it. You'd be surprised at how many anonymous letters we get. I just wanted to clean out the old stuff."

I fumed inwardly as I glanced around the office, whose neatness suddenly struck me as obsessive. Old stuff indeed—a letter that had generated newspaper headlines across the world. "Do you have any idea who wrote the letter? Could it have been a prankster?" I asked.

"It was definitely not an outsider, and not a crazy guy. You have to understand that after the fall of the Wall in 1989, not all the Stasi people found new jobs. Those who retired got their pensions cut. Many want to make some money, and many know something interesting, but not quite enough to make a complete version, which they could sell to a newspaper for a decent sum. That's because of the way the Stasi worked; it was so compartmentalized. So these guys give you just a tidbit, a teaser. Then it's up to you to get extra details from the other people in the know. For me, that's what happened in the Estermann case: one guy knew a small part of the story and wanted it to come out."

"What was it about the letter that convinced you Estermann was a spy?"

"The fact that it gave such precise details, and the reason for Estermann working for the Stasi—money."

"What happened when you tried to verify what it said?"

"The Stasi guys clammed up. When this kind of stuff breaks, they phone each other, they say to each other: 'Shut your mouth.' If one of them starts to tell you the story, you have to go to the next guy, and the next. And the second or third guy you contact will just play dumb.

Usually if you want to get any further, you have to offer money, a lot of money. That's the only way you can solve the puzzle."

"How many people did you talk to?"

"A lot. None of the ones we spoke to denied it; they were very unsure. There was just one guy—I was told that he was the officer in charge of Werder—he told me that maybe Werder was Estermann."

"What was his name? In your article you mention a Stasi major; you don't give his name, but you call him only 'H. Sch.'" I handed him a copy of his article that I had brought with me.

Brinkmann read it through, then thrust it back to me. "I can't remember. I've thrown away all the names. And these guys are not in the phone book, you know."

I was making little progress fast. I tried a different approach. "Let's assume that the letter was a hoax. Do you have any idea why it was sent to you, and who might have wanted to play a trick on you?"

"I've thought about that, believe me. It's possible that one, or several, ex-Stasi guys got together and decided to do this letter to show the world how stupid newspapers are. They're very bitter about the way they were treated by the press after the Wall collapsed. I was working that beat at the time; I exposed a lot of Stasi people and what they had been up to. It's possible they wanted to get their own back on me. Call it a vendetta."

There was nothing more I could hope to obtain from Brinkmann, so I thanked him and got up. He put his hand out to stop me and fished in a drawer before pulling out a copy of his memoirs. He scrawled something on the title page and handed it to me. "I hope you will find out whether Werder was Estermann," he said. "We called our people off the story after a few weeks because it was taking up too much time and we were getting nowhere. It was costing too much, and we had no joy with trying to identify the Stasi spy in the Vatican."

Out in the street, I glanced at the inscription Brinkmann had written. It read: "Good luck in finding out more secrets." I wondered how much the Estermann story had cost the *Berliner Kurier,* and what my chances were of finding more pieces of the puzzle—without paying a pfennig for any of them.

❖

IF ANY DOCUMENTS testifying to Estermann's work for the Stasi had survived the collapse of the Wall, I was most likely to find them in the headquarters of the Gauck Authority, the commission set up by the government of the new, unified Germany to sift through the secrets of one of the cold war's most potent spying machines. The commission's job was no easy task. Placed back-to-back, the files were rumored—no one had been able to check—to form a continuous line more than a hundred miles long, and to include more than 40 million index cards. That amounted to more than twice the population of East Germany.

Feeling discouraged after seeing Brinkmann, I walked a few blocks and reached the lobby of the main Gauck building. There I met Rudiger Stang, a senior researcher at the commission with whom I had made an appointment. Stang, a slight, birdlike man with designer stubble on his gaunt face, took me up in the elevator and guided me through a series of corridors, each nightmarishly identical and sterile, as we weaved our way into the heart of the building.

We walked for some time, but met no one. As we trudged down the endless corridors, I learned that Stang had worked in a publishing house in East Germany before the Wall came down, checking translations of novels by authors from Bulgaria, a fellow-Soviet-bloc member. Now in his early forties, he was in charge of several research teams that focused on the Stasi's spying on various religious groups in East Germany and elsewhere, including the Catholic Church.

At last, Stang stopped to unlock the door to his office. It was bright and airy, with potted plants and neatly stored box files on the shelves.

Through the open window came the sound of children on a playground. It could have been the office of any mid-level civil servant, anywhere. There was no trace of the deceit and suffering, of the psychological and physical violence, that the files he spent his days studying must document.

On a square Formica table near his desk lay a thick file marked in big black letters: VATICAN. We sat on either side of the table. The folder, which I hoped would prove a Pandora's box of secrets, lay closer to him than to me. He opened the file a fraction, fished out the top piece of paper, and closed the file again.

"For you," he said. "The only document we found with Werder's details on it."

He noticed my bewilderment, and explained: "It's a copy of the index card that bears the agent's cover name, in this case Werder. It's part of a catalog known as F22. There's another index, F16, which is the most important one. Everything is in it. The real names of anyone on whom the Stasi has a file. That means all the agents, and all the victims of the Stasi's spying. Plus the details of what the Stasi did to these people."

I eyed Stang expectantly, but he disappointed me. He failed to pull out the appropriate document from the folder and instead said: "I'm sorry. The F16 reference to Werder is missing. It was probably destroyed when the people of East Berlin stormed the headquarters."

Much as Stang himself must have sympathized with the anger of his countrymen, who had set fire to piles of precious documents and sprawled graffiti proclaiming STASI-GESTAPO-KGB all over the Stasi headquarters when the Wall fell, I had the impression that he would have preferred an orderly handover of the hundreds of thousands of papers that now enabled him to make a living.

I looked more closely at the card that Stang had given me. I asked him about the number in the top right-hand corner of the card: XV/3764/79.

"That's the registration number under which all Werder's output was classified."

At last I was onto something. "Surely all we need to do is find the file which bears that registration number," I said.

Stang looked at me with a pitying expression. "That also is lost. But don't despair. There are some things that you may find useful."

The card described Werder as an IM, an *Inoffizielle Mitarbeiter* (unofficial collaborator), one of the tens of thousands of valuable informers who had helped to make the Stasi the most pervasive intelligence-gathering apparatus of Eastern Europe. The date of his recruitment was August 29, 1979—but the *Berliner Kurier,* I remembered, had given it as October 29, precisely two months later.

The card also showed that Werder had initially been attached to a section that looked after East Germany's central bank and other financial and economic institutions. This department, Stang assured me, had nothing to do with either military or religious institutions. Much later, in January 1985, Werder was transferred to the section responsible for counterintelligence.

I asked Stang what he made of the little information at his disposal.

"We looked for Werder and we looked for Estermann. The only thing we found on Werder was this index card. We found nothing on Estermann. So we can't check anything out. We can't establish, on the basis of our files, whether Werder was Estermann."

"You have any advice for me?"

"Find the officers who handled Werder and ask them. You may be lucky; perhaps they are still alive. I can give you two names—Hans-Peter Schippmann and Werner Lucke." He slid across the table a photocopy of a document entitled *Most Secret! For Internal Use Only!*

The first thing I noticed was that Stang's black marker pen had already been at work, deleting about a dozen lines on the document. The second was Schippman's name on the form and his date of birth. Both matched the reference—"H. Sch. (age 57)"—in the *Berliner Kurier*. And Schippmann had the rank of major, as the newspaper had said.

The document was Schippmann's Stasi personnel form. But the marker pen had wiped out the information about his parents, wife, children and relatives, and, more frustratingly for me, the name of the street where he lived. Even his passport photograph had a wide black line across his eyes, part of his forehead, and his nose. All I could see was a thick head of neatly combed hair, a thin mouth, and a square jaw. He wore a jacket with large checks and a tie.

"Sorry," said Stang. "I had to delete the street name: I think he's still alive. I have to delete anything that is not relevant to the researcher's purpose, and any information on the individual's private, sexual, or financial affairs. That is the rule."

I was grateful that his censorship had spared the name of the city: Berlin. It was a start, but not much more. Brinkmann had warned me that Stasi veterans kept their names out of the phone book. I asked Stang whether he had anything on the other officer, Lucke, but he shook his head.

Stang reached for the folder once more. He pulled out a thick sheaf of pages. "My guess is that this isn't about Werder. This is everything we have about an agent whose code name was 'Lichtblick'—the name means both a flash of light and a moment of joy. He was the Stasi's main source on the Vatican."

"What do you know about him?"

"Not a lot. His real name is not in the files, but the most likely candidate is a Benedictine monk called Eugen Brammertz. He's dead. This is a list of the reports he sent to the Stasi from Rome; we don't have the reports themselves. They were probably destroyed."

I was beginning to wonder whether enough files of importance had survived the 1989 cataclysm to keep Stang and other researchers in business. I picked up the thick wad of documents, but before I could open my briefcase, Stang grabbed them back. There was a look of panic on his face. "I can't possibly give you these documents like this," he said.

My heart sank. I saw myself trapped in the cavernous building for hours taking as many notes as I could in case a single detail, a reference number or a name, proved important later on. Assuming that Stang would agree to let me study the papers.

"The papers have to be stamped. I must certify that they come from here," he explained.

He fetched a stamp and an ink pad from his desk. With a dull thud, he branded, in red ink, the words KOPIE BstU precisely in the middle of the first page. Then on he went. "BstU," he informed me between thuds, "stands for the official name of the Gauck Authority. This is not really my job. But I forgot to ask my assistant. You see, people might think you obtained these illegally. And then you wouldn't be able to use any of the pages. It won't take long."

Two hundred and nine thuds later, Stang finally looked up with a satisfied smile. "Now you have to pay for them. That is the rule," he said. He waved me out, locked the door of his office, and guided me through the corridors until we reached a door that, like all the other doors, was identical to that of his office. A cashier handed each of us a form to fill out and sign, and then, after paying, I was free to leave, clutching my papers with their handprinted seals of approval. The newborn Germany was selling the secrets of its discredited elders, but only to cover the operational costs of bureaucracy.

✦

IT WAS STILL RAINING OUTSIDE. I caught a tram down Karl-Liebknecht Street, named after the revolutionary who was executed in 1919 along with his comrade Rosa Luxemburg. The street had long sold out to the capitalist enemy, with giant posters for Coca-Cola and McDonald's. The tram was painted bright yellow, and a poster on its side proclaimed: THE LOTTERY MAKES MILLIONAIRES.

Off the Unter den Linden boulevard, I sheltered from the rain in a café with Art Deco statues of small silver nudes holding globes of light. I pored over the list of Lichtblick's reports, which stretched from 1974 to 1987. Most of the material focused on the Vatican's policy toward the two Germanies, especially after the cataclysmic election of the pope from neighboring Poland. File after file detailed the Vatican's reaction to elections in West Germany, the influence of the Polish contingent in the Vatican, ties between the Church and the Reagan administration, between the Church and the CIA. Even the background to the pope's visit to Liechtenstein was worthy of interest.

There were only two reports on the attempted assassination of the pope in 1981. They touched on the trial of the gunman, Mehmet Ali Agca, and on the claims that he had been sent by the KGB. But there was nothing that Estermann, as a witness to the shooting, could have contributed. Nor was there anything on the pope's security, his daily routine, or his travel arrangements—all subjects that Estermann was well qualified to describe. Besides, Estermann was only twenty years old, and still attending business school in Switzerland, when the reports had first started flooding in from the Vatican.

It was far more plausible that the author of these reports was the spy whom Stang had identified, the late Eugen Brammertz. A former prisoner of war in Russia, he was fluent in Russian and had worked until 1986 as a translator for the German-language edition of the official Vatican newspaper, *L'Osservatore Romano*. Estermann was definitely not Lichtblick, but were Estermann and Werder one and the same person?

To track down the two ex-officers who knew the answer, Schippmann and Lucke, I enlisted the help of an independent Berlin researcher, Wolfgang, who was recommended to me by German colleagues. When we spoke on the phone, I was relieved to learn that he did not believe in paying for information. He told me that he would do his best to find out where the officers lived.

While I waited to hear from him, I went to see the former Stasi headquarters on the Normannerstrasse, the heart of which was now a museum. The statues of Marx and Engels, gifts from the Soviet secret police, still stood in the entrance where, early every morning for almost three decades, they used to welcome General Erich Mielke, the minister for state security.

Mielke's suite of offices had been spared the destructive fury of the mob, and was as dust-free as if he were expected to return at any moment to command what the state propaganda machine described as "the Sword and Shield of the Party." A panel quoted Mielke's motto: WHO IS NOT WITH US IS AGAINST US. WHO IS AGAINST US IS AN ENEMY, AND ENEMIES WILL BE ELIMINATED.

But the steel safe built into the wall gaped open behind his chair and the shelves under the oppressively low ceiling were empty. The guidebook handed to visitors described the antiquated typewriters and Bakelite dial telephones, rather euphemistically I thought, as "basic office technology of the German Democratic Republic." The only personal memento Mielke left behind lay on top of his otherwise shiningly bare desk: a white plaster death mask of Lenin, eyes closed and a goatee beard so precisely rendered it looked lifelike.

Late that night, Wolfgang called me at my hotel. He had already found the addresses I needed.

CHAPTER TWELVE

THE NEXT MORNING as we drove through sprawling housing developments to Schippmann's home, a long way southeast of the center of Berlin, Wolfgang revealed how he had found the addresses. A couple of friends at the central post office—"Call them my agents"—had raided its database of ex–directory subscribers and plucked out the details on Schippmann and Lucke. But they had been unable to supply him with telephone numbers. In any case, Wolfgang added, this was hardly the kind of thing that could be tackled on the phone.

While Wolfgang drove, I studied Schippmann's life and career as outlined in his personnel form. The son of a bricklayer, he spent two months in the Soviet Union training with the Komsomol youth movement. A model apparatchik, he joined the Communist Party at the early age of nineteen, and like Werder started his Stasi career as an unofficial collaborator. He was promoted steadily, collecting bronze, silver, and gold medals and several trips to the Soviet Union as rewards for his loyalty.

It had started raining again just as we pulled up outside Schippmann's apartment building, close to the river Spree. One glance was enough to see that wealth was certainly not among the perks of a lifetime dedicated to "the Sword and Shield of the Party." The building was composed of prefabricated concrete slabs piled on top of each other, a construction typical of the vast depressing housing developments of East Berlin. In the untended grass stood a bronze statue of a busty young mother, her brood of three children clutching at her skirt, a throwback to the Communist ideal of human fertility.

We pressed the buzzer and waited. We stared up at the empty windows. A middle-aged man came out onto his balcony and stood there, arms akimbo, his belly bending the petunias on the ledge. A child's multicolored plastic fan, the kind sold at public parks and fairgrounds, which had been stuck among the flowers, turned limply in the rain. The man stared at us, and we looked away.

Wolfgang cursed under his breath. "Doesn't look old enough to be Schippmann, but the guy is probably ex-Stasi himself. They tend to live in the same buildings. Sometimes they just stare, sometimes they take pictures of you. Old habits."

We pressed the buzzer once more. This time a sleepy male voice answered. After some hesitation, whoever it was clicked the door open for us and we made our way up a staircase that reeked of damp. Awaiting us wasn't Schippmann, but his teenage son, Olaf. He showed us into a sitting room with dingy wallpaper and a brown, mauve, and yellow sofa. I had expected the flat to be full of Stasi and hammer-and-sickle relics, but there were none on view, nothing that spoke of the past apart from a black-and-white wedding photograph.

We asked whether we could speak to Schippmann, but Olaf said his father was not at home. Could we perhaps have a few words with him on the telephone now? No, that was not possible. I explained that I had come a long way, and Olaf agreed to pass on a message. After I had scribbled it out on a scrap of paper, he gave me their home telephone number to try later.

✦

MY ONLY OTHER LINK to the mysterious Werder, Werner Lucke, lived a short drive away. I knew nothing about him, apart from his address and the fact that he had worked for the Stasi. Wolfgang dropped me off on the street where Lucke lived. Lined with chestnut trees and detached houses set among tiny gardens, it was smarter than Schippmann's. Among the spotless cars parked along the curb, only a fluorescent-yellow Trabant, the people's car of the former East Germany, lowered the general tone. As did Lucke's home: his building, again of the drab prefabricated variety, sat oddly on the street and must have been the shame of its neighbors.

Alone, I walked up to the front door. This time the buzzer was answered immediately. "What do you want?" a gruff voice barked out.

I started explaining, in the German I had learned at school, but did not get very far.

"Not good," the voice interrupted me. "Now is not a good time. We are going out now." A click. Lucke—assuming it was he—had hung up.

At a loss what to do, I waited for a few moments. Then the door opened, and a stout woman wearing glasses, her silver hair tied back, stepped outside. Before she could challenge me, I reached out to stop the door from closing behind her, thanked her, and crossed the threshold. She looked startled but did not try to stop me.

I was just in time to see a thin man with greasy hair, dressed in faded jeans and a denim jacket, scoot down some steps and make his way out of the entrance lobby through a back door. I guessed he was in his seventies—old enough to have risen to a significant position in the Stasi before retiring.

I had not come all this way to lose one of the two people who could tell me whether Estermann had indeed been a spy and a traitor. If this man in a hurry was Lucke, I had to go after him. If he was not Lucke, all I risked was a little embarrassment. So I rushed after him, down the steps and out into the garden at the back.

"Herr Lucke," I chanced when I got within earshot of the elusive figure.

Before I could say any more, the man waved me away with a scowl on his worn face. I had no doubt it was Lucke. As he marched on, shouting *"Nein! Nein!,"* the woman who had unintentionally helped me to spot him hurried up to me and asked what she could do to help. She introduced herself as Frau Lucke.

Her manner was not hostile, simply cautious, so I pulled out my copy of the index card with Werder's name on it. Perhaps Stang's official-looking red stamp would help my cause. I asked Frau Lucke whether she remembered the newspaper stories about an agent called Werder and the commander of the Swiss Guard at the Vatican.

"Ah yes, we saw the story in the paper at the time," she replied as she led me off in pursuit of her husband through a path that led to the main street.

"Do you remember what your husband said about it?"

"Yes. That it was rubbish. That Werder worked in Section XVIII/4, that it dealt with economic and industrial espionage, and that it had nothing to do with religion."

"Did your husband work with foreign agents?"

"All the people under him were East Germans."

I apologized for upsetting her husband. Not to worry, she said, and tapped her head. Herr Lucke had been a little moody ever since he had a tumor removed from his brain. Although the Stasi had allowed him to retire because of his health, the pension was not very generous, and "to help make ends meet" he worked four days a week at a Mercedes-Benz factory.

We reached the nearby street and walked up and down for a while, with Frau Lucke muttering to herself, "Where is he, where is he?" I felt a twinge of guilt at ruining her outing. Eventually she suggested we call off the chase and scribbled their home number down for me. "It is better if you telephone; it is easier that way," she said.

When I dialed the number that afternoon from my hotel, Frau Lucke answered after the first ring. Her first words were hardly encouraging: "A moment, please. I think I cannot help you."

It was a while before her husband came to the phone. "Yes, this is Lucke." His voice was, thankfully, less sharp than it had been that morning. But it was nowhere as friendly as his wife's.

I started telling him about Werder and Estermann, but he cut in quickly.

"The section I worked for had nothing to do with the Vatican. We didn't deal in espionage abroad; we were a domestic service. Only the foreign espionage service could work with foreigners. It was forbidden for us. We would have had our heads cut off if we had done so."

It was no joke. Lucke sounded perfectly serious, and I had no doubt the Stasi had persuasive means to enforce its internal rules. "So Werder was not Estermann?" I asked.

"Of course he wasn't. What the *Berliner Kurier* wrote was complete nonsense."

"Do you remember who Werder was?" I asked.

"No. You'll have to ask someone else. I have no idea."

Before I hung up, I offered an apology. "Herr Lucke, I'm sorry for this morning. I didn't have your telephone number."

He gave a throaty chuckle. "We can talk about anything you like. But I don't like being assaulted, you know."

A few days later, after several attempts, I managed to reach Schippmann through his son. I still hoped to identify Werder. Schippmann started by telling me that I was the first person to ask him about Werder, and that he could rule out any link with Estermann or the Vatican. And yet, in the newspaper article, "H. Sch."—as Schippmann was referred to—had been misleadingly quoted as saying he had nothing to do with Werder.

"So who was Werder?" I asked. "Is he still alive?"

"I'd rather not give you his real name. But I can tell you that he had nothing to do with any foreign country. He used to live in the town of Gosen near Berlin, and I came across him when I was in charge of overseeing security for a training center being constructed by the Stasi. Werder was a restaurant manager; he helped us solve a small problem, something to do with discipline among our construction workers."

"Doesn't sound as if it had much to do with spying."

"It didn't. The only espionage link was the Stasi training center. Basically the workers had gone on a rampage in Werder's restaurant, and we had to pay him for his help in dealing with them. We wanted to be discreet about why we were paying him, so we put him on our list of collaborators."

Although I insisted, Schippmann refused to give me any more information that might help me to track down the real Werder. But there was no room for doubt: Estermann had never been Werder, there was nothing to show that Estermann had spied for the Stasi, and in any case, the Stasi's spy had nothing to do with the Swiss Guard. I was satisfied that my visit to Berlin had been worthwhile, but this was spoiled by the frustration I felt at the journey's having been prompted by an anonymous letter that was full of lies. I was impatient to return to Rome and resume the hunt for the mysterious priest I had been told was definitely a Vatican spy—Father Yvan Bertorello.

CHAPTER THIRTEEN

THE EEL WAS AS SLIPPERY as ever. Back in Rome it took me six weeks, and twice as many phone calls, to persuade Bertorello to meet me for lunch. When he finally did agree, he suggested we meet at St. Anne's Gate. But then he hastily backtracked and suggested we meet instead outside the Congregation for Bishops, the body that oversees episcopal appointments and is located off St. Peter's Square. Apparently he had little desire to be seen near the barracks of the Swiss Guard.

"I presume you are waiting for me" were Bertorello's first words when he came up to me.

A short, nervous-looking man whose left temple was dotted with teenagelike pimples under mousy-colored, crew-cut hair, he had a prominent Adam's apple and was so thin that his pale cheeks appeared sunken around his thick upper lip and lantern jaw. Small gold-rimmed glasses perched on his aquiline nose, and instead of a priest's garb, an unfashionable knee-length coat hung on his frame. He looked older than his thirty-seven years, to all appearances a cadaverous clerk belonging to one of the more obscure Vatican departments who had been allowed out for a little fresh air after weeks of seclusion with some crinkly parchment as his only company.

His complexion turned as bloodless as white marble when I suggested we talk at the Caffè San Pietro, a bar across the street, the Via della Conciliazione, which was also close to the Vatican press office. He told me he had no desire to bump into anyone from the Vatican press corps and marched me off toward the Borgo Pio neighborhood, saying he knew a good trattoria where he used to go with "my dear friend Tornay." I resisted the temptation to start asking Bertorello there and then about that friend's last night. Perhaps eating lunch would make him more ready to talk.

Not that it was easy to get a word in edgewise. Bertorello led the way at a brisk pace and talked, in French, as fast as he walked, pointing out the black Mercedes that he said the German embassy loaned free of charge to Cardinal Joseph Ratzinger, the head of the Congregation for the Doctrine of the Faith, because he was not happy with his Vatican-issue Lancia sedan. Hardly pausing to breathe, he then told me that years ago the pope, on the CIA's recommendation, had a nuclear bunker built under the Pontifical Library.

He interrupted this flow of tidbits of information to which he apparently attached great significance only to reprimand a street hawker who had called out to him in English. Bertorello haughtily informed the man that he did not speak English or Italian, only French. Which was untrue, but fighting for the French language against Anglo-Saxon cultural imperialism was a Bertorello hobbyhorse.

The trattoria he had picked was as long and narrow as a railway car, and as soon as we sat down, Bertorello cocked his head to eaves-drop on the conversation of the two people at the next table. After a while he turned back to me. "Tourists, American. It's all right, we can speak," he said.

But I still had to bide my time while Bertorello sent back a bottle of Frascati wine that he said had been spoiled by a defective cork, telling the waiter that he came here often with "important men of the Church." The waiter obliged, muttering that there was no need to name-drop to have the wine changed in this establishment.

The diversions over, Bertorello said he had agreed to our meeting only because De Villiers, the author of the spy novel loosely based on the Swiss Guard deaths whom I had met in Paris, had put in a good word for me. De Villiers had invited him to his luxurious villa on the French Riviera and given him the manuscript of his book to read before publication. Despite the distractions offered by the villa's grand piano, where he sat himself down to play, with the maid as his only audience, and the swimming pool—De Villiers lent him a pair of swimming trunks—Bertorello's blood had boiled at the way he was depicted as the murderous Father Hubertus.

"I'm sure that De Villiers would have liked me to make a public protest, because it would have given him publicity. But I never did complain. I stayed mum," he said.

I asked Bertorello to tell me about his background. He had started out as a student of engineering, but switched to law and then to theol-ogy. He described himself as an "international consultant" for the sale of gold and jewelry to heads of state and other VIP clients. He was also involved with a nongovernmental organization that was active in Armenia. He ended by saying that he used to have three passports, but now he had only two: a French one and an Italian one.

I remembered that the Vatican issued its own passports, and guessed that perhaps he had been stripped of that privilege, although I had no idea why this should be so. "Did you have a Vatican passport, too, and was it taken away from you?" I asked.

Bertorello took a minute sip of the white wine that was as thin as he was. "You are saying so. Not me," he said.

It was going to be a long and cryptic haul. "I've been told you are known as Father Yvon. How long have you been a priest?" I asked.

'People say ridiculous things about me, that I'm a priest, a monsignor. In fact, I'm a deacon, part of the order below priests. I mean 'was,' not 'am.' I demanded to be freed of that obligation. It took a long time, but in the end I got an authorization from the pope. You need his signature to be allowed out. They were scared that I would speak. Anyway, now I am a layman."

He smiled as he awaited my question. "Scared that you would speak—about the Swiss Guard?" I said.

Bertorello half covered his mouth with his hand, as if he regretted having spoken. I had the uncomfortable feeling that he was playing a game with me. "Let me give you a scoop," he said. "Did you know that John Paul is thinking of bringing back the ceremonial throne on which his predecessors were carried so he can be seen by the faithful?"

I'd seen the story in the newspaper a couple of weeks earlier, and was unimpressed. Besides, he hadn't answered my question. "What's the link with the Swiss Guard?" I asked.

Another tiny sip. "None. I'm often told I sidestep questions on certain matters," he answered, looking not the least bit apologetic.

"What was the problem with the Vatican?"

"I was suspected of being a member of SISMI, the Italian military secret service. That's the reason for my problems. I was put on trial. There was talk of transfers of funds worth several million dollars, of drug trafficking. They just couldn't understand why I was traveling so much on my Vatican salary of thirteen thousand francs a month. Then I was acquitted. So now I have told the Vatican that I want not only a letter clearing my name, but also a job, even a phony job at the French foreign ministry. I've waited three years, but you have to be patient in life. In the end I'll get the letter, I'm certain of it."

The Vatican's concern was understandable. After decades of excellent relations with the Italian government across the Tiber—the seven-times prime minster, Giulio Andreotti, was a frequent guest of several popes—the prelates had been shocked to discover that SISMI intelligence had committed the blasphemous indiscretion of spying on the Holy City in the late 1970s and early 1980s. The Italian spies, aided by paid informers among men of the cloth, had reported not only on the Polish pope's backing of opposition forces in his homeland, then part of the Soviet empire, but also closer to home on several more liberal monsignori who were critical of John Paul.

The "friendly" SISMI discovered it was not the only one spying on the Vatican at the time. The Kremlin also had an ear in the Vatican, in the shape of a listening device hidden in the apartment of John Paul's right-hand man, the then secretary of state, Cardinal Agostino Casaroli. The bug was in a glass-cased statuette in the dining room, its signal picked up at the Villa Abamelec, the Soviet ambassador's residence not far away on the Gianicolo Hill. When told about such devices, John Paul commented that he would recite the rosary aloud wherever bugs might be hidden: "I will convert them," he added with gusto.

"So do you work in intelligence?" I asked Bertorello.

"I used to. But not for SISMI."

"For the Vatican?"

"I won't answer that one. But bear in mind that the Vatican knows everything, even things that are beyond its spiritual mission. It is interested in everything. Its secret service goes back centuries. It was dissolved by Benedict the Fifteenth in the 1920s, but Pius the Tenth reestablished it to chase the modernists. Today there's a counterintelligence service attached to the Vigilanza police force. Few people realize this, but as an intelligence organization, the Vatican rivals the CIA. Once you understand the Vatican, the CIA, and the Mossad, you understand the world."

Although he had spoken in a hushed voice, there was suddenly so much fire in his eyes that I was reminded of De Villiers's description of Father Hubertus, the character he had based on Bertorello—"a zealot, an apprentice martyr who literally burns with exaltation."

I guessed that the Vatican's moves against Bertorello had more to do with his involvement in the events that followed Tornay's death than he was letting on. I had quickly grown tired of his reserve, and was determined now to ask him about the last moments of his "dear friend': "Tornay's mother says you told her that her son was murdered. What grounds did you have for saying that?"

Bertorello held my gaze and remain tight-lipped. But he swallowed hard, and his prominent Adam's apple bobbed visibly.

I fumed, and tried again. "Tell me what you think of this scenario. You're involved in delicate Vatican missions, and one of them is finding out about Opus Dei. Specifically about Opus Dei and the Swiss Guard. You recruit Tornay to help you understand the way Opus Dei has penetrated the Guard, but he finds out too much for his own good. And he is murdered. Is that what you believe happened?"

His eyes blazed again. "It would make a good thriller. But I won't talk." His voice suddenly rose slightly. "Are you playing devil's advocate? Did the Vatican send you to me? Because if you are secretly recording me, I would like to say for the benefit of anyone listening that all I have said was on a personal basis and does not commit the Vatican. And you can tell them to get stuffed!"

I kept a straight face, but I was amazed by his outburst. All I could do was assure him that I had only a pen and a notebook with me. He seemed to accept this, so I continued. "Why did you speak so freely with Tornay's mother, but refuse to speak now?" I asked.

"I was offered six hundred thousand francs by *Paris-Match,* the French magazine, to write a book. But the Vatican has made it very clear to me that it doesn't want me to write a book."

"You haven't considered going ahead anyway?"

Bertorello's eyebrows shot up in horror. "You have no idea of the power they have. They could destroy me. The Catholic Church is mother and father to me. It would have to treat me very badly before I could even dream of going against it. My lips are sealed. As God is my witness."

I turned away, pretending to be interested in our neighbors. I was annoyed and did not want Bertorello to see it. I was again reminded of a phrase from De Villiers's book: when Father Hubertus proves particularly uncommunicative, his questioner muses that "he would have willingly knocked [the priest's] head against the wall, but his moral code prevented him from doing so."

Bertorello's resistance reduced me to silence for a while. Eventually, I tried a gentler approach. "Do you agree, or don't you, that Tornay committed the two murders and then killed himself, in what the Vatican called 'a fit of madness'?"

He looked sullen and took his time finishing his mouthful of veal and mushrooms. "If the Vatican says so, it must be so." A mischievous twinkle appeared in his eyes. "I've got a dossier on Tornay, with photographs of him. I knew Tornay before he joined the Guard. Imagine if that got out, what people would say. The dossier is my bargaining chip while I wait for the letter clearing my name. But I have an idea for your book; perhaps we'll discuss it some time in the future. In the meantime, here's one piece of advice: Find out what really happened in St. Peter's Square when the pope was shot. You'll soon realize it's not true that Estermann shielded him from the bullets, which is what the Vatican claimed after he died."

My attempts to get him to say more proved fruitless. All he would tell me was that he had decided to stay silent "out of respect for Tornay." He brought our meal to a quick close, telling me he had to go and see the Lebanese ambassador "about his bloody diplomatic pouch," and after that he had to organize a trip to Brunei, where he was to meet the sultan, who is "perhaps the richest man in the world." Then he stood up and rushed away, without even pausing to put on his coat.

I was left alone to finish my espresso, feeling immensely frustrated. With his erudition and passion for espionage in the Vatican, Bertorello must have fascinated Tornay. But although Bertorello appeared to sincerely believe that something was seriously amiss with the Vatican version of the deaths, he had given me nothing to back his initial conviction—that Tornay had been murdered. I had no idea whether he still held it. I still needed to find out what, if anything, he knew about the deaths that was so much at odds with the Vatican's official version.

CHAPTER FOURTEEN

ON MAY 6, 1981, on the eve of the annual swearing-in ceremony, Estermann, a captain at the time, was among the officers present when John Paul gave the Swiss Guard his traditional blessing. "We pray to the Lord that violence and fanaticism may be kept far from the walls of the Vatican," the pope told them. A week later John Paul was fighting for his life after being shot in St. Peter's Square.

The role that Estermann played immediately following the shooting was mentioned by the Vatican again and again after his death. From Cardinal Sodano downward, officials praised Estermann's heroism in shielding the pope's wounded body from further attack. John Paul himself, however, had made no public mention of Estermann at the time of the 1981 assassination attempt, saying only: "One hand fired the gun, and another guided the bullet."

Bertorello's suggestion that Estermann's role had been misrepresented tantalized me, because it was an episode that, to all appearances, had been exploited in order to create a wide gulf between a worthy Estermann—portrayed as the pope's guardian angel—and an undisciplined Tornay. After scouring through newspaper clippings from the time of the assassination attempt, I found an eyewitness who could tell me exactly what had happened in those tumultuous minutes: Francesco Pasanisi, who had served for several years as the Italian chief of police acting as liaison with the Vatican for the pope's security. As such, he had escorted the pope on dozens of visits to Roman parishes and on longer journeys across Italy. And he had been walking right by the pope's Jeep in St. Peter's Square when the shots were fired on the afternoon of Wednesday, May 13, 1981.

When I neared the Bronze Doors for our meeting on a sunny spring morning, Pasanisi, gray-haired and looking frail, was resting on a stool, framed in the shaded doorway of the nearby Italian police station—a space like a cramped porter's lodge, which was its only toehold on Vatican territory. He stood up with difficulty and leaned heavily on my arm as we moved slowly out into the sunshine.

"I have trouble walking because I had an accident while I was fooling around on my scooter, a Vespa, the other day," he joked, before adding: "The truth is, I'm not the chap I was twenty years ago. I was born in 1920, like the pope. But I mustn't complain."

Despite the warm Roman weather, he wore a reversible raincoat and a brown corduroy beret pulled to the side at a rakish angle. He clutched a battered brown briefcase in his big chubby hands. Long retired, he had taken to writing books and had published several on the nineteenth-century brigands who had infested the hills around Naples, where he was born. We had taken only a few steps when I felt his hold on my arm tighten.

"The assassination attempt was committed at five twenty-one P.M. and thirty-four seconds," he announced out of the blue, with the clipped precision of a police officer testifying in court. Then he dropped his formal tone as abruptly as he had adopted it and confided: "I know because my watch dropped off my wrist when I jumped into action. I found it later and it had stopped at precisely that time."

He launched into his story without further ado. "So . . . that day the pope comes out into the piazza, standing in his white Jeep. He looked radiant, as he always did. The driver and the pope's valet, Angelo Gugel, sat in front. The pope's secretary, Dziwisz, sat on a little white seat facing him. He was holding a briefcase with speeches and things. The square was packed. There were two rows of barriers marking the pope's route around the square, and the Jeep started down it slowly, very slowly. There wasn't a breath of wind; the flags were all dead still. The pope goes around a first time. He wanted to say hello to everybody, so on the first tour of the square the Jeep hugged the left side of the route. Then he starts going around a second time, and the Jeep hugged the right side."

"Where was the Swiss Guard?"

"The ones in dress uniform were in their usual places back at the Bronze Door and around the square. Then there were a couple in dark suits, among them Estermann, who, like me, were walking alongside the Jeep. I was by the rear left wheel. We were supposed to stick close to that wheel and follow the Jeep around the square. As far as the steps in front of Saint Peter's, where the pope would get out and address the pilgrims from his throne on the esplanade. We were watching the pope the whole time. It sounds crazy, I know, but at the time the rule was that we keep our eyes on the pope and not look at the crowd. Of course that changed afterward."

He pointed a few yards away to the obelisk in the center of the square, where a rotund middle-aged bishop was posing for photographs with some young Japanese tourists. One of them had thrown an arm around the bishop's shoulders. The bishop looked startled at such familiarity, and then smiled fixedly for the camera.

"The Jeep had just gotten past the obelisk and was turning back toward the Basilica. The car had stopped because the pope wanted to take a little girl in his arms—she was blond, with a puffy face, and she was carrying a balloon. He handed her back to her mother. That's when I heard the first gunshot. Hundreds of pigeons flew off all over the place. I knew immediately that it was gunfire because I had been an officer in the war. The first shot wounded the pope in the hand. The second struck him in the stomach."

Pasanisi was tiring in the sun, his brow covered with beads of sweat. Engrossed in his tale, he took no notice of his discomfort. "Immediately I jumped onto the back of the Jeep and threw myself over the pope's body. Gugel and Dziwisz—who had dropped his briefcase—were also close by. I grabbed the pope under the armpits, to stop him falling. One of the bullets landed at our feet. The pope said something in Polish; I could only make out 'Częstochowa'—he was praying to the Black Madonna of Poland. I said to him 'Holiness, Holiness, courage.' He answered me in a very faint voice: 'Thank you, inspector.'"

"Where was the Swiss Guard? Where was Estermann?"

"I have no idea."

"What do you mean, you have no idea? Wasn't Estermann the closest to the pope? That's what the Vatican said, that he shielded the pope from the other shots."

Pasanisi spoke in a deadpan tone: "I didn't see him; he must have been behind me. Anyway, there weren't any more shots, so how could Estermann have shielded the pope from them?"

To give Pasanisi a chance to rest, I led him back to the shade of the colonnade. We perched uncomfortably at the base of a column, with Pasanisi breathing heavily for a while. Then he fumbled inside his briefcase and pulled out a wine-colored folder. He glanced briefly at a black-and-white photograph and then handed it to me. It was an extraordinary picture. Taken from only a few feet away, it showed the pope seconds after the shooting. He had collapsed to his knees as if in prayer, the white skullcap visible on his bowed head. Three people were fighting to keep him upright.

Of the three, the one that stood out was Pasanisi, his face distorted by a snarl-like grimace as he seized the heavily built pope from behind and strained to bear his weight. Gugel was standing in front of the pope and had hooked his hands under the pope's arms just above the elbow. The pope's face, inches from Gugel's stomach, was invisible. Dziwisz was on his knees at the pope's side, trying to steady him. And as Pasanisi had said, Estermann was behind his right shoulder. He looked panic-stricken and was open-mouthed, perhaps shouting an order or an appeal for help. But he was too far away to be touching, let alone shielding, the pope.

"So you were the hero that day, not Estermann?" I asked.

Pasanisi grunted. "Don't know about heroes. What I do know is that Estermann was behind me."

He stuffed the photograph back into the briefcase. "Ninety kilos," he continued. "That's what His Holiness weighed, and at that moment it was a deadweight, believe me. I could feel the pope dying in my arms. His eyes were half-closed, and a bloodstain as big as my fist appeared on his white robe, under the wide sash he wore around his waist. It spread fast. His blood stained my trousers, the blood of His Holiness. I haven't washed that pair since; I keep them like a holy relic. It was only when I grabbed hold of the pope's left hand to try to comfort him that I realized he had also been shot in the index finger. There were streaks of blood running down from the nail."

He was staring out at the square, his gaze slowly sweeping over the cobblestones, but his mind was not on what his eyes saw. "You have to imagine, it was like a battlefield out here. People hugging each other and crying, people on their knees and praying. Broken cameras lying on the ground where people had dropped them. There were even dentures jammed in the cracks between the cobbles. The driver was so terrified when he saw that the pope had collapsed that he got out of the Jeep. But he left it in gear or something, so it rocked back and forth. I had to shout to him 'Let's go!' to bring him back to his senses. I had no idea if there were more shots coming, I just had to get us moving again. I stuck with the pope. We took him to an ambulance near the Basilica and then I followed it all the way to the Gemelli Hospital. The ambulance raced up one-way streets; it almost crashed into a Land Rover which was overtaking another vehicle and heading our way. I signaled I wanted to get in front of the ambulance, but there was no way I could manage it because of the one-way streets. I just couldn't get in front."

"Did Estermann or any other Swiss Guard come with you?"

"No. They'd been close to the Jeep and then they disappeared. Estermann wasn't in the Jeep when we reached the ambulance. He'd gotten off before. And he definitely wasn't in any of the cars that went to the Gemelli. The pope was in the ambulance with Dziwisz and his doctor, Buzzonetti. Took us eight minutes to get to the hospital, and when we arrived I ran so fast up ten flights of stairs that I got to the top before the elevator which was bringing up the pope. He was wheeled past me into the operating room. I knelt down. He looked at me; his eyes were dull but he was still lucid."

The great bell of St. Peter's rang a sonorous peal for midday and Pasanisi stood up. Again leaning on my arm, he led us away from the Bronze Doors and across the square. I asked him what he thought of the pope's security, and the role of the Swiss Guard.

"The Vatican relies on faith. On the day of the assassination attempt, I had fifteen guns at home but none on me. I didn't feel the need, and besides, the pope doesn't like to have them anywhere near him. At his summer residence in Castel Gandolfo, we'd patrol the grounds with dogs, not with guns. As for the Swiss Guard, it's only for parades."

"But the Guard claims it's responsible for protecting the pope. It's the only security in the pope's palace!"

"You want my opinion? You can't save a life with a halberd. The Guard is part of the decoration. It may have been useful in the sixteenth century, but certainly not today. And in any case, this pope is indefensible."

"That's quite an admission for someone who was in charge of his security," I said, startled at his frankness.

Pasanisi shrugged, in no way offended. "Maybe so, but it's true. That old black Mercedes with the SCV-1 license plate, the one the pope uses—it's not bulletproof. He wants to stand in the back of the car, to be seen, and to shake hands with people even though he risks being pulled off balance. He wouldn't be able to do that in a bulletproof car with a sealed roof. People grab at him, but that doesn't worry him in the slightest. I've seen him return to the palace in the evenings with ugly, bloody scratches on the backs of his hands."

"Didn't you make any suggestions to him, try to persuade him to improve his security?"

"Of course I did. He wouldn't hear of a bulletproof car. I begged him to be more cautious, not to take bunches of flowers or gifts from people because they could have a bomb hidden in them. He always gave me the same answer: 'I want to go among the crowd, like a man among brothers. My defense is my cross.'"

We were standing by the wooden barriers marking the Vatican's border with Italy on the eastern edge of the square when Pasanisi

LEFT Cédric Tornay takes the Swiss Guard oath in the St. Damasus courtyard in May 1995, swearing to "serve the Supreme Pontiff John Paul II and his legitimate successors, sacrificing my life to defend them if necessary."

BELOW St. Peter's Square, showing the Apostolic Palace (right). Pope John Paul II was in his private apartment on the top floor when shots were fired in the Swiss Guard barracks below his windows.

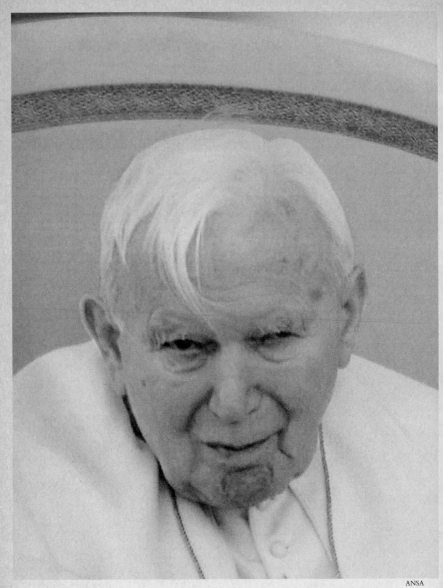

June 2002: During a weekly general audience held in St. Peter's Square, the toll that age and ill health have taken can be seen on the pope's face.

LEFT Alois Estermann photographed shortly after the pope named him the new commander of the Swiss Guard. Estermann saw in his promotion "the hand of God." Hours after this picture was taken, he was found dead in his apartment.

BELOW Estermann and his wife, Gladys Meza Romero, are received by the pope in May 1997, before the annual swearing-in ceremony for new recruits.

ABOVE RIGHT The Apostolic Palace soars above a small square just outside the Estermanns' apartment. The windows on the top floor are of the pope's bedroom.

RIGHT A detachment of guards marches back into the barracks. The Estermann apartment is on the second floor of the building.

LEFT The Estermanns' neighbor Sister Anna-Lina Meier, the nun who raised the alarm after finding the body of the new commander's wife.

BELOW Monsignor Alois Jehle, the chaplain of the Swiss Guard, to whom Tornay appealed shortly before his death. It was Jehle who swore all members of the Swiss Guard to silence about their lost comrade.

ABOVE In March
1998, two months
before the Swiss
Guard deaths, the
pope names his
personal secretary,
Stanislaw Dziwisz,
a bishop—
a virtually
unprecedented
move that
prompted much
envy in the
Vatican village.

BELOW The pope
embraces Cardinal
Angelo Sodano,
secretary of state
and the Vatican's
"prime minister."

SERVIZIO FOTOGRAFICO DE L'OSSERVATORE ROMANO

SERVIZIO FOTOGRAFICO DE L'OSSERVATORE ROMANO

ANSA

LEFT Sodano, who said of the Swiss Guard deaths: "In times like these, we feel above all the need to be silent."

BELOW Monsignor Gianbattista Re, named a cardinal by the pope, pays homage shortly after his appointment in St. Peter's Square. Re was among the senior Vatican officials who helped to stifle talk about the deaths.

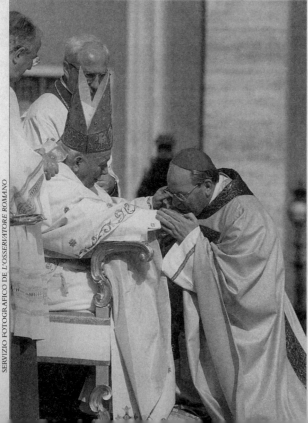

SERVIZIO FOTOGRAFICO DE L'OSSERVATORE ROMANO

Joaquín Navarro-Valls, the pope's spokesman, fields questions on the morning after the bodies were found in the barracks. Within five hours of the tragedy, he produced an official version of events that he labeled "a moral certainty."

SERVIZIO FOTOGRAFICO DE *L'OSSERVATORE ROMAN*

Tornay and his mother, Muguette Baudat, are received by the pope on the day he took the recruits' oath. After her son's death, the pope refused to see her again and turned a deaf ear to her appeals.

Tornay poses in front of the monument to the fallen in the main courtyard of the Swiss Guard barracks.

RIGHT Tornay on a flight to Venezuela, where he vacationed with his friend Steve Kellenberger and another fellow guard, in May–June 1996.

BELOW Tornay and Kellenberger relax during their vacation.

Tornay on a beach in Venezuela.

The pope prays before the coffins of Estermann, his wife, and Tornay. The pope said Tornay was now before the judgment of God, "to whose mercy I entrust him."

A rare photograph of Yvon Bertorello, a deacon and Tornay's so-called spiritual confessor.

LEFT Muguette Baudat, Tornay's mother, believes that her son did not commit suicide, as the Vatican maintains, but was murdered.

BELOW Baudat with Tornay's two sisters, Mélinda (left) and Sara (right).

The pope, moments after being shot in St. Peter's Square in May 1981. Supporting him are police chief Francesco Pasanisi (left) and Dziwisz (right).

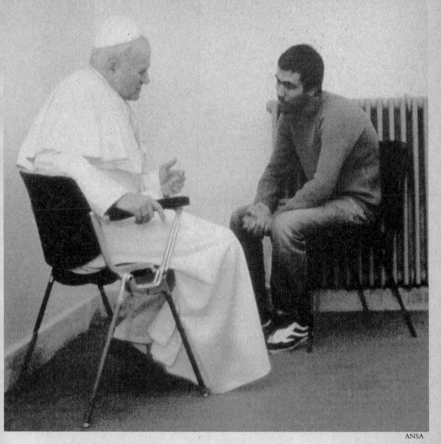

December 1983: the pope in hushed conversation with the man who tried to kill him, Mehmet Ali Agca, at Rome's maximum-security Rebibbia Jail.

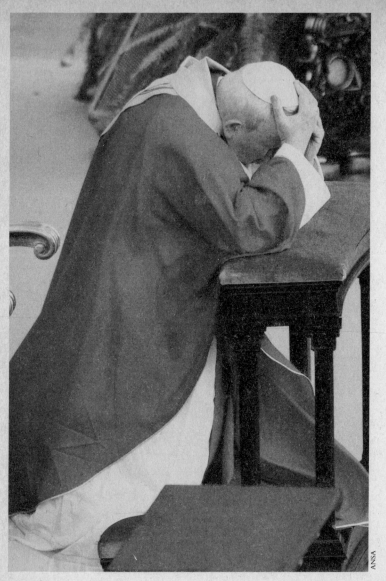

ANSA

May 2002: The pope prays after proclaiming five new saints of the Catholic Church in St. Peter's Square. During the ceremony, he asked the faithful to pray for him "so that I may continue my service."

tapped me on the chest with his index finger. "Listen, my friend. You know what happened to the bullet that hit the pope in the stomach? After he recovered, he sent it to the village of Fatima in Portugal, so that it could be mounted on the crown of the statue of the Virgin Mary. It's in Fatima that the Virgin is said to have appeared to three shepherd children in 1917. And her appearance was on May thirteenth—the same date that the pope was shot, and survived. That tells you what the pope thinks about his security."

As I watched him walk slowly away, I wondered why the Vatican had gone to such lengths to mislead public opinion over Estermann's role during the assassination attempt. It was as if the Vatican needed to depict Estermann as a hero, for reasons that were a mystery to me. But if it could distort the truth about Estermann, it was more than likely that its much less flattering portrayal of Tornay was also deceptive.

✦

A FEW DAYS LATER I called at the home of Professor Massimo Lac-chei, a writer and art historian. Lacchei had caused a scandal when he published a collection of short stories, or rather with just one item in the collection, a story entitled "Mass in a Private Chapel." It is an account, spiced up with a couple of lewd anecdotes, of an all-male party he attended at the luxurious palazzo of a Roman politician, where the two most eagerly awaited guests were a couple of officers of the Swiss Guard. The pair were lovers, and they were struggling to keep their relationship as secret as possible. The book would certainly have passed unnoticed had not Lacchei called a press conference, in February 1999, on the very day it was released by a small Roman publisher, to announce that the two officers—"Major Jörg" and "Lieutenant Kaspar" in his book—were in fact Estermann and Tornay.

The short story opens with the guests waiting expectantly for the two officers. They arrive, Mass is celebrated, and then, over a meal, the guests sit in rapt attention as the officers relate their love story: a first meeting on a rainy evening in Lausanne in Switzerland, a twenty-four-hour escapade to Amsterdam, where they link themselves to each other with handcuffs to symbolize their love, and then Kaspar/Tornay's decision to follow the older partner to Rome and join the Guard.

But the two officers are visibly distraught, and it emerges that Jörg/Estermann has a girlfriend, who has followed him from Switzerland to Rome. The two men fear that she may suspect something, and could cause a scandal that would wreck their careers in the Guard. "For sure," says Jörg/Estermann in the last line of the story, "everything would be resolved if I married her and we became one big family."

Lacchei's short story rode roughshod over a Vatican taboo: the idea that homosexuality could exist within its walls. The Vatican was tight-lipped about Lacchei's book, and the sole comment came from an unidentified official who dismissed it as "only shameful speculations."

I found it hard to believe the idea that Estermann and Tornay, whom so much divided, were not only lovers but also that they had confided so freely in complete strangers. But I wanted to find out why Lacchei, an avowed homosexual, had decided to write such an account, and whether he could come up with any evidence to prove its veracity.

Lacchei was waiting for me at his home near the river Tiber, an attic three floors up—no elevator, as is common in Rome's historic center—with a jasmine-strewn terrace. The sitting room was dotted with ancient Roman statues, the stone capital of a column, and Renaissance paintings of the Virgin in heavy gilded frames. On a paisley sofa, Lacchei sat nursing a tiny fluffy white dog. He wore a goatee and small round glasses, and was dressed in black from head to toe. Filling the window behind him was the dome of St. Peter's and the Gianicolo Hill.

He saw me staring at the view. "Tornay didn't like it," he said. "When he came here, I said to him, 'See, you can't escape Saint Peter's.' He muttered to me, 'Enough,' and then he turned away."

I was surprised. There was no mention in the short story of Lacchei seeing one of the officers before or after the party. "Tornay visited you here?" I asked.

"Yes, I was out walking Honey—that's my dog—and we met by chance on Via della Conciliazione a year after the party where I saw him with Estermann. We sat down for a chat and then he came back here with me. He liked to fool around. Sexually, too."

Lacchei was going too fast for me. "Hold on," I said. "Let's go back to the first time you met the officers you called Jörg and Kaspar. Why had you been invited?"

"It was a Sunday brunch in the spring of 1997. The host invited me because I was supposed to do an appraisal on two of his paintings. By the way, he wasn't a politician. That was an invention, just like the handcuffs. He was a Roman nobleman, part of a family with historic ties to the papacy. I can't tell you his name or those of the other guests; I've been warned not to. After the book came out and I said who the officers were, the nobleman sent his chauffeur around to my front door to tell me that if I revealed any names, I'd get my legs shot up. And that would be the least that would happen to me."

Lacchei's reference to "a family with historic ties to the papacy" was so vague as to be meaningless. Such families were a dime a dozen in the Eternal City, as many aristocrats had popes in their family trees, including the Aldobrandini, Borghese, Chigi, Farnese, and Della Rovere dynasties, to name only a few.

"How do you know the two officers were Estermann and Tornay? How do you know they were lovers?" I asked.

"I was introduced to them. There was also an American priest, an Italian monsignor, and a student at the Catholic University in Rome. The nobleman was showing off by inviting the officers. No one told me that Estermann and Tornay were together, but I was struck by the great gentleness with which Tornay stroked Estermann's neck. This very handsome young man was almost massaging Estermann, and Estermann let him do it. Remember that homosexuality was the coagulant of the party."

A strange choice of phrase. I carried on: "I find it very hard to believe that someone like Estermann, if he did have a relationship with Tornay, would have risked his career by behaving himself like that in public."

"Well, in fact, Estermann was the more discreet of the two. He hardly spoke to me or anyone else. Tornay tried to talk to everyone. So much so that Estermann slapped him lightly on the thigh to make him shut up."

"If the two characters in your short story are Estermann and Tornay, why didn't you give them real names in the text rather than wait until after publication?"

"It just goes to show, doesn't it? No one asks why I wrote that collection of short stories. My book is about homosexuality in the Church, about the hypocrisy of the Vatican. People say I just wanted to get out the story about the Swiss Guard. But it's the shortest story in the book, it's the last one, and the names are invented. If I'd wanted publicity, I would have put it first, and I would have put their real names in from the start."

His explanation was less than convincing. "Do you have any evidence at all to show that there was a relationship between Estermann and Tornay?" I asked.

"If you mean letters or documents, no, nothing. But I can show you my diary," he said. He got up to fetch it from the drawer of his desk. "Here, look, that's a list of all the medication I had to take after meeting Tornay again."

I looked at him blankly.

"Tornay. I told you. I met him again a year later, at the end of April 1998. It was just a few weeks before he died. He was a soul in torment then, but he'd lost none of his gentleness. He was going through a spiritual crisis; that was my impression. We talked about my passion for art, about how he could help me to get into areas of the Vatican that are usually closed to the public so that I could see some wonderful things. Then I brought him back here."

Lacchei paused, but it was for effect. He needed no prompting to continue. "One thing led to another, certain items of clothing got a bit loose, and we had just the beginnings of oral sex. I got a tremendous infection in my throat after that; the doctors had never seen anything like it. Tornay asked me for payment, he wanted a million lire, but we didn't get very far because someone rang the doorbell and he had to rearrange himself very quickly. When he left, he said that now that he knew where I lived, he would come back to see me. I knew what that meant: we had some unfinished business. But he never did come back."

He thumbed through the diary. "See, I wrote down the list of antibiotics I had to take. I had sores down my throat, I could eat only mashed potatoes, I even had difficulty breathing at one point. I never found out what the disease was." He showed me the entry for May 4, 1998. It was in red ink: "They killed each other." It was an odd way to put it. The entry for the next day read: "Poor Cédric."

"If Tornay was homosexual," I asked, "what were the former girlfriends who turned up at his funeral? Figments of someone's imagination?"

"I think Tornay was a homosexual who every so often looked to women to console him. When I met him the second time, the time he came up here, the thing with Estermann was over. Estermann had already betrayed him. All I know is that Tornay saw Estermann in an embrace with another guard in the changing rooms at the barracks. He was pretty shaken up. I remember him saying: 'I forgive, but I don't forget.' Tornay was unhappy with the Vatican, he was keen on returning to Switzerland. But he wasn't someone planning a murder. I see the

Swiss Guard as a kind of hothouse, whose flowers are picked by homo-sexual bishops and cardinals. People in the Vatican tell me the guards supplement their tiny wages with the money they make that way."

Over the next few days, I tried to establish some firm basis for what Lacchei had told me, and piece together Tornay's apparent "other nature." At first I felt discouraged. No one wanted to talk. I would try to coax something out of the people I met, only to come up against a law of silence as solid as the bastions of the Vatican. Never had the Holy City seemed more like a fortress. The difficulty I encountered reminded me of the silence with which it had greeted the murder of Enrico Sini Luzi, the Gentleman of His Holiness who had been beaten to death by a Romanian male prostitute five months before Tornay's death.

If the catechism published by Italian bishops was any guide, Sini Luzi had violated the sixth commandment—thou shalt not commit impure acts—not once but twice. The catechism branded homosexual acts as a sin on a par with prostitution, masturbation, fornication, rape, incest, contraception, adultery, divorce, polygamy, and all "carrying out of genital sexuality," as it called it, outside marriage.

I looked outside the Vatican for some possible leads. With the help of Roman gay associations—none of whom wanted to see their name in print—I discovered that Tornay had been seen regularly at several gay bars in Rome. A member of one of these associations told me that he had also gone many times to a fitness club on the Via Aurelia west of the Vatican, which was popular with Italian and foreign prelates. Tornay had on one occasion met a young Italian police officer there and the two had had sex together shortly afterward. The police officer had refused to talk about Tornay, fearing that he would lose his job if his homosexuality became known.

"Gay people in the Vatican live their homosexuality in a crazy, schizophrenic way," my source told me. "They believe they are serving the Catholic Church to the best of their ability, but at the same time the pope is telling them that homosexuality is 'morally disordered' and their superiors are preaching from every pulpit that the Devil is inside them and leading them down the path to eternal damnation.

"Let me tell you a story. We were never able to act on it because the people involved were too terrified to have their names made public. A couple of years ago, a prelate who works at the Vatican Museums had a hand in recruiting staff—both cleaners and security staff. This prelate would ask candidates to come for an interview, then he'd tell them that he wanted to get to know them 'more intimately.' Which meant sexual favors. The staff he recruited were all good-looking; some of them looked as if they'd stepped straight out of the frescoes in the Borgia Apartments."

According to authoritative research published by Father Andrew Greeley, 25 percent of priests under the age of thirty-five are gay, with half of them sexually active. For the American writer Garry Wills, homosexuality forces such priests "to observe a discipline of deceit lest their secret slip out. They are in their own prison of falsehoods. Nothing could be further than this from the gospel ideal of 'open speech.'"

Even members of the clergy who try to minister to homosexuals are punished by John Paul. In January 1995, the pope stripped Bishop Jacques Gaillot of his French diocese of Evreux and forced him into retirement at the relatively early age of sixty. The Church had been reprimanding Gaillot for years for urging the use of condoms in order to prevent the spread of AIDS, giving interviews to gay magazines, and lobbying on behalf of illegal immigrants. The pope wanted to send him to Partenia, in the Sahara Desert in southern Algeria. Gaillot's comment was: "I hope to work with the poor and the outcast. I feel particularly close to them now." He stayed in France and, undaunted, continued campaigning for the poor and the outcast through a Web site.

From a former Vatican employee who did agree to a furtive conversation away from the city-state, I found out that a former chaplain of the Swiss Guard was a homosexual. He'd had several affairs with members of the corps, and whenever his advances were rebuffed, he would dress himself in civilian clothes and go to Rome's Termini railway station to find male prostitutes. The ex-employee told me that a Swiss Guard plucked up his courage and complained about him to the elderly, wheelchair-bound Cardinal Andrzej Maria Deskur, who has been the pope's closest friend ever since they studied at a seminary together. "We will do nothing," Deskur muttered. "The chaplain is digging his own grave." Two weeks later the chaplain died of AIDS. The scandal never became public knowledge.

SOME DAYS AFTER my meeting with Lacchei, I had a stroke of luck. One of the *vaticanisti* journalists who work at the Vatican's press office told me that a former guard had opened a flower shop in Rome. "Interesting thing is," the journalist confided with what was almost a wink, "the chap's a homosexual, and doesn't bother to hide it anymore."

Franz Steiner's smart boutique is in the heart of Rome, in a narrow alleyway close to the lower house of the Italian parliament. When we sat down for tea at a chic coffeehouse a few doors away, he told me that his business was thriving; he was called on for official functions in the parliament, for the city's nobility, and for the big names of fashion when they showed off their collections.

Tall and thin, with a short-cropped sandy beard, Steiner is in his early thirties and has lived in Rome since joining the Guard in 1995. Despite his many years in Italy, he has lost little of his guttural German accent. He told his most vivid memory of what it had felt like to serve in the Vatican: once, on a night patrol, he had flashed his light on the face of a crucified Christ near the Sistine Chapel, and quickly shifted the light because at that desolate hour the statue had struck him as so lifelike that he feared he would wake up Christ Himself.

"I'd always dreamed about joining," he said. "Ever since I was a child, I can still remember seeing the Swiss Guard in their uniforms close to the pope when I watched the Christmas Mass on television with my parents."

"And when you got there? Did it live up to what you'd imagined?"

He made a wry face. "At first it felt as if I was doing my national service all over again. The times when I was stuck with the halberd, forced not to move even one muscle, I would pray that a cardinal would pass by so that I could do the salute and get a tiny bit of exercise. Sundays were the worst because all the offices were closed and hardly anyone ever came by. After six months I called my mother, I told her how arrogant the prelates were. I felt as if I had Big Brother watching me all the time. We found out that one guard, who stayed only a year in the barracks, had been planted by Cardinal Sodano to spy on us. There was so much pressure on us."

"What kind of pressure?"

"Physical, like the pace we were forced to work at. And psychological, too, which was the worst. Some people choose to live in the Vatican because for them it is like living under a giant, protective cocoon. But for many people life in the Vatican is just a big pretense, because the truth is that under all the cassocks and the robes there are individuals who want to live normal lives, who have desires that are absolutely normal—including sexual ones."

I took this as my cue. "How are homosexuals treated in the Swiss Guard?" I asked.

"Ask the commanders and they'll tell you there are no gays in there. Right at the start, the first time the commander, Buchs, summoned me and the other new recruits to his office for a welcome speech, he told us that three things would get us expelled and sent straight back to Switzerland: first, if he found out that one of us was gay; second, if we failed to respect curfew; and third, if we were caught drunk on duty."

He stroked his beard for a while, apparently debating whether or not to say more. Then he continued: "So I had no choice but to hide my homosexuality. I soon realized that the only way to survive as a homosexual in the heart of the Church was to keep it invisible. I was a loner, I didn't feel I fitted in. Whenever I could, I'd escape from the Vatican to go and see the art in the museums and the churches of Rome."

"Did you confide in anyone?"

"No, I didn't; there was no one I could go to. We were supposed to go to Monsignor Jehle, the chaplain, if we had a problem, but I wouldn't have dreamed of going to him. He's a bigot; he'd insist on us going to Mass all the time. I couldn't stand having to enter the chapel in single file with the other guards. I got tired of it all, and I left after the second year."

I did some quick addition: Steiner's departure from Rome occurred a year before the shootings. I asked him what he remembered about Tornay.

"He struck me as immature, like a young dog with big floppy paws, discovering the world around him in a clumsy way. He started in the Guard a month before me, but we weren't close enough for us to discuss anything in any depth."

"Is it true that Tornay was particularly undisciplined?"

"No more than the others. I got on okay with Estermann, but he was more strict with the younger guards. I don't know why. The thing about Estermann was that he was always in control. He was very different from the other officers: when there was a decision that had to be made, they would look around to see if someone of a higher rank could make it for them. Estermann wasted no time; he just went ahead and made the decision there and then."

"Do you know anything about Estermann and Tornay having been together for a time?"

"No, I'm sorry, I know nothing about that," he answered, putting down his cup and saucer. He had been friendly and relaxed until now, but his tone had suddenly become dismissive. With a mumbled apology that he had to get back to his boutique, he gave me a hurried handshake and strode away.

All the Vatican's worldly and spiritual powers could not stamp out homosexuality within the ranks of the corps that guarded its gates, so instead it made a priority out of presenting an acceptable public front.

With the help of a friendly priest who works in the Vatican, I tracked down a retired officer of the Guard who had served some years before Steiner. The ex-officer, who insisted I keep his identity secret, is a homosexual and confided to me that Dziwisz, the pope's private secretary, had told him four times during his career at the Guard that he should get married.

"Dziwisz told me it was the only way to ensure I'd have a decent future in the Guard," said the former officer. "It was his way of saying that even if I was gay, I had to show I wasn't. I was outraged. There's nothing in the rule book that says unmarried officers can't be promoted. Imagine, celibacy is a requisite in holy orders, but in the Swiss Guard they want you to get married because they're so scared of gays—even though canon law says the faithful are free to choose whether to get married or not.

"When Estermann, who was still unmarried at the time, was promoted to the rank of major in 1983, the commander told me that the Secretariat of State had agreed to his promotion only on condition that he get married very soon. And sure enough, in December of that year, he married Meza Romero. Before that, he'd come up to me and said that rumors were going around that he was gay."

"Why were people saying that?" I asked.

"I've no idea why people were saying it," the former officer answered. I suspected he was being disingenuous and did not want to admit to knowing about Estermann's homosexual leanings because he feared the Vatican would punish him for being indiscreet. Perhaps, I reflected, Estermann was trying to find out what other officers in the Guard knew about his homosexuality. He had taken a risk in broaching the subject, but then again, he must have been fully aware that it could jeopardize his career in the Guard.

CHAPTER FIFTEEN

IT TOOK SEVERAL WEEKS of punching out the mobile phone number I had reluctantly come to know by heart before Bertorello could, or would, agree to meet me again. He was forever traveling, shuttling between Rome and Paris, or flying as far as Hong Kong. Always on business, he assured me. He did not believe in vacations. I had almost given up hope when he announced that he was in Rome for a few days, and suggested we drive out to the hills south of the capital. An evening meal al fresco on a lakeside terrace would be pleasant, he said. He turned up dressed in a green polo shirt and faded blue Bermuda shorts that floated about his thin legs like slack sails. I took the casual look as an encouraging sign.

The trattoria was decorated with photographs portraying its

rotund owner, Daniele, performing amateur theatricals and wrapped in the toga of an ancient Roman. Bertorello told me he often took guests here, including the French ambassador and his wife, and—he added as a throwaway remark—Tornay, several times.

Bertorello chose a table in a corner of the terrace and again, just as had occurred the last time we'd met, I had to wait and listen as he chatted, unprompted, about how he had managed to get a French couple, both of whom were freemasons, into a private dawn Mass celebrated by the pope in his palace, how he would use his Vatican contacts to obtain a visa for a Cuban friend of Daniele's to come to Italy, and how he would soon be seeing Saddam Hussein in order to seal a petroleum contract with Iraq.

We had ordered, and eaten most of the first course of Daniele's homemade ravioli with a sauce made of boar's meat, by the time he paused for breath. I seized the chance to ask if there was anything about Tornay's death in the dossier he had mentioned to me at our first meeting.

Bertorello started as if I had uttered a blasphemy. He clutched the edge of the table, his thin fingers white against the checked tablecloth. "You must be crazy! It's an affair of state! I can't possibly tell you what's in it. I'm very careful: I've made three copies. One is with a relative, and two are with friends I can trust. In case something happens to me. I've received death threats."

"Who from?"

He ignored me and suddenly developed a keen interest in the colorless sunset across the lake that was shrouding the waters and the pine trees in an ever-darker shade of gray. His head shifted slowly from side to side as he took in the scenery, staring at length before speaking again. "I've finally gotten the letter I asked for. The one from the Vatican clearing my name after I was acquitted on the spying charges. It's signed by Jean-Louis Tauran, the foreign minister. But you have to be very careful with the Vatican. You'll go into some prelate's office, he'll be all sweetness and light to you, but by the time you walk out of the office he's already cleaning his knife."

The fact that Bertorello had managed to obtain what was effectively a written indulgence from such an authoritative source despite having had to stand trial said a great deal for the enduring influence of his Vatican connections. I tried to drag him back to the night Tornay died. I told him I was skeptical about the material he had at his disposal being as explosive as he seemed to believe.

"I know sixty percent of what happened," Bertorello replied. "There's what I know, there's what I've been told, and there's what I think. I will tell you everything if you give me five million francs, and if you get me into a witness protection program with a new identity. I will do this only for money. You have no idea how much power these people have."

I was reminded of Michelangelo's reply after the fierce Pope Julius II told him to use gold and rich colors on the figures in the frescoes of the Sistine Chapel. "Holy Father," Michelangelo said, "in those days men did not bedeck themselves in gold, and those you see painted there were never very rich. They were holy men who despised riches."

Bertorello gave me no time to respond. Again he was going off on a tangent. "Did you see the pope's face after the Swiss Guard deaths? I saw him close up when he went to the chapel to see the bodies, and I can tell you he was completely overwhelmed. I could see from the ghastly look on his face that this was one of the worst things that had happened during his pontificate, and he knew it."

Bertorello's remarks tore to shreds what little faith I had in his conspiracy theory. Not only because he had confessed much of his ignorance, but also because he had nonetheless demanded payment. Perhaps Bertorello's claim that Tornay was murdered had been prompted by the despair he must have felt at the loss of his friend. But there was at least one respect in which Bertorello could help me—piecing together Tornay's last evening. If Bertorello was Tornay's spiritual adviser, it was reasonable to suppose that Tornay would have tried to contact him in those last hours. I asked Bertorello if he had.

Bertorello answered without hesitation. "I was one of the last people he tried to reach. I was away; I was in a plane on my way back to Rome at roughly the time everything happened. Tornay left me two messages. One was on my mobile phone, at eight-thirty in the evening."

"That's half an hour before he died!" I exclaimed. "What did he say?"

"Something like: 'Please, call me back. It's urgent.' I wasn't able to call him back until ten past nine, but by then it was too late. And then, when I got to the place where I was staying in Rome, I found out that he'd called there, too, just after a quarter to nine. He left a message for me. He gave his name, said he was from the Vatican, and that he was a friend of mine. He said something very serious had happened, it was really urgent, and I must call him back immediately. He repeated it several times; he was very insistent. And despite all that, the girl who took the message gave it to me only the next morning. I found out that Tornay was dead when I saw the front page of a newspaper as I was walking to the Vatican."

"Why were you one of the last people, perhaps the very last, Tornay tried to contact?"

He shrugged. "Tornay told me once that I was the most important person for him after his mother, that he trusted me more than any other friend of his. I suppose he appreciated the fact that someone who worked inside the Vatican treated him like a normal human being. Most Vatican people are very snotty toward the guards. And I helped Tornay to find a job; he was due to start working in September as a bodyguard for a bank chairman in Geneva who is a friend of mine."

Tornay had been so eager to leave the Vatican that he enlisted

Bertorello's help in finding a way out. No doubt, like many who had dealings with Bertorello, Tornay must have been impressed by Bertorello's knack for obtaining favors for himself and his friends from the Vatican hierarchy, but I suspected there was more to Bertorello's relationship with Tornay than he was letting on. It was as I listened to Bertorello chatting with Daniele, the owner of the trattoria, that the coin dropped. Daniele was saying that he missed his *"caro, carissimo amico"* (dear, very dear friend), a young Cuban man who was finding it hard to get a visa to visit him in Italy.

As Bertorello promised Daniele that he would look up someone at the Cuban consulate the very next day, I wondered furiously how I could pose the question I wanted to ask. I could find no delicate way to phrase what I was after, so as soon as Daniele had moved away, I stared straight at Bertorello.

"There's one thing I haven't asked you. Were you and Tornay together—I mean, did you have a relationship?" I gabbled.

He looked stung, and played for time by raising his glass and sipping from it with pursed lips. "Perhaps you should start by asking whether I am homosexual," he said.

I obliged, and waited.

"No." There was a twinkle in his eye; I guessed he was playing a game and not telling the whole truth.

"All right, then, are you bisexual?" I persisted.

"Yes. What about you, are you bisexual?"

We were making slow progress. "No, I'm not."

But Bertorello would not let go. "Do you realize how many people are bisexual? Many more than you think. Haven't you even been tempted?"

What a strange conversation to be having with a defrocked deacon, I thought. I was in no mood to humor him. "No, never. And I don't think this has got much to do with what we're talking about," I replied.

As I stared at him, struggling not to give him the satisfaction of betraying my frustration, I was taken aback by the transformation he had just undergone. Until a few moments earlier, he had sat as taut as a wire, like a suspect in a crime fearing that his words would be used against him. But now he slumped back in his chair, smiling. It was as if, having confessed to what many in his church considered a sin, he felt more at ease. "You know," he said, "I have never paid for sex. I almost did, though, just once. I was in what we'll call a special place; I'd drunk quite a lot. I was about to start negotiating a price with the person concerned, and my mobile phone rang. I'm rather pleased it did ring, because it put an end to the matter."

In the hope that sharing confidences might make Bertorello more cooperative, I told him about my meeting with Lacchei. "So what am I to believe?" I concluded. "That Tornay was heterosexual, or that he did have a relationship with Estermann?"

Bertorello hesitated, but only slightly, before answering. "Tornay liked women mainly, and he was very well hung to boot. But he also liked men, sometimes. He didn't go all the way, though; he just liked to try things like oral sex. It's true that he was with Estermann; it lasted two years. They broke up in January of their last year. But I don't think saying they were 'together' for all that period is the right word. It would be better to say that they were together occasionally during that time."

I did not try to ask how Bertorello could be so well informed on Tornay's anatomy and sexual preferences. The degree of his intimacy with Tornay took second place to what he was saying about Estermann and Tornay.

Bertorello was eyeing me smugly, savoring the effect of his bomb-shell. He was the first close friend of Tornay to admit not only to the latter's apparently occasional homosexuality but also to mention Tornay's relationship with Estermann, a relationship that had ended four months before their deaths.

Bertorello's remarks cast the deaths in a new light and tore a great hole through the Vatican inquiry for its failure even to consider the possibility of a *crime passionel,* a crime of passion, committed by a jilted lover. There was little escaping the conclusion that that failure had been intentional, given the Vatican's knowledge of Estermann's affairs.

Perhaps this was what Monsignor Alessandro Maggiolini, the bishop of Como in northern Italy, had been thinking of when he challenged the official version hours after the deaths with the enigmatic remark that even under the uniforms of the Swiss Guard, there are men of flesh and blood, "with their passions and failings."

"Why did the relationship end?" I asked.

"Because Estermann had relationships with other guards as well. I'd say a quarter of the guards are gay, and another quarter are bisexual. Many of them are young, handsome, virile. They've got gorgeous uniforms. And what's more, they come from the Vatican—a mark of purity. It's a fascinating combination."

There was a hint of lust in Bertorello's remark. "Were Estermann's relationships the reason why his promotion to commander was blocked for such a long time?" I asked.

"Yes, they were. Estermann tried to be discreet—he and Tornay went out for a drink together only a couple of times. But people in the Vatican knew what Estermann was up to. The pope knew, and he blocked the promotion. But Cardinal Sodano lobbied and lobbied until he finally got what he wanted."

Then the veil came down again as suddenly as it had been lifted. "I don't want to talk about these things," Bertorello said with a churlish tone, snapping out of his relaxed stance. "I don't think it helps the

Church. Would you say your mother was a prostitute if you were writing a book about her? I hardly think you would. Well, neither would I."

The sun had long sunk behind the hills on the other side of the lake by the time the meal ended. Over coffee, I brought up one last time what Bertorello had told Tornay's mother on the day after his death. "Don't you have any regrets for leading her to believe that her son was murdered?" I asked.

"All I can say is that I didn't put it that directly. Anyway, Tornay's mother has a lot to answer for. I remember she complained to me that I cried more than she did over his death. That's not surprising, since she ignored him when he was alive. He went through hell because of her. In the last months Tornay and his mother became very distant. My only regret is the way she was treated when the funeral service was held in Saint Anne's near the barracks.

"I was supposed to be her minder. After the service, the coffin was whisked out of the Vatican in a normal van, not one of those hearses with a cross on it, through a gate which is near the pope's helicopter pad and which is rarely used. And off it went to Switzerland. The mother wasn't told, and she was furious that she was prevented from following her son. I told her I had no choice; I was only obeying orders. I told her that the Vatican didn't want paparazzi chasing the coffin. But she was upset all the same."

Bertorello got up to go. Whether I liked it or not, our meeting was over.

CHAPTER SIXTEEN

FROM THE VALLEY of the river Rhone, the road due south through Switzerland zigzags up the mountains toward the Grand-Saint-Bernard Pass, which is the oldest of the Alpine pass routes. For thousands of years, tribes and armies have marched along that route to cross the border with Italy—Hannibal and his elephants, Julius Caesar and his legionnaires, Napoléon and his troops. Today the road is the gateway to the Valais, a mostly Catholic enclave of glaciers, dead-end valleys, darkwood chalets, and cow-fighting championships. A virtual Berlin Wall runs across the region, dividing the western and fiercely French-speaking area from the German-speaking section. The locals nickname this barrier the "*Rösti* curtain," after the grated and fried potato dish that is popular among the German speakers, but despised on the other side.

There was certainly no *Rösti* on the menu at the roadside auberge some miles short of the Grand-Saint-Bernard in the French-speaking area where Muguette Baudat, Tornay's mother, had agreed to meet me. As I waited for her, trucks rumbled past a few feet from the windows of the smoke-filled inn, which was lit by naked bulbs. From a television set in a corner, the sound of horns blowing during a ski championship competed with the noise from the trucks.

I had decided to travel to Switzerland to track down Tornay's friends and acquaintances, to see whether they could shed any light on his time at the Swiss Guard. But first I wanted to tell Baudat about my inquiries so far, and about my talks with Bertorello.

She strode in, wrapped in a jacket that she held tight to her body. She wore her hair, which was now dyed a reddish brown, in stiff strands, which gave her an odd, almost eccentric appearance. She said hello to me in a voice that was even more throaty than I remembered, kissed me three times on the cheeks, apologized for being late—she worked in a café and a couple of regulars had stayed on and on—and then had a noisy coughing fit. When she had recovered, I asked her whether it was a smoker's cough.

She sat down without taking off her coat and shook her head impatiently. "No, it's bronchitis. But I don't have a fit of madness coming on." She grinned, ordered a coffee, and lit one of her designer-thin Vogue menthol cigarettes.

I found her remark in poor taste, but took it as a sign that she was still refusing, as she had told me in Rome, to think of the dead Tornay as her son, Cédric. I wondered how much greater the shock would be when the realization did at last hit home. I began by asking her whether she had made any progress in her attempt to see the Vatican's files on its investigation.

"None at all. I've tried and tried, but I've gotten nowhere. Now I've lost my confidence in Vatican justice, and in the pope. You remember I told you about that letter I sent out to Tornay's friends asking them if they would talk to me about his time in Rome? No one talked to me, but afterward, a monsignor representing the pope's envoy to Switzerland asked to see me. He wanted to find out how much I knew and what I planned to do about it. He gave me a rosary, but he also threatened me in the name of his superiors, telling me I should stop asking about Tornay's death and think of my surviving children. He said he was sure I wouldn't want anything bad to happen to them. That's a threat, isn't it? So I decided to appeal to the pope himself. I wrote to him, twice, but I got no answer."

She gulped down the rest of her coffee and ordered a hot chocolate. Then she sat quietly for a while, staring at her chapped fingers as she worried the three gold rings she wore on each hand.

"You didn't try anything else?" I prompted her after a time.

She looked embarrassed. "Well, there is another thing. It may seem strange to you, but I might as well come clean now. You know the Vatican performed an autopsy on Tornay's body? Well, it was a butchery. I know because once he got to Switzerland, I stole his body to have a second autopsy done here."

I was dumbstruck. I knew the Vatican had done an autopsy on Tornay, but had come across no mention of a second one. "What on earth made you do that?" I asked, not sure whether to believe her or not.

"I'd spoken to my lawyers; we were angry that the Vatican had told us nothing about its autopsy. So four days before Tornay was due to be buried, I got my two daughters and a couple of friends to help me get him out of the morgue at the hospital in Martigny. The place is run by nuns. I told them that I had to close the lid of the box in which the coffin was placed because there was a disgusting smell from the body and I had to spray some disinfectant inside. The nuns believed me. I told them the lid had to stay closed for three days and they shouldn't touch anything. They never knew that we'd emptied the box and loaded the coffin into a black van. And the people who prayed there over the next three days had no idea that he was gone."

Again, I was surprised by the clinically detached way she spoke of her son and his corpse. "Why did you have to do things in such a cloak-and-dagger manner? Didn't you get any permission for all this?" I asked.

She looked a little shamefaced. "I found a judge who gave me an authorization for the autopsy. Legally you're not supposed to shift a body from one Swiss canton to another, but we did just that. Call me a body snatcher if you like, but it was my son. Apart from anything else, I wanted to be certain that it was my son in that coffin. And I wanted the autopsy done by an expert of great authority in Geneva, to find out if there was anything strange about the body."

"And the expert's conclusion?"

Before she could answer, the rotund owner of the inn who had been doing the rounds of the tables, dressed in what looked like a doctor's white blouse, ambled up to us. He held a very mature white cheese in his hand as reverently as if it were the local skiing trophy. He delicately sliced off two runny morsels, speared them with his knife, and offered them to us.

After Baudat had licked her fingers clean, she turned back to me. "He concluded that the cause of death was a shot from a gun placed in Tornay's mouth. For it to be murder and not suicide, he would have had to be completely incapacitated, drugged or something. We put him back in the morgue, and a day or so later we buried him in his dress uniform."

At first I was shocked that a mother could even think of such a macabre subterfuge, much less carry it out herself like a thief in the night. All I could see her having achieved was confirmation, as if this had been necessary, that it was indeed her son's body in the coffin whose lid had been prised off. But then I realized that it was her frustration with the Vatican's silence that had caused her to act as she had. I kept my thoughts to myself. There was no point in annoying her and risking an argument on that score when what I really wanted to talk about was Bertorello's comment that she had "ignored" her son when he was alive, and that Tornay had "gone through hell" because of her.

Without mentioning Bertorello by name, I told her that someone close to the Vatican had told me that Estermann was a closet homosexual, that he had affairs with his men, and that Tornay had been among them.

Baudat's brown eyes flashed with fury. "That's a line planted by the Vatican; it's part of their attempt to drag Tornay's name through the gutter. They crucified him after his death, that's what they did. They wanted to make him sound like a prostitute. Tornay's family and his friends know that he was not homosexual."

She pronounced the word "homosexual" as if it were a disease. At the risk of angering her even more, I mentioned something else I had heard in Rome: that some people believed she was partly to blame for what had happened to her son.

Another flash of rage. "What they forget is that although I'm a Protestant, I brought him up a Roman Catholic because that's what his father wanted. I'm sure they go on about my two marriages, but my first divorce occurred when Tornay was only three years old. He was too young to realize what was happening. I just took him aside and told him: 'Mum and Dad don't get on anymore.' I didn't want to tell him lies. It was better for us to split up rather than go on fighting all our lives."

"How did you bring up the kids?"

Her anger abated as quickly as it had flared. She simply arched her thin, almost transparent eyebrows. "Why do you want to know all this?"

"Because I'd like to know what your son went through," I said.

"Okay, I'll tell you. I brought the kids up on my own. I had to work to get the money to feed them, and I found a job as a cashier at the Coop supermarket. I sent them to a school run by Catholic nuns, but I never abandoned them. It was the nuns who told me to get my first divorce, when my husband went off with another woman. The nuns also told me that I was young and that I shouldn't sacrifice everything for the kids. I'd go the village ball, try to meet someone."

"When did you get married again?"

"In 1986. Tornay was twelve years old. But things turned out badly. My second husband beat me four times, and every time the local magistrate had to come to the house. After the last beating he said to me: 'I have a wife and child, I don't want to live with you. You should divorce him.' Both times I got divorced, it was other people who told me to do it."

"Was Tornay at home when the beatings happened?"

"We had a strategy worked out. Mélinda's role was to stay with me to protect me. Sara, the youngest, would go down to the cellar so she would not see anything. And Tornay was to worm his way out through a door or a window, any way he could, and scramble to fetch help."

Baudat had long stopped worrying her rings, but now she started on an earring, stroking between thumb and forefinger a tiny silver chain that dangled from her lobe. She smiled weakly to herself. "Once, it got so bad that a friend of mine called the police. But they said they could only intervene if I called them myself. My friend told them I was in the process of being beaten to death, how the hell did they think I could go to the phone? The police came in the end. The fourth time my husband beat me, Mélinda was sick of it. She stepped in between us and said: 'If you want to beat someone, beat me.' She got hit."

She pulled at the chain on her earring, so hard that I thought she would hurt her earlobe. "I've no idea why my second husband was like that. He'd change completely after one glass of wine, just like that," she said, snapping her fingers. "Afterward he'd go down on his knees in front of me; he'd say he loved me and that he'd never do that to me again. Of course it was my fault. I should never have married him."

"And Tornay, how did he come through it all?" I asked.

"We had a talk about my second marriage after it was all over. Tornay told me that if there was one thing I shouldn't apologize for, it was getting married to that guy. Tornay was an adolescent then, and he told me that he'd needed to have a father figure at that time. We were like that, straight with each other. I always told him the truth. When he was a child, I'd switch on the electric hot plate; I'd put it on low and make him touch it so that he realized he could get hurt. Instead of telling him that a glass could break, I'd have him knock it off the table and see it break. When he was a teenager, we talked about sex quite openly. Once I said to him that if his girlfriend ever came to me and told me she was getting no pleasure out of having sex with him, that it was all over in two minutes flat, I'd give him a clip on the ear. I told him that he had to think of the girl's pleasure, not just his own, otherwise it wasn't love."

"Did you ever talk about death with him?"

"Yes, I did, several times. Once, when he was only eight years old, I asked him and his sisters what they wanted to happen to them after they died. Sara said she didn't know, Mélinda said she wanted to be cremated, and Tornay said he didn't want to be burned. That was all that mattered to him—not to burn."

"Did you ever talk about suicide?"

"I remember teaching him that the worst thing he could do was to take his own life. I told him that even Hitler, who killed so many millions of people, would not have as much to atone for as someone who took their own life. That's my faith: I believe in spiritual respect for oneself. So I can conceive of Tornay killing someone else, but I can't conceive of him killing himself."

I let pass the grotesque parallel with the Holocaust, but wondered what impression such ideas had made on her young son. "Did you ever think of committing suicide yourself?"

She froze, then reached for her cup, without looking down. "Tornay and I spoke a lot about suicide. I did think of suicide when the kids were small, when I was on my own and I couldn't make ends meet. It was such a difficult time. But then I picked myself up and made a fresh start."

✦

THE ANCIENT TOWN of Saint-Maurice, where Cédric Tornay was born, squats on the floor of a narrow gorge, hemmed in between a bend in the west-running river Rhone and a rocky crag. In Roman times the town was an imperial customhouse, on the road leading from the heart of the empire to the far-flung provinces. Still of strategic importance, Saint-Maurice is today a garrison town, ready to ambush any invader with artillery and explosives hidden in a mazelike fortress of tunnels and caverns that run for miles inside the rock face.

It was midafternoon by the time I arrived, and already the crag was shrouding the sun's rays from the town. The town looked deserted. An old couple hurried down the high street that winds through the town, parallel to the river's glacial waters. But when I reached the end of the street, where the rock face leans so close to the river that the town is pinched to an abrupt stop, I discovered that festivities were under way: a large white tent filled a small field, and as I approached I could hear the sounds of Mass coming from inside. I looked in and saw an elderly bespectacled figure leading the service before rows of children and teenagers dressed in scout uniforms.

A woman in the flowing skirt and embroidered bodice of the local folkloric dress was setting out bottles of red wine with military precision on a red-and-white-checked tablecloth for a post-Mass aperitif outside the tent. She explained that the town was celebrating the seventy-fifth anniversary of its Boy Scout group, and that the gray-haired cleric leading the service was Monsignor Henri Salina, the abbot and himself a former scout—"a few summers ago," as she put it.

It was Salina who had given the sermon at Tornay's burial service in the town, a few days after the funeral at the Vatican. At the time he had struck a note that sounded like a rebuke to the prelates in Rome who had rushed to blacken Tornay's name like vultures tearing at a carcass. Quoting Saint Paul addressing the Corinthians, Salina had urged: "Yea, I judge not mine own self . . . he that judgeth me is the Lord. Therefore judge nothing before the time, until the Lord come, who both will bring to light the hidden things of darkness, and will make manifest the counsels of the hearts: and then shall every man have praise of God."

I waited until the Mass was over and approached Salina as he stood in line to have his glass filled. He was chatting amiably to others in the line. Despite his ready smile, his face had a sad, weather-beaten look about it, with untidy eyebrows and deep bags under his eyes. When I mentioned Tornay's name, the heavy crucifix on Salina's gold chain jerked as he abruptly squared his shoulders, and he spilled a little of his wine. He soon recovered his composure and agreed to talk to me. "But not here; it's better if we go to the abbey," he said.

I followed him as he marched through the alleyways, his long black robe flapping about his ankles. As we walked he told me that he had been a member of the scout movement during World War II and had helped to welcome refugee children who had crossed the border from France.

The abbey, which Salina said was the oldest north of the Alps, was directly beneath the overhanging rocks I had seen on my arrival in the town. Inside, Salina showed me into a small room off a vaulted corridor of bare stone. The room was empty save for two wooden chairs with backs whose ornate carvings guaranteed discomfort. The shadow of the lead lattice of the single stained-glass window cast a shadow across the floor like that of prison bars, and I thought of the heavy mass hanging unseen over our heads. Salina pressed a booklet into my hands, murmured an apology, and promised to return soon, then disappeared through the door, his steps ringing down the flagstones of the corridor.

I glanced through the booklet, entitled "Saint Maurice; the Martyr and His Abbey." According to the ancient chronicles, Maurice was an officer with the legions of ancient Rome who mutinied when Emperor Maximian ordered him to fight against his fellow Christians in Gaul. Maurice sent a messenger back to the emperor to explain his act of rebellion: "We are your soldiers, O Emperor, but we freely acknowledge that we are also the servants of God . . . To you is due military obedience, but to God, justice. Our hands are ready to wield weapons against any enemy, but we would be wrong to stain them with the blood of innocent people . . . We have ever fought for justice, loyalty and the protection of the innocent. If we do not keep our pact with God, how can we keep it with you?"

The emperor's answer was to put Maurice and more than six thousand of his fellow legionnaires to the sword. The mutineers, or so the chronicles record, "never resisted in any way. Putting aside their weapons they offered their necks to their executioners." The booklet compared Maurice, who legend says is buried on the abbey's grounds, to the saints Thomas Becket and Thomas More—all three were forced to choose between the service of God and the service of their earthly rulers.

Perhaps the abbot, in giving me the booklet, was trying to tell me something about Tornay? As a Catholic growing up in the town, Tornay would have heard again and again, both at school and in church, about Maurice's act of defiance in the name of faith. And there was a strong echo of the Roman soldier's message in Tornay's last letter to his mother in which he complained of the injustices he was forced to endure. He also announced his intention to give his life for the pope, saying it was his duty to "render this service . . . to the Catholic Church"—as if he were embracing what he might have seen as martyrdom.

I heard steps resounding again down the corridor, and then Salina reappeared. This time he sat himself down, so straight-backed that his body did not even graze the uncomfortable carvings on the chair. I began by asking how well he had known Tornay.

Salina stroked the crucifix on his chest with a bony hand as he tried to recollect. "Tornay lived in Saint-Maurice for thirteen years, but I met him for the first time at the Vatican. I remember he was taking part in the swearing-in ceremony in 1995. He was a new recruit. I was the head of the Swiss bishops' conference at the time, so attending the ceremony was one of my duties. I can tell you he struck me as a very open, cheerful, pleasant young man. A lively chap."

This was strange. Here was a member of the clergy, the leading religious authority in Saint-Maurice, with something positive to say about Tornay—something discordant with what the Vatican had led everyone to believe. "What did he tell you about his commitment to the Swiss Guard?" I asked.

"We spoke about it briefly. He told me he wanted to serve for just two years, and he asked me whether I would help him find a new job when he finished. Then two years later, in the late summer of 1997, we met again in the barracks. He wasn't sure whether he should reenlist or not. I told him the job market in Switzerland was very tough. The rate of unemployment is around six percent in the Valais region, which for

Switzerland is very high. I told him he should do another two years, and try to learn a couple of languages in his spare time."

"So less than a year before he died in May 1998, he was thinking of quitting the Guard," I said, as much to myself as to Salina. "Did he strike you as particularly unhappy? Did he talk of anything going wrong?"

"No, no complaints, never. The last I heard from him, he was planning to leave either in August or December 1998. He got in touch to ask whether I would help him apply for a job back here in Saint-Maurice with the special defense unit that looks after the military fortifications. We're not supposed to know about it, but this place is pretty much armed to the teeth, with secret installations all over the place. Guns in the grottoes, bridges all wired up to explode at a flick of a switch, that kind of thing. Tornay probably found out about it at the firing range; the instructors there are often in the defense unit. He thought I might put in a good word for him."

"And did you?" I asked, making a mental note to visit the firing range later.

The abbot gave one vigorous nod. "I would have if—"

He broke off in midsentence. "If . . . ?" I prompted.

"If he hadn't died. I told him to let me know once he had sent in his application, and then I would intervene. You know, whatever some people say, I didn't think there was anything odd about him wanting to leave. It was already first-rate of him to reenlist and agree to serve as a lance corporal. Saint Maurice is small place, the population is only six thousand. So to have even one local boy in the Swiss Guard is something we can be particularly proud of. Anyway, I put his request away in my pending file, along with the Christmas greeting he sent me. Then he died."

The bony fingers ran up and down the crucifix, the taut skin almost translucent over the knuckles, as Salina stared absentmindedly out of the window.

I waited. It was a long time before the abbot spoke again. "I was right here," he said. "I remember getting a call at about ten o'clock in the evening. I was dumbstruck. The Swiss Guard had called the central Church body in Switzerland, who then called me because they were desperate to get in touch with Tornay's mother. They wanted to get to her before she heard the news on the radio, and to make sure she would have time to let any relatives know, too. I called the priest who lived closest to her; I told him to grab his knickknacks and get to her fast. Already during that first phone call, I was told that the word from Rome was: Tornay shot the other two and then killed himself."

The Vatican machine had moved even faster than I had thought. Within an hour of the deaths, it had not only determined the sequence of events in the Estermann apartment, but had also started spreading its version within the Church bureaucracy. I reminded Salina of his words at Tornay's funeral, and asked him why he had chosen to quote Saint Paul about judging nothing "before the time, until the Lord come."

"It wasn't easy finding the right words. I would have preferred to do Estermann's funeral. My feeling is that you can't explain the unexplainable. The gospel says: 'Do not judge, lest you be judged.' Saint Paul says: 'I judge not mine own self.' But for us it is difficult; we associate the sin with the sinner. I simply think that Tornay learned of the nomination of Estermann, saw that Estermann had refused him the medal for three years' service, and that was it."

It was the most levelheaded explanation I had heard so far from a clergyman, and all the more refreshing for the abbot's failure to peddle any of the Vatican's talk of a "fit of madness," cysts in the brain, or even cannabis use.

CHAPTER SEVENTEEN

THE FIRING RANGE was a short distance out of town, off the main road and across some fields. I parked outside an ugly red building shaped like a small aircraft hangar. It looked deserted at first, but after I had called out a couple of times, a young woman emerged and showed me into the main office. She was the secretary at the range, and had no hesitation in telling me the name of Tornay's instructor: Rémi Wiesel. He was not there, but she let me use the telephone to call him. Wiesel sounded friendly and cheerful, and I was relieved that his good humor did not vanish when I mentioned Tornay's name. He told me he had taught Tornay for three years, from 1991, when Tornay was sixteen, until he had moved to the Vatican. Wiesel agreed to come and meet me there and then.

That Tornay should learn to shoot at such a young age was not unusual in Switzerland. It was typical of the extreme militarization of the country, which goes unnoticed by most visitors. Around a host of inoffensive-looking towns like Saint-Maurice, the granite insides of mountains have been gouged out to make space for invisible bunkers, barracks, hospitals, and even runways for fighter jets.

To preserve its five-hundred-year record of peace, Switzerland maintains one of the world's largest armies, on a per capita basis—a militia composed of 650,000 people, or 10 percent of the population, which can be fully mobilized in less than forty-eight hours. Young men who refuse military service, whether for religious or other motives, are simply jailed for up to six months. Military service is highly regarded by banks and businesses, and some demand that their staff seek the highest possible rank in the militia. For a young man like Tornay, a military career such as one with the Swiss Guard is considered a strong career move.

Wiesel, who lived nearby, arrived after only a few minutes. A short, stocky figure, he walked me onto the platform from which the teenage Tornay, lying on his stomach, must have spent hours aiming and firing at the targets three hundred meters away. Wiesel sang the praises of the TG2000 electronic wizardry that instantly measures a shooter's skill.

I asked him how good a shot Tornay had been.

Wiesel beamed. He was both proud and fond of his former pupil. "I don't mind telling you he had a passion for it. At the start he came here for the same reason that most youngsters come—they get a free course here; the army pays. The aim is to prepare them for national service. But Tornay concentrated more than most. He wanted to get everything into his head, and he didn't want me to have to repeat anything. It was a matter of self-respect for him. He started out with a Faas-90; that's an assault rifle the boys use during their military service.

Delicate piece of Swiss work, that, you have to clean it every thirty shots. But it's nice and light, and precise—you can kill a man at three hundred meters, no problem. Tornay became not the best shot, but one of the good ones. Good enough to take part in competitions at a regional level."

"And discipline? The Vatican said that Tornay quarreled with his superiors, that he broke curfew a couple of times."

Wiesel scoffed. "I never had any problems with Tornay, whether it was discipline or anything else. He was always punctual. Any time I'd mention a competition coming up, he'd be game for it. And he liked the military. That's why he wanted to sign up to guard the fortifications. He saw me wearing the uniform of the defense unit once; he was seventeen at the time. He asked me all about it. It's a bit of a military secret for us, pretty hush-hush, so I didn't tell him things like where the machine guns and the ammunition are hidden. But I put him in the picture all the same."

"Would the unit have recruited him?"

"Of course. He was a great guy, and he was all right with weapons. He took his gun home like everyone else, and he took proper care of it. After his military service, he could have signed up as a weapons instructor. But the unit wasn't recruiting at the time, so he went off to Rome."

In the barracks of the Swiss Guard, Tornay and the other junior officers had kept their ordnance guns in their apartments. This practice has its roots in the Swiss military: army planners wanted men to feel comfortable with weapons, and to ensure a speedy mobilization of the militia army. An estimated six hundred thousand Swiss homes have assault rifles lying under beds or stacked away in cupboards. Swiss soldiers even keep gas masks at home.

Wiesel stared at the targets across the field. There was a pained expression on his face. "Tornay was completely reliable, not at all harebrained. That's why the news of his death shocked me. If there was this snag about the medal, he must have been really burned up about it. The medal is very important for those boys; it's a great honor for them. And the worst possible thing for Tornay would have been to find out on the eve of the ceremony that he wasn't going to get it. But there has to be more to his gesture than that medal."

"What more?"

"I don't know; I lost touch with Tornay when he left for Rome. I'll tell you someone who might have an idea, though. Chap called Jo Georges. He's got a training school for security personnel and body-guards not far from here; it's quite well regarded in Switzerland. Tor-nay asked him for help to find a job. Make sure you ask Georges about it. Tornay told him why he was unhappy with the Swiss Guard, profes-sionally speaking at least."

In the hours following the deaths, the Vatican had been at pains to insist that the tragedy in no way reflected badly on the Swiss Guard. The Guard could not be faulted, Navarro-Valls had stressed repeat-edly—a view that might be disproved by Georges, should he prove willing to reveal what criticism Tornay had made.

Before leaving, I found out from Wiesel that the training school was in the town of Sion, farther up the Rhone. When I called, Georges agreed to see me, but he was busy and the soonest he could free himself was in two days' time.

"Ever seen Tornay's handwriting?" Georges asked me on the telephone.

"No," I replied.

"Well then, I'll bring something you'll want to take a close look at," he said before hanging up.

CHAPTER EIGHTEEN

GIVEN WHAT THE VATICAN had said about Tornay, I had expected the town of Saint-Maurice to be somewhat anxious to forget that he had ever lived there. But the opposite was proving to be the case, and no less an authority than the Abbot Salina had spoken up in his defense. In an attempt to sound out those who might have known Tornay better than he did, I called the next day on François Mottet, a primary-school teacher. As we sat on a bench in the empty playground where Tornay had run about as a child, I asked Mottet, bearded and soft-spoken, what he could remember of him.

"He was average as far as marks went, but then that's typical of kids who are a bit restless. Oh, and his spelling was no good."

That was certainly true of the last words Tornay had penned: the letter to his mother was full of spelling mistakes, I remembered. "What about discipline?" I said.

"He wasn't a problem in class, but in the corridors and in the playground he'd jump around a lot. He was so lively that I had to keep an eye on him. And he'd get himself noticed because he liked to stand up for younger boys whenever they got bullied."

"Did you have to punish him often?"

"No more than his classmates. He respected authority. Whenever I gave him odd jobs to do in class, like putting things away or cleaning the blackboard, he did them willingly. He never played truant. Nothing like that. I just had to remind him to stop playing soccer when it was time for lessons, and not to make too much noise. He was pretty much a team leader, and his classmates liked him, especially the boys. He didn't have much time for the girls."

"How did he take his parents' divorce?"

Mottet thought for a while. "There was one thing. Sara, his younger sister. He was very concerned about her, very protective. He behaved as if he was playing the part of the father. He would always walk her home even though it was a short distance up the hill. He lived in a small apartment house by the railway, close to the railway depot."

"Did you stay in contact with him after he left school?"

"No, I didn't. But then I met him one year on All Saints' Day at the cemetery in Martigny, when he was seventeen. He'd gone to pay his respects at the grave of a relative. I remember him as a tall young man, relaxed, smiling. He told me that he was working as an apprentice mechanic. He looked genuinely pleased to see me."

Across the street from Mottet's establishment was the secondary school that Tornay had also attended. Inside, I asked a secretary whether I could talk to the school head, Lisianne Parchaix. While I waited, the secretary told me that Tornay had studied there for only a year when he was thirteen, before moving on. It was in that year that his mother had remarried and moved out of Saint-Maurice to a smaller town nearby.

There was still no sign of Parchaix, so I asked the secretary to pull out the file on Tornay. She hesitated, then brought me a thick binder for his class, which listed his marks. They were average, with the best result in mathematics—he received a four out of a maximum of six, according to the Swiss system.

Then Parchaix emerged from her office, and the secretary swiftly slammed the file shut, but she was not quick enough. Parchaix stared angrily at her. "Tornay's school results belong to him," she snapped before I could say anything. "We are a school, not a news agency. There is nothing special to say about him." With that, she turned and vanished back into her office.

Chastened, I walked back toward the historic center of the town.

◆

DURING MY STAY in Saint-Maurice, I found three of Tornay's friends who were willing to talk about him. All of them were upset at what the Vatican had said about him after his death.

"We're all pretty cut up here about the way the Vatican has dragged Tornay through the mud," said one. "We're prepared to accept that he committed the crime, but it's a bit much to make him sound like a madman, and drugged up to his eyeballs as well. And they could have had the decency to call him a suspected murderer rather than condemn him without even waiting for the inquiry to start.

"Tornay was a believer, but not devout. He received his first Communion like most people around here, but he wasn't the kind of guy who goes to Mass every Sunday. You could joke with him about the Church and religion, but there was one thing you couldn't crack a joke about, and that was the pope. He had this huge admiration for the pope. One of the things he was most proud of was having kissed the pope's hand before his swearing-in ceremony. We went to visit him three months after he'd arrived in Rome, and often when he was off duty, he'd go and listen to the pope speak at an audience or a service. And he gave me a framed papal blessing as a wedding present."

"How did Tornay fit in with the Guard?" I asked. "Did you see any signs that he wasn't completely happy there?"

"He was very open and proud. We could see that that didn't go down too well at the Vatican. Especially with the Swiss Germans, who make up most of the Guard. He took us round the barracks once and he said hello to a few Swiss Germans, but they didn't acknowledge him. Basically, the Guard was divided into two clans. Tornay saw that the tensions that exist here in Switzerland are even more intense in the Guard. And the Guard is much stricter than the Swiss army. Tornay said the French speakers on sentry duty were often watched over by the Swiss Germans. Even if it was raining, the French speakers weren't allowed to move an inch, not even to take shelter in the sentry box at the Arch of Bells."

Another friend said: "Tornay told me there was a problem with Estermann only once, one of the last times we were in touch. It was in March, two months before his death. He just mentioned that there was tension with Estermann. Nothing more specific. Tornay wasn't the kind of guy who complained, not about the Guard, not about anything. It was a question of pride. I'm convinced that he wanted us to have a positive image of him.

"Tornay was unable to unburden himself, he just bottled things up. Practically the only thing he ever complained about in his letters was back pain. By the way, he was a lousy speller—I'd go through his letters with a red pen like a schoolteacher, and then pull his leg about them. He was very popular with the Italians. When I saw him in Rome he'd made masses of new friends. It was amazing, especially given the fact that he didn't speak a word of Italian when he got there. But then, they were more acquaintances than real friends.

"It was obvious that he was homesick. He was very attached to his family, to his mum especially. His dad ran off to Mauritius with another woman and married her. Once Tornay drove all the way here in his old Fiat Ritmo, with the Vatican City license plates and a card with a picture of Jesus stuck to the rearview mirror, just to spend two days helping his mother when she moved to a village near here. He really was the man of the family."

According to the third friend, "Tornay could have left Rome after the first two years, but he wanted the promotion to lance corporal. He wanted something impressive to show for all the work he had put in. There's an examination that all guards have to take two months after joining. It's a tough one. They have to learn where all the offices are in the Vatican, the names of the important people, even their phone numbers—all by heart. Tornay studied hard for it, he didn't go out at all, and he made it.

"The medal for three years' service would have meant a lot to him. When he was a Boy Scout, he would show us his new badge every time he went up a grade. The medal would have been a matter of self-respect. Estermann's decision not to give it to him was unfair, and Tornay had a strong sense of justice. If a friend was picked on at a party and got bullied into a fight, Tornay would jump right in and defend him. He was never scared of getting hurt.

"At school he always spoke his mind, and that got him into trouble. On Wednesday afternoons, when there are no classes, he would get detention and have to spend three hours copying pages from the dictionary or sweeping leaves on the playground. Always because he didn't keep his mouth shut. It was the same during his military service. If an order was fair and logical, fine. If not, he'd speak his mind. I'm sure that if Estermann had picked on him and ridiculed him in public, Tornay wouldn't have stood for it. He wanted his superiors to be fair.

"But he wasn't very fair with women. He was always flirting with other men's girlfriends. He was good-looking, and that attracted a few homosexual priests. Once Tornay wrote to one who had been harassing him. The priest wrote back all high-and-mighty, saying how dare Tornay think that he was sexually interested in him.

"When I heard the news from Rome, that Tornay was among three people found dead, the first thing I thought was that he'd died committing a glorious feat. I thought he'd jumped in to shield someone from an attacker. He had a heroic side to him. I have absolutely no doubt that he believed in the oath. Tornay really would have given his life to save the pope."

CHAPTER NINETEEN

THAT EVENING I checked into a hotel off the main street and stayed indoors, unwilling to venture out because after the early sunset imposed on the town by the rock face, the air had turned ice-cold. In any case, I knew I had enough reading to keep me busy for the whole evening. Tornay's friends had allowed me to photocopy the letters they had received from him.

Tornay wrote so many that they had trouble keeping up with him. He wrote most of them when he was on the night shift, and there was little else to help keep him awake. I imagined him in his uniform, scribbling away as he sat at the desk in the frescoed antechamber outside the pope's apartment while the rest of Vatican City slumbered.

The letters stretch from February 1994, shortly after his arrival in the Eternal City, to April 1998, a month before his death. Many are stamped in the top left-hand corner with the image of a stern-faced guard in gala uniform, complete with breastplate, pleated white collar, and plume-topped helmet. Tornay's name and address are stamped on the envelopes in ornate script, next to the papal miter and keys.

As I began to read by the poor light of a bedside lamp—the hand-writing was sloped, unjoined, and the letters were riddled with spelling and grammatical mistakes—I realized this was the first time I was hearing Tornay speak for himself. I found it a little disconcerting that I was doing so in the town where he grew up.

The earliest letters are full of optimism. All is well, he reports two months after reaching Rome. He is burning the candle at both ends, he likes the job, and he is slowly learning Italian. "In two or three months' time, I'll speak it well enough to flirt with the chicks." And yet, as he boasts, he has also found time to write a hundred letters since joining the Guard—more than ten a week.

There are other signs of homesickness. He has stuck photographs of his Saint-Maurice chums above his bed so he can see them often. His friends back home "must have a bit of a hangover because if my calculations are right it's carnival time for you lot." During ten years with the Boy Scouts, he had helped many times to decorate the colorful floats used in the carnival procession through the narrow streets of Saint-Maurice. I imagined the main road, which had been deserted when I arrived, jammed with floats, and a young Tornay perhaps perched on one of them, or more likely jumping constantly on and off, pausing only to flirt with a girl.

A year into his service at the Vatican, he says again, "all is well in the best of possible worlds," and for him there are few sights more impressive than a dozen guards presenting arms in perfect unison. On the downside, the curfew is very strict, which means that he has to be back in the barracks by midnight, apart from three days a month when he can stay out until one o'clock in the morning.

But this does not stop him having a busy social life, drinking until late at night with his comrades-in-arms, and then fighting a hangover to cope with sentry duty at dawn. Once, after a party in the barracks that ended at three o'clock in the morning, he reported for sentry duty at "Cardinal"—as the guards call the apartment of Cardinal Sodano, the secretary of state—just before eight o'clock "in a bit of a state."

The alluring city outside the Vatican's gates is, of course, much richer in temptations: "The women here are superb. I've rarely seen the like elsewhere. But the problem is they're not after the same thing as I am and what's more I've got to polish my Italian. Then eventually we can look for something more."

In a rare confession, Tornay admits that despite all the company, he still feels lonely: "What I miss a lot are my friends. I've got a few here, there's a good atmosphere but it's not the same thing. The problem is that I've realized I can count my real mates in Saint-Maurice on the fingers of one hand."

In June 1995, life in a sweltering Rome is a whirl of parties, and trips to the beach or the swimming pool whenever he has a day off. But half of one letter contains a detailed explanation of how to reach him by telephone, which is only possible during mealtimes in the canteen. "Phone me bang on time otherwise they call me in my room and I've got to run. And if you call too late when I'm supposed to dress for duty I get stressed," Tornay fusses. "If you've got the blues or you've got some problems a phone call is so easy," he adds in a postscript that sounds more like an appeal than an offer of help.

On his return to the Vatican after celebrating the New Year in 1996 with his family in Switzerland, he admits to feeling depressed for a whole week. No sooner has he made this confession than he takes it back, dismissing his feelings with platitudes: "As the saying goes everything's got a price. Living in Rome is a privilege so you've got to suffer a bit."

From then on, the stamp with the proud guard disappears from the writing paper, perhaps, I thought, a sign of his growing dissatisfaction. Not that this can be inferred from his writing: in the spring of 1997, he is "a little stressed" but partying so much that "the hours of sleep can be counted on the fingers of one hand . . . The most important thing is that I'm having fun and that I live my life as I mean to."

As I read on into the night, my eyes feeling strained in the weak light, I realized that Tornay was deceiving not only his friends but also himself. When his superiors made him a lance corporal in August of the same year, it is clear that he did not welcome the trade-off that forced him to remain with the Guard. "The promotion means I will stay at the minimum one more year," he wrote. He commented unconvincingly: "But the work's pretty interesting. Much more contact with the tourists."

Even when he finally announced that he had decided to leave Rome, Tornay was still pretending that all was well. "For my part everything's fine," he wrote, adding: "I've made a big decision. I am returning to Switzerland. I don't know when yet. It could be in a year or in six months. I'm starting to look for a job and when I've got something firm which allows me to take a flat in Saint-Maurice, I'll pack my bags and *via* [away]."

There is little explanation for his decision, apart from the fact that he had been worked to the bone recently and all his days off had been canceled. There is only a hint of regret: "Rome really is a superb city, and I think I'll miss it."

By the time he wrote the last letter, on April 14, 1998, Tornay had made up his mind. He would show the Roman sights to a group of friends from Saint-Maurice who were due to visit him a month later, and then in the summer he'd pack his bags, hand his uniform back, and leave. "It's over," he wrote.

One thought struck me when I finished reading. Nowhere, in all the letters that Tornay wrote from the Vatican to his closest friends in Saint-Maurice, was there any mention of the name Estermann.

CHAPTER TWENTY

THE NEXT MORNING, I followed the Rhone upstream toward Sion, the capital of the French Valais region and home to the training school for security personnel that Tornay had contacted about a possible job. From several miles away, two rocky hills topped by medieval castles stuck out from the otherwise smooth floor of the valley. The hills looked incongruous and bleak, and reminded me of something I had heard in Saint-Maurice: conventional wisdom pronounced the people of Sion bizarre, clannish, and as silent as the grave. I hoped this would not prove too accurate.

Jo Georges, the training school's director, had suggested breakfast at a hotel bar on the town's outskirts. All I knew about him was that he had previously served as a senior police officer and had headed the local branch of Switzerland's domestic intelligence agency. The bar was empty, and I had no trouble spotting him. Dressed in an open-necked shirt and crumpled jacket, the sad-faced Georges sat at a table facing the door, a large brown envelope lying in front of him under a plate that contained a half-eaten croissant. He beckoned me over as soon as I walked in, we shook hands, and without further ado he slid the envelope across the table.

I fished out a few sheets of paper that had been clipped together. On top was a letter, the handwriting instantly recognizable after my reading the previous evening. Dated "Swiss Quarter, Vatican City, 27th February 1998"—a little over two months before his death—it was a letter by Tornay in which he proposed his services for a security job in his homeland. There was no doubt what Tornay was proudest of about his time in Rome: in his very opening sentence, he said he had spent several years "close to the Holy Father." He went on to explain that his first year of pay as a noncommissioned officer would end in the summer, and from then on he would be free to leave the Guard with two months' notice.

Attached to the letter were various certificates and a curriculum vitae, which put his knowledge of both French and Italian ahead of his knowledge of German, of which he had only "scholastic notions"— something that must have created serious difficulties for him in the German-dominated Swiss Guard. The CV said he had left school at the age of sixteen and worked as an apprentice mechanic at a railway company in a nearby town before leaving for Rome. His proficiency with guns was mentioned twice, both as a skill and as a hobby, along with skiing, running, hockey, and soccer.

I looked up at Georges, who was steadily munching his way through the rest of his croissant. He stopped to hand me another piece of paper, then returned to his breakfast. I wondered whether he would ever speak. The document was about Georges's training school and listed the subjects covered by the course for bodyguards, ranging from bomb alerts and booby traps through self-defense and coping with stress to kidnappings and first aid. There was also a section on an attack as seen through the eyes of the assailant.

Georges broke his silence at last. "Take a close look. I sent that to Tornay after he first called me in November 1997. A couple of weeks later, we discussed the list in detail on the phone, and believe it or not, most of it was gibberish to him. His senior officers had never covered those things with him. I remember exactly what he said. He told me: 'We're supposed to protect the pope, but in fact we're here just for show. It's all folklore, we might as well be working for the tourist board.' He was really disappointed with the Swiss Guard. But not bitter. He didn't make it into a personal thing."

"Did he tell you why he had joined in the first place?"

"Yes, he did. He had an ideal, like all those who join the Swiss Guard. I mean, it's not as if you're taking a job as a bricklayer or something. He thought that he would be working as a bodyguard for the Holy Father and get up close to him. And all he got was a lovely uniform."

"How did he sound when he called you? Depressed, desperate, anything like that?"

Georges slowly shook his head. "He wasn't a manic-depressive, if that's what you mean. He was a perfectly normal guy who wanted to get the hell out of Vatican City. He was sick of playing the quaint toy soldier, and he thought I could be his ticket out of there. After he phoned, I asked him to send me his CV. I was eager to talk to him, I'd have given him a job interview anytime. Partly because I was intrigued by what he had to say about the Swiss Guard. I quizzed him the couple of times that we spoke on the phone. Lots of things shocked me."

"For example?"

"I like the way Tornay put it. He said to me that militarily, the

Guard is at least one war behind the times. These guys have no idea what to do if someone starts shooting. You'd think they'd have learned a lesson after the pope was shot. But not at all. Tornay was given shooting practice only once, in a cellar on Vatican territory. The guards aren't taught to think things out like an attacker, to put themselves in his shoes so they can work out how best to neutralize him. They're not properly briefed before they're deployed. And those sentry duties— pointless, completely pointless. The guards stand without moving a muscle for up to five hours a day. We know for a fact that after two hours of sentry duty, you're too exhausted to be of any use. You can't concentrate anymore, and all you're doing is putting the target in even greater danger."

"Did Tornay pass on your comments to his superiors, perhaps without saying who they came from? Perhaps he tried to change something."

Georges's look of surprise showed he had never asked himself the question. "All I know is that he wanted to make the Swiss Guard more professional. He had his own ideas; he'd read up on the subject. I asked him whether there was at least some dialogue between the men and the senior officers. He said there wasn't. The men were there just to receive orders. Like youngsters doing their military service. The last time Tornay called me was in March. He said he'd be over in April and I agreed to meet him then. But I never heard from him again. It's a pity. I'd have gladly found him a job."

Georges was not finished. He stabbed at the crumbs left by his croissant, trying to collect as many as he could on his index finger.

"I'll tell you something else," he said. "Those deaths should never have happened. Not if the Swiss Guard was run properly. Sentry duties and curfews aren't enough to protect someone like the pope. It's crazy that the commander of a military corps has no protection, that people can just walk up to his flat. And it's just as crazy that NCOs and officers are allowed to walk around carrying guns all over the Vatican, and don't hand them back when they go off duty. Common sense dictates that you establish security perimeters, and that in the zone closest to the target—in this case, the pope—anyone who is armed is accompanied by a colleague, at all times. The guards aren't supposed to trust each other. Do you realize? If Tornay really had been a madman, he could have shot not Estermann, but the pope. I mean, what does the Vatican think it's doing? Relying on divine protection from the Holy Spirit?"

CHAPTER TWENTY-ONE

IN ROME, the Swiss Guard's commander had blocked my attempts to talk to Tornay's closest comrades-in-arms. But here in Switzerland, I set out to find any of his former companions who might have left Rome since his death and returned to their homeland. Although they had been sworn to silence by Monsignor Jehle, the chaplain, within hours of the deaths, the fact was that as ex-soldiers, they were no longer under the Vatican's authority, and this might make them more ready to defy Jehle's gag order.

I had brought with me a yearbook of the Swiss Guard that a contact in the Vatican had obtained for me. Published in three languages—German, French, and Italian—it was for the most part very dull, and I could not imagine even more than a few guards wanting to read it. It contained a chronology of the past year, as well as the speeches given by dignitaries from the pope downward at the swearing-in ceremony. The one thing in the yearbook that was of huge interest to me was a list of all the members of the Guard, including those who had recently left. The list contained not only the names and ranks of guards and officers, but also the Swiss cantons in which they were born and in which they had resided before joining the Guard.

I concentrated on the French-speaking veterans who had joined the Guard at the same time as Tornay and who had left it since his death. There was a good chance that among them I would find the companions who had been closest to him in Rome. Given the hostility between the French Swiss and their German rivals, it was unlikely that Tornay would have made friends among the latter. One name stood out: an ex-guard called David Tissières. He had not only been born in the same town as Tornay, but had also been sworn in on the very same day. He had been promoted to the rank of lance corporal, like Tornay, and had left Rome in late 1998, a few months after the deaths.

Tracking down Tissières was easy. Switzerland has such a small population that a call to directory assistance amounts to a nationwide search. He was at home when I telephoned and quickly agreed to see me. He lived only a short way out of Sion, on a bend in the road that leads up the mountainside to the village of Savièse. The road weaves through steeply terraced vineyards that produce a local wine derisively labeled in my guidebook as "Switzerland's best-kept secret," because most Swiss vintages fail to travel abroad.

When Tissières showed me into the sitting room of his apartment, which had a magnificient view over the vineyards, my first impression was that he nurtured fond memories of his time in Rome. A Swiss Guard halberd stretched at an angle across an entire wall, as if ready, at a moment's notice, to slice through the air and chop off the heads of guests sitting on the sofa beneath it. The sword worn with the gala uniform also hung in its sheath nearby, as did a framed papal certificate bearing the signature "Joannes Paulus II," and a photograph of Tissières shaking hands with the pope. Tissières, who now worked as a police officer, explained that he had been nine years old when he caught his first glimpse of the pope during the latter's visit to Sion. The sight planted the seed that brought him to Rome years later.

Like all the other guards, he enlisted without any need for an interview. He could still remember his arrival at St. Anne's Gate with the regulation thirty-five kilos of luggage, and his exhausting first day of duty: three shifts each one and a half hours long, during which he had to stand sentinel, motionless, at the Arch of Bells. Despite his complete lack of experience, he could just as easily have started out at the pope's front door, as shifts were assigned at random.

The pace had never let up: working days lasted an average of nine to eleven hours, often as many as thirteen, while days off could be canceled at a moment's notice. All of this left little time for his hobby of jogging in the Vatican Gardens, one of his few privileges, or for the parties celebrating the return to Rome of guards who, as tradition dictated, brought fresh supplies of chocolate, wine, and easily meltable raclette cheese from their vacations at home.

Tissières pointed to the smallest of his Roman relics hanging on the wall, a gold medal tied to a ribbon with the Vatican colors of white and gold. There was no nostalgia, and plenty of bitterness, as he spoke barely above a murmur: "And that, friend, is the cause of three deaths."

I leaned forward for a closer look. The medal seemed very ordinary, rather cheap, and was less well crafted than the Vatican's famed postage stamps. It bore the arms of John Paul II in one corner. This was the *benemerenti,* the award for three years' service with the Swiss Guard. This was the medal that Tornay had been refused a few hours before his death. That morning I had noticed an announcement in the obituaries of the local newspaper that mentioned the medal as one of the highest achievements of the deceased, an elderly pensioner.

I had expected it would take some time for Tissières to feel comfortable enough to talk about Tornay's death, but given how he pointed out the medal without any encouragement, I decided to take the plunge. I asked him whether Tornay had ever spoken to him about the award.

"Yes, the last time I saw him. It was on the morning of the day he died. Tornay was on duty at the gates that lead to the papal Audience Hall. There was a synod, a meeting of bishops in the auditorium, and his job was to direct the bishops when they arrived. He was really upbeat; he told me that the medal would be pinned to his chest in two days' time. He said to me: 'Then I will leave.' He'd made up his mind to go back to Switzerland."

Judging by Tissières's words, Tornay had no suspicion that he could be refused the medal. "And then? Did you hear what happened after he discovered that he wouldn't be given the medal after all?" I asked.

"All I know is that I went to see the list for myself early that evening, just before I was set to go out with my parents. They'd come down to Rome because I was due to get the medal, too, and they wanted to attend the annual swearing-in ceremony at which the medals would be handed out. It's a good time for families to come to see us, because it's the only time of the year when we're allowed to show them all over the Vatican, even the inside of the Apostolic Palace. Except for the third floor, where the pope lives. Of course, that's always off-limits."

"And the list?"

"I went to the canteen, I found the list on the bulletin board. I saw that my name was on it, as I'd expected, but the thing that really hit me was that Tornay's wasn't. I was with a friend at the time, and I said to him: 'Tornay's going to fly off the handle.'"

"What made you think that?"

"The medal meant a lot to him because he wanted to go back to Switzerland with his head held high. It was pride, but it was understandable because he had had a difficult childhood and he wanted his years in Rome to be a success, an achievement. He wanted to make a fresh start, to prove himself. But Estermann was always hounding him."

Tissières had spoken the last sentence as if he'd been talking to himself, staring out of the windows at the vines that carpeted the slopes rising from the valley. As he fell quiet, I tried to remember the words that the former commander Colonel Buchs had pronounced at Tornay's funeral—how Tornay was sensitive to the way he was treated, and how he suffered from heartrending tension. I reminded Tissières of what the Vatican had said about Estermann and Tornay in the hours following their deaths—Estermann, a faithful and tireless servant, and Tornay, undisciplined and unpredictable.

"Tornay was a great guy, and the Vatican blackened his name when he could no longer speak for himself. The truth is that he was no better and no worse than the others as far as discipline went. When Tornay was promoted, Estermann was the only senior officer who voted against it. A promotion was a collegial decision by the senior officers, not like the medal, which was only up to Estermann. He liked to humiliate Tornay publicly. Once, Tornay and some friends were sitting on a bench in the courtyard of the barracks, and Esterman's wife, Meza Romero, walked by. She was the wife of a senior officer, so they all said hello to her. The next day Estermann punished Tornay because he had failed to stand up when she passed. None of the others had gotten up either, but Tornay was the only one who was punished."

"Was there any particular reason for Estermann picking on Tornay?"

"I don't really know. Perhaps the fact that Tornay would often answer back when he was reprimanded. In any case, Estermann couldn't stand having French speakers around; he'd always tell us: 'You Swiss

French are completely out of place in the Swiss Guard. There is no room for you here.' We didn't like him either; he made the Guard so strict, much stricter even than the Swiss army. For him, the ideal guard was a guy who did his duty without thinking, who kept his mouth shut, and who went to Mass every day. Every time we came up with an idea for something, we knew what Estermann's answer would be: '*Nein*.' We were always mimicking the way he said that; it was so hard."

Tissières paused for a moment. "Estermann is not the only person I'm angry about. There's also Monsignor Jehle. I heard that he refused to see Tornay after evening Mass, only a couple of hours before he died. It doesn't surprise me: Jehle was supposed to be our confidant, the person we'd go to with our personal problems, but he was monitoring us all the time. He never took up our complaints with anyone. Tornay also tried to see Cardinal Schwéry, who's from Sion and who was always friendly with us, but I don't know what came of that. My impression is that Tornay had no one to talk to."

Again he fell silent, fingers playing a martial tattoo on the coffee table.

"What about his health? How come the cyst in Tornay's brain wasn't known to the Swiss Guard until after the autopsy?" I asked.

"Because the medical checks are nonexistent. When you start out as a guard, you get four medical visits in three weeks; they examine you all over—they do X rays of your whole body, they stick things into you, the works. But all the years after that, nothing. It's up to you to ask to see the doctor if you're not feeling well."

While Tornay was at the Vatican, there had therefore been no chance of him discovering the tumor, and no chance of him being able to do anything about it.

Tissières stood up and searched through a bookshelf. He picked out a videocassette. "You might like to see this. It's Tornay's swearing-in ceremony. It was also mine."

The small flat suddenly filled with the sound of a long drumroll as a sergeant major, carrying the red-and-gold banner of the Swiss Guard high above him, led the detachment of new recruits into St. Damasus Square, below the windows of the pope's apartment. A commentator struggled to make himself heard above the din: "The ceremony starts on time, as precise as a Swiss watch, which is no surprise given that these men are the Swiss Guard."

The date was May 6, 1995. Applauding the detachment and sitting on plastic chairs was a kaleidoscopic assortment of diplomats in dark suits and military attachés in uniform, marines from the U.S. embassy with close-cropped hair, Italian carabinieri police officers in gilded finery, priests and nuns in more somber garb, and the guards' parents. Several of the mothers wore Swiss folk dress. I knew that Tornay's mother was in the crowd, but it was impossible to pick her out. A clutch of senior prelates sat, smug and unsmiling, in throne-like chairs that blocked the view for many of the lesser members of the audience behind them. The drumroll came to a crashing end and was followed by the pontifical march, the Vatican's national anthem.

Tissières offered his own commentary. "Eleven and a half kilos, not counting the sword and the halberd. That's what the boys have got strapped on: the breastplate weighs nine kilos, and the helmet two and a half kilos."

I recognized a fresh-faced Tornay standing rigid at attention in the second row of the detachment, shining breastplate strapped tightly over his dress uniform, helmet rammed down over his forehead. A look of furious concentration was stamped on his face. Estermann, one large medal under his neck and another under his left breast, snapped at them in Swiss German to present arms, and twenty-seven halberds clutched in white-gloved hands came to a rest on the cobblestones with a dull crash and a clang of metal. I asked Tissières to guess what was going through Tornay's head at the time.

"We're so scared of getting something wrong that we don't think about anything at all. The previous days were a mad rush to get everything perfect. We make one mistake, we let the team down in front of everyone—there's always a chance the pope might be watching from the windows of the third loggia. Not only that: we also get punished. It's as simple as that."

"Doesn't the oath mean anything, then?"

Tissières looked incredulous. "You must be joking. Like all of us, Tornay thought about very little else for weeks before the ceremony. Can you imagine, dying at the service of the Holy Father? It's our ideal, the height of honor. It's why we're there. In the two months before the ceremony, Jehle prepared us for the oath; we talked about the spiritual side. When we swear, we make a sign with the right hand which symbolizes the Holy Trinity—the Father, the Son, and the Holy Ghost are all there with us."

He pointed to the screen. Jehle, the only figure among the senior prelates clad in black from head to toe, stood at a lectern reading the text of the oath: "I swear I will faithfully, loyally, and honorably serve the Supreme Pontiff John Paul II and his legitimate successors, and also devote myself to them with all my strength, sacrificing my life for their defense if necessary.

"I take on the same duties with regard to the Sacred College of Cardinals whenever the See is vacant. Furthermore, I promise to the Commander and to my other superiors respect, fidelity, and obedience. This I swear! May God and our Holy Patrons assist me!"

Moments later Tornay shook himself out of his deathly stillness. In a gesture he must have practiced for days, he thrust his left foot forward, then marched stiffly with clenched fists through the center of the square, the blue, red, and yellow bands of his jacket twisting in the air as he bore down on his commander. All eyes were upon him. His own gaze was fixed on Estermann, who returned the stare from his close-set eyes, unblinking. Without a word being spoken, Tornay came to an abrupt stop a few paces away from his superior.

All that separated the two men was the standard of the Swiss Guard, which writhed languidly in the slow Roman breeze as a junior guard held the flagstaff horizontally. One more jerky left step forward and Tornay thrust his left hand forward to grab hold of the flagstaff with such force that the banner shook. Then he punched the air with his right hand, three fingers extended to symbolize the Holy Trinity.

Estermann's thin lips, which had been pressed tightly shut, parted. "Swear!" he commanded. Still gazing into Estermann's eyes, Tornay shouted the oath in a voice straining with tension: "I, Cédric Tornay, swear to observe faithfully, loyally, and honorably all that has now been read out to me! May God and his saints assist me!"

I reflected that three years later, two days before the same ceremony was due to take place, that oath would return to haunt him in the last hours of his life.

The image of Tornay vanished. The screen went blank. Tissières had pointed the remote control at the set and switched it off. Eventually he broke the awkward silence: "I'd say that almost all of us are ready to die for the pope. Tornay was definitely among those. And I defy you to find anyone who was not granted the medal after three years in the Guard. The rule is that it rewards the length of service, period."

I was so taken aback by his outspokenness that I felt I had to mention the silence imposed by Jehle. "Weren't you and all your companions sworn to silence right after the deaths?"

"It's true that we were told not to speak, but even worse for me was the fact that nobody in authority ever came to us to tell us precisely what had happened to Tornay. The Vatican hushed everything up."

I noticed that Tissières looked drained, clearly tired by our talk, so

I pulled out the Swiss Guard's yearbook and asked him who else among the corps' veterans could speak to me about Tornay's time in Rome. Tissières jabbed a finger at a name on the list of recruits. "Steve Kellenberger is your man. He joined six months before Tornay, and they were very close. He left Rome some time ago. I don't know where he is now, but he's probably back in Switzerland. That's where almost all of us end up after the Vatican."

As I left, Tissières had one last recommendation for me. "Go and see Tornay's tomb. You'll see that even today, people still leave medals and flowers for him. They think he was a victim. They know it could all have been avoided. Don't misunderstand me: I don't justify his act, I'm not an apologist for murder. But I understand Tornay's gesture."

CHAPTER TWENTY-TWO

WITH THE HELP of the ever-efficient Swiss directory assistance, I quickly found out that there was only one Steve Kellenberger in the whole country. On the phone, he told me that he lived near Zurich airport, where he worked for Swissair. He suggested we talk at his home after he finished work. It was only after I put the phone down that I realized he had spoken English with more than a hint of an Australian accent.

Kellenberger lived in a pristine residential complex of low apartment buildings and tree-lined streets. Fair-haired, tall, and athletic, he still had his Swissair badge clipped to his well-ironed white shirt when he opened his front door. I was half expecting another sitting room full of Swiss Guard relics, but all I saw at first was a pair of African lances fixed to the wall, a piece of patchy black-and-white animal skin stretched between them—the trophy he had brought back from a safari. There was only one small memento of Rome: on discreet display on the corner of a bookshelf lay the brass belt buckle from the gala uniform.

As he rummaged around in the kitchen, Kellenberger summed up his background. His parents were Swiss but had emigrated to Australia, and his mother had sent him to Roman Catholic schools. They divorced when he was still a teenager. A former altar boy, he had at one time planned to spend a lifetime with the Swiss Guard, but instead he left after two years. "I got a bit of an overdose as far as the Church goes," he said.

He emerged from the kitchen clutching two tall cans of beer and handed me one before flopping himself down into an armchair. I asked him whether he had kept a diary in the Vatican.

To my surprise, he looked hurt. "A diary? You must be joking. Only poofs do that kind of thing. Do I look like a poof?" he asked.

I reassured him that no, he didn't look like a "poof," and reflected that however close he and Tornay had been, there was little chance that Tornay had confided his homosexual leanings to him. I was beginning to wonder whom Tornay could have confided in, apart from Bertorello.

With a friendly smile, Kellenberger launched into an anecdote. "It was the biggest scare of my time in Rome. I was on night patrol in the Apostolic Palace, on my own. Everything was dark; I just had a flashlight with me. Every step you take echoes on the marble; there are no carpets, no furniture. Anyway, there's a chapel on the floor beneath the one where the pope sleeps. That night I found that the door of the chapel was open, which was unusual. Guess what I found inside? A velvet-covered box on a pedestal. And inside the box was a human skull. I'm not kidding. Didn't look too good. Turned out it was the skull of a second-century saint. Someone had forgotten it there. There, that's the Vatican for you."

He eyed me with a keen stare. "But you want to know about Tornay, don't you?"

Thrown by his story, I could only nod.

"Okay, I'll tell you about Tornay. We learned Italian together; we were in the same class. I'll be honest: at first I couldn't stand him. I thought he was a bigmouth, he bragged a lot about women and what he'd done with them. He was always trying to tag along with me in the evenings. After a bit I ran out of excuses for shaking him off, so we went for a drink together in a bar not far from the Tiber. We just talked and talked, mainly about his family troubles. I'd say we identified with each other—imagine, we were the only sons of divorcées in the Swiss Guard. Tornay's stepfather was a cop, a hell of a brute. He beat Tornay's mother. Tornay was only a kid. He got hit, too. For me, what Tornay went through goes a long way to explaining why the Guard mattered so much to him."

"What about Tornay's real father, the one who went off to Mauritius to marry a woman there? What was he like?"

"Tornay was completely devoted to him. He kept saying what a good, generous guy his old man was. In fact, his old man was a complete idiot. He'd ended up in jail for a bit for some small crime. I thought, God, what a combination for a member of the Swiss Guard: a divorced Protestant mum and a dad who's done time. I met the dad one summer in Castel Gandolfo, the pope's summer residence. The guy was about to fly off to Mauritius. I'd expected someone pretty impressive. But really, just the look of him—he was in jeans and plastic sandals, no socks, looked a real tramp."

"How did he treat his son?"

"He never said a single nice thing to Tornay, never asked him how things were going at the Guard, nothing. We were out on the piazza, having an evening drink. Don Salvatore, the local priest, came up to me to say hello. He didn't know Tornay, but he could see Tornay was in the Guard like me. Just to be nice, I suppose, Don Salvatore told Tornay's dad that he was lucky to have a son in the Swiss Guard, and that Tornay was doing a great job and was very respected. Tornay was too embarrassed to translate, so I did it. Afterward, Tornay's dad turned to his son and said: 'Your job, any damn fool could do it.' Which wasn't a very tactful thing to say, given that he was with not just one guard but two at the time. I remember I paid for all the drinks, and Tornay paid for the dinner. But the worst thing was the way his dad spoke about women: he said they were all whores, and that when he went on holiday to Brazil, they were cheaper than his meals there. He told us that he picked up this woman, and that when she was eating his breakfast, he said to her: 'Hey, if you're hungry, eat what's between my legs, not my breakfast.' He was so proud of that. What a savage."

Kellenberger took a sip from his can of beer. "There was something odd about the mother, too. The way Tornay spoke about her was incestuous; it was the way we'd have spoken about a girlfriend. He'd say, 'My mum's got a really good-looking arse,' or tits. It was weird."

I tried my luck. "Was Tornay bisexual?" I asked.

"He had sex on the brain, I'll say that about him, but it was sex with girls. On the walls of his room, he stuck dozens of pictures he'd cut out from magazines. You'd look at them and only after a while you'd realize there was a picture of a naked woman in a corner, showing everything. The officers who were supposed to inspect our rooms never spotted them."

"Is it true he was undisciplined, or were the senior officers picking on him unfairly?"

"Tornay was a victim. He wasn't a violent nature, but he was the victim of bullying for three years. He was made to swallow shit all that time, and he never forgot any of it. For the Swiss Germans, he was the Devil in person. Right at the start, the first December he was in Rome, it was raining badly and the Swiss Germans forced him to stand in the open for hours at the Arch of Bells. They didn't allow him to put a cloak on or to step into the sentry box. He caught bronchitis because of that. He wrote a report to complain, but it was just flushed down the drain. And another time, we broke the curfew together, we spent the night out, and we got back at eight o'clock in the morning. The whole Swiss Guard already knew that he'd been out, and the Swiss Germans were waiting for him, ready to pick him to pieces."

"You were both punished?"

Kellenberger banged his beer can down on the coffee table. "No! Nobody did anything to me. But Tornay was dragged before Colonel Buchs. He wasn't allowed to go out at all for several evenings. He was ordered to return by midnight instead of the normal one o'clock in the morning for weeks afterward. And as if that wasn't enough, he was made to work in the kitchens. The Swiss Germans hate the French speakers so much, and they took it out on Tornay. But he wasn't incapable, like some people say. He was even respected by our rivals, the Vigilanza police. They thought so highly of him that they wanted to poach him. Once, Tornay came up to me and said: 'Imagine Estermann's face if I went and joined the Vigilanza!' "

"And Estermann? Did he side with the other Swiss Germans against Tornay?"

"You bet he did. Estermann made sure that Tornay had more than his fair share of work. Estermann's whole approach was crazy. He wanted to turn all of us into combat monks. He'd charge down the corridors in the mornings and shout, 'Wake up! There's no one in the chapel, you must come and thank God that you are here! You are here to serve all day, either on duty or in the chapel!' And Tornay was the only one who stood up to him. When Estermann robbed Tornay of the medal, right at the last minute, he was just amusing himself. The medal was a big deal for Tornay. I once asked him whether the rank of lance corporal wasn't enough for him. He told me: 'I want to serve three years and I want a medal.' I said I could buy him one, but he didn't want that. He'd done so much to get that far."

The term "combat monks" reminded me of the way the sect-like Opus Dei saw its members as soldiers at the service of Christ. I asked Kellenberger whether he had come across any evidence of Estermann's sympathy for the movement.

"We all knew that Estermann was in Opus Dei. There was a Spanish monsignor who was a senior member of Opus Dei; he often came around to the barracks and asked for Estermann. One day they organized an outing to Villa Tevere, the headquarters of Opus Dei in Rome. Except they didn't say it was the headquarters, they just said there would be a barbecue at this villa. I stayed away because for me, Opus Dei is like a sickness inside the Church, but lots of guards went."

"Did Estermann ever talk about Opus Dei with the guards, with Tornay?"

"I don't know about Tornay specifically, but I heard that Monsignor Jehle, the chaplain, told Estermann off for trying to recruit guards into Opus Dei. Publicly, Estermann denied he was in it. Once, when we were gathered in the courtyard, he told us that he had heard rumors that he was a member of Opus Dei. Then he started shouting: 'I am not Opus Dei, I am not Opus Dei!' again and again. It was so bizarre. I thought he was protesting too much."

"Tornay must have known that Jehle stood up to Estermann, so did Tornay ever try to confide in Jehle? After all, Jehle was the Guard's chaplain," I asked.

Kellenberger shook his head. "Nobody went to Jehle. We hoped at first that he'd be a friend and an ally, but there was only one thing he was worried about: that we should dress properly and wear ties for

Sunday Mass. It's as if a passenger on the *Titanic* complained that a fork was not properly polished. He was so obsessed by Mass at his chapel that he stopped Tornay taking a day off for his girlfriend's birthday. We were going to go together and we told Jehle that we'd go to Mass near where she lived, but Jehle said that all the guards had to be with him in the chapel. He said that every Sunday, God sent a blessing to all the guards in the chapel, and if you weren't there you wouldn't get the blessing. When I heard that, I thought to myself: God must be pretty busy, then, giving his blessings to people attending Mass all over the world."

"Was Tornay the only one who thought the Guard needed reform?"

"Many of us kept asking ourselves: What on earth are we doing here? The officers think they command an elite corps, but that's rubbish. All we're taught is how to stand still. Dziwisz, the pope's secretary, told us his master gets very nervous if he sees guards moving around; he thinks something's wrong. He's afraid of crowds; the assassination attempt has stuck in his mind. We've got small containers of tear gas, but we're not allowed to take them with us to events where there are large crowds. The monsignori are worried that using them would create panic. So the tear gas is out most of the time, as are guns. If there's serious trouble and the pope is sitting on his throne, the guards of honor who are on duty next to him are supposed to pick it up and run."

It sounded absurd to me. I imagined two guards in their dress uniforms struggling not to hurl the pope out of his chair as they made their exit as fast as they could, which, it was safe to assume, would not be fast enough to shake off an attacker. I told Kellenberger that I had seen no cupboards for storing weapons in the guardrooms on the upper floors of the Apostolic Palace, including the pope's third loggia.

He gave a loud guffaw. "That's because there aren't any. The weapons are kept several floors down. They're in locked cupboards, but it doesn't need a Houdini to get to the key: it's in an envelope which is stuck to the inside of a desk drawer with a piece of tape. In any case, a lot of them are wooden machine guns dating from the 1930s that were banned ages ago in Switzerland because they're too dangerous. They could just explode in your face."

The security would have been laughable had the pope's life not been at stake. "But surely anyone with the rank of lance corporal upward has his own ordnance weapon?" I asked.

"Yes, they do. But they're not allowed to carry them when they're dressed in their gala uniforms. They can carry them only when they're wearing the blue uniforms—but those uniforms are worn only at night, and at Saint Anne's Gate. Not much use then, is it?"

"Did Tornay ever try to persuade Estermann to make some changes in the way the Guard was run?" I asked.

"Yes, he did. He drafted a report. It was like a battle plan: a new system of shifts and assignments to help the Guard cope with the shortage of recruits. Estermann shoved the report in a drawer and that was it. But the report did help Tornay get promoted to lance corporal."

Kellenberger got up, saying he wanted to show me a photo album. The pictures were all from his two years in Rome, and many were of his dead friend. There was Tornay clowning about in his room, the walls plastered with sheets of aluminum foil and countless photographs cut out of magazines; bleary-eyed after a late-night party around a cheese fondue and beer; laughing as he strung reams of toilet paper across a companion's room in a practical joke; and playing the piccolo, with the band of the Swiss Guard.

"Tornay learnt how to play the piccolo in just a few weeks; he was so desperate to be in with the lads," Kellenberger said. "He was a strange guy; I never understood him completely. He did odd things, I don't know why. Once, after we'd had a late beer together, he did his washing in the laundry of the barracks, and because there was room in the machine, he offered to put in my stuff as well. I went to bed, but at three o'clock in the morning he stormed into my room. He woke me up and told me that I owed him two thousand lire for the washing. I told him to help himself from my wallet on the table and to get the hell out."

Nothing in the photographs hinted at the tragedy ahead. I asked Kellenberger whether anything he knew about Tornay and his plight in the Swiss Guard would have led him to expect that he'd meet such an end. Had Tornay, when venting his frustrations, ever hinted at an extreme reaction—either revenge, or suicide?

"Revenge, no, never, although he did keep a list with the names of the people who had slighted him. And he was always the first one to step in and defend you if someone treated you badly, even if it meant taking a few knocks for you. He only once mentioned death to me. We were in his car near Saint Anne's Gate, and he was driving recklessly. I told him to calm down. His answer was: 'I'm not afraid of death. When it comes, I will just accept it.' He told me his only worry was the life insurance policy he was paying for through the Vatican. He said to me: 'If ever I have to kill myself, I'll have to make it look as if it was an accident so that my mother and my sisters get the money.' But that was three years before he died."

A couple of the photographs showed Tornay smoking cigarettes. At the risk of upsetting Kellenberger, I asked him whether it was true, as the Vatican had claimed, that his friend smoked cannabis.

Kellenberger knitted his brows. "Some other guys, yes," he fudged.

"But Tornay?" I insisted.

There was no answer. Kellenberger was as mute as a guard on sentry duty at the Bronze Doors. But his embarrassment told me what I wanted to know.

Kellenberger flicked impatiently through the photo album, stopping to stare at the picture of Tornay with his flute. After some time, he continued: "If he did smoke cannabis, I wouldn't tell you. In any case, the Vatican inquiry concluded that he wasn't under the influence of cannabis when he died. And what's more, it's not cannabis that makes you lose your sense of time, as the Vatican claims. It's the crazy pace of the shifts."

"In his last days, was there anything else, apart from his professional frustrations, that might have been preying on his mind?"

Kellenberger relaxed again. "I'll say. Violetta," he said with a grin.

It was the first time I had heard that name. "Who was she? A girl-friend of his?"

"'Is,' not 'was'—she's not dead, you know. And she was more than a girlfriend. He had a series of girlfriends in Rome, even though Jehle doesn't want you to have a life in Rome and would rather your girl-friend was far away in Switzerland. Actually he'd rather you didn't have a girlfriend, period. Violetta was the only woman Tornay ever wanted to marry. The first time they met—it wasn't long after he'd enlisted—they fell for each other straightaway. We were at a party and I had to lend them my car because he wanted somewhere where he could screw her. Imagine, a car with Vatican license plates. When they brought it back to me, the windows were all steamed up. I got into the back; Tor-nay was driving with Violetta next to him. I started dozing off, but then I noticed that the car was swaying and swerving. I saw that she was performing oral sex on him. I said, 'Stop that right now, not in my car.' Then Tornay turned around and said: 'Maybe we could do some-thing all together.' He was suggesting group sex, but Violetta refused. They each had other relationships after that, but he was devoted to her. Then, shortly before he died, she came to see him in Rome. She told him she was pregnant by someone else. That must have been a strain for him."

"Any chance of my getting in touch with her?"

"None, I'm afraid. I've completely lost touch with her, and I never found out her surname. The last time I spoke to her, she asked me to keep an eye on Tornay. I told her I wasn't his nanny, there was nothing I wanted to do or could do."

Kellenberger had spoken the last words with a harsh edge to his voice, and it suddenly occurred to me that perhaps he felt some responsibility for his friend's fate. I asked him whether he felt guilty about Tornay's death.

"I do feel a bit guilty. I remember that on the platform at the railway station in Rome, when I quit and was about to leave for Switzerland—Tornay served for another two years—he was in tears and he asked me five times to stay. He kept saying he wouldn't have any friends left. I told him that I couldn't stay just to hold his hand until he got his medal. And when I went back to Rome for his funeral, Colonel Buchs, the former commander, came over to me and said: 'You see, you went away and this is what happens.'"

"It was hardly your fault," I offered.

"Well, the whole thing need never have happened. If the senior officers had used a little bit of psychology. And if there had been someone who understood him a bit."

He folded his arms and leaned forward. "I had a dream on the night that Tornay died. More like a nightmare. I was on the military course that we all have to do once a year in Switzerland, and I was up in a fortress above Saint-Maurice. We're supposed to simulate war conditions. We were completely isolated, with no news from the outside world.

"That night I dream of a grassy Alpine field. There's a white barrier across the field, and beyond the barrier it's pitch-black. There's a flash; it lights up a guard's helmet on the other side of the barrier. I recognize Tornay; he's marching away from me. I shout to him to come back, but he doesn't even look at me; he just marches on. I was sleeping in a dormitory, and one of my neighbors woke me up. He told me to shut up. I must have been shouting in my sleep. In the morning I was told that Estermann had been killed. Nobody knew anything else. I thought I'd phone Tornay when I got out of the fortress to find out what had happened. When I came out, I saw his face on the front page of a newspaper in a rubbish bin. That's the first time I ever fished a paper out of a bin. It's the last time, too."

CHAPTER TWENTY-THREE

BEFORE I LEFT, Kellenberger lent me the letters Tornay had sent him after he left Rome. He told me I would find several references to Ester-mann, who had been completely absent from the letters Tornay sent his friends in Saint-Maurice. I sat down in a café near Kellenberger's home to read through them.

The first letter in the pack was a draft of a resignation letter that Tornay had written after he was severely punished for breaking the curfew, more than two years into his service. In it, he says he is sorry to leave what he still calls "our" corps, and would have gladly stayed for a third year or even longer, but he has no choice. His first complaint is odd: Tornay protests that he has not been awarded the *benemerenti* medal a few months before he completed the statutory three years. I had found out from the ex-guards I had spoken to that medals could be awarded in advance, and Tornay notes: "I was willing to sign a commitment that I would finish the year."

When Estermann struck Tornay from the list on the day they died, it was therefore not the first time that the lance corporal had been refused the medal. And yet the Vatican had made no mention of this, insisting that the shock of learning that he would not be awarded the medal had been enough to cause Tornay's "fit of madness."

But there are other grievances behind Tornay's resignation letter. The behavior of the Swiss Germans toward the French speakers, and especially toward himself, is, he says, unacceptable. So is the unseemly rush by fellow guards to rat on their companions in order to gain advancement, and the unsuitability of noncommissioned officers who are promoted simply to fill the shoes of those who have left. Nor does Tornay spare the senior officers: they are too cowardly to defend the Swiss Guard's interests and take a stand against senior Church prelates "because they are scared of getting thrown out of the Vatican."

Tornay never did hand in the resignation letter to his superiors. According to Kellenberger, he decided to stay in Rome because he wanted to be promoted to the rank of lance corporal, and to be awarded the medal the following year. The "bumpkins," as Tornay calls the German speakers in one of the letters, continue to make life hard for him. In a single month, one of them picks him out again and again to do overtime, for a total of twenty-five hours. "The bumpkins are still as moronic as ever," he notes.

None of the letters reveals any sign that Tornay wanted to confide in anyone of authority. Quite the contrary. He is summoned by Monsignor Jehle for "a big discussion" but has no wish to go. "And what's more, Jehle can't even be bothered to offer you a drink," he writes. Two months later he does go to see Jehle, but it cannot have been a very satisfactory encounter. Tornay's verdict: "I still mistrust him."

I found the first direct reference to Estermann in a letter dated October 1997, almost three years after Tornay's arrival. There is a long-running staff shortage and "at the pace we're going everyone's going to leave because we're working like dogs." The real piece of news is that Buchs, the commander, is leaving and the successor has not yet been chosen: "I hope the new guy will be a bit better, and that he'll bring some solutions to all the problems. But between ourselves, let me tell you that if it's Estermann who gets the promotion I'm leaving."

The following month Tornay outlined his hopes after taking the "great and wise" decision to leave the Vatican. He made up his mind at a time when Estermann had not yet been appointed commander. Tornay writes: "I'll have totaled three years in December 1997 and I believe that I've accomplished my mission. That doesn't mean I'll leave in two months. I'm starting to look for a job and it's possible that before finding something I like I may serve one more year. But the important thing for me is to have a goal and above all not to return to Switzerland to go on the dole. I want to have a salary which will allow me to stand on my own two feet."

In January 1998, he wished Kellenberger "a year full of joy and pleasure." Tornay had four months left to live.

Much of this letter is devoted to Estermann: "Nothing special here apart from the fact that Estermann is making a few changes so that he can keep a closer watch on us. The first change is the night patrol—one every two hours and what a patrol! Imagine, an electronic system that you've got to activate at all the guardhouses, and the computer can see whether you've been everywhere . . . And the next novelty will be that they put the telephones on a computer so that they can keep tabs on how long the conversations last, say between the guards on the second and third loggia. Which means that's the end of phone calls while on duty. I'm impatient to see what the next changes will be. As you can see we're going to have fun."

The final mention of Estermann is in the last letter, dated March 4, 1998, precisely two months before his death. Tornay is in the town of Ariccia outside Rome, where he is attending a spiritual retreat under the leadership of the Swiss Cardinal Schwéry—"this year a Cardinal and next year the P——[Pope]!" he jokes, adding: "He's very friendly and what's more he makes us laugh."

After apologizing for the fact that his duties as a lance corporal leave him little time to write, Tornay confides: "My days at the Guard are numbered. It's not only that I want it that way, but also that Estermann is insistent. He knows he cannot kick me out but I too know that I've got to cool down a bit so that I don't hand him on a plate any reason to punish me or to try to dismiss me. It's very hard but it's important to me because it has to be said that I can't allow myself to go back without a job."

KELLENBERGER DID ME ONE MORE FAVOR when I returned Tornay's letters to him. For some time now, I had been trying to identify, and trace, the friend to whom Tornay had entrusted the last letter he ever wrote, with the request that it be passed on to his mother "if anything happens to me." The Vatican had done its best to foil any attempt to find this witness, one of the last to see Tornay alive. At his press conference, Navarro-Valls had revealed only that Tornay had given the letter to "a guardsman." At least this had the benefit of limiting the number of possible recipients to under a hundred. Unlike the text of the letter, which was leaked to the press within hours, the name of the friend remained secret. So secret that he was not even mentioned in the final report that marked the closing of the city-state's inquiry.

It was Kellenberger who lifted this particular veil for me. The guard's name, he told me, was Claude Gugelmann. I checked the year-book: Gugelmann had left Rome after Tornay's death, which heightened my hopes of being able to talk to him. Had he still been in the Vatican, he would be highly unlikely to break Monsignor Jehle's law of silence.

Like virtually all veterans, Gugelmann had returned to Switzerland on leaving Rome, and I was able to find his address and telephone number. He lived in the French-speaking part of the country, near the border with France. When I called him, I simply told him that I wanted to ask him about his time at the Vatican. I was careful not to mention his friendship with Tornay.

But Gugelmann wasn't eager to talk with me. He was courteous but firm, and told me that he was about to leave for three weeks' service with the army. He would be in barracks, completely isolated, for all that time. I wasn't sure I believed him, and I guessed that he had realized why I wanted to see him. But he did agree to give me the number of his mobile phone so that I could reach him more easily when he resurfaced. I hoped he was not simply trying to buy time.

CHAPTER TWENTY-FOUR

GUGELMANN WAS STILL FULFILLING his military obligations when Kellenberger telephoned me in Rome a few days later. He sounded jubilant. "Guess what?" he said. "I met Violetta yesterday!"

I was puzzled. "Didn't you tell me you'd lost touch with her?" I asked.

"Yes, it was a coincidence. It was so strange it gave me a chill. I was in Lausanne for the day, and I went to the Café des Artistes for lunch. They started playing this song, 'I Will Survive'—it always reminds me of Tornay. Years ago, the song was playing when I went out for a drink with Tornay—my ex-girlfriend Linda was there, too—and the two of them started kissing in the bar in front of me. Anyway, yesterday in the café when the song ended, someone tapped me on the shoulder from behind. It was a girl; she asked me if I recognized her. I didn't at first; she'd had her hair cut real short. But it was Violetta. We were so moved we both started crying. We had to go outside in the street to talk."

"Did you mention that I'd like to talk to her?"

"Yes, I did." I could imagine the smile on his face. He was enjoying keeping me guessing.

"And?"

"And it's okay; she's happy to talk to you. I'll arrange for you two to meet. She lives in Montreux, on Lake Geneva. By the way, she hasn't even been to Tornay's tomb yet. So I'll take her to see it soon."

By the time I traveled back to Switzerland, Gugelmann's three weeks had ended. I hoped to kill two birds with one stone. I would see Violetta and then contact Gugelmann again. I flew into Geneva, and from there drove along the crescent-shaped lake, a slow wind thinning out the morning mist over the water. I reached Montreux with a couple of hours to spare, so I drove on, past the atmospheric castle of Chillon, which seems to rise out of the depths and which was visited by Byron and Shelley, past the less notorious Saint-Maurice, and on to Martigny.

Near Martigny, I saw a sign indicating a turnoff for Salvan. I felt a lurch in my stomach. The name brought sinister memories back to me: some years earlier I had been sent from Paris, where I was working for the Reuters news agency, to report on a collective suicide by dozens of members of the Order of the Solar Temple—"Lucky you, the biggest story in Europe today," my boss had said to me—and I arrived in the mountain village in time to see bodies being swung into cardboard coffins outside a burned-out chalet as some cows looked on from a nearby field. The local rescue services had run out of body bags.

Martigny's old town was tiny and I had to ask for directions only once before it became obvious that I was on the right road, given the high number of undertaker's premises among the timbered auberges that flanked the alley leading away from the Church of Notre-Dame-des-Champs. The cemetery was a few hundred yards down the alley, packed tight into a narrow strip of land at the foot of a wooded hillside with a view of the peaks that encased the valley. Nearby were the ruins of the town's Roman amphitheater, which dated from the second century—perhaps Saint Maurice himself had seen it before his martyrdom a few miles away.

It was only as I walked through the cemetery's open gate, which was flanked by two stone pavilions, that I realized I had no idea where Tornay's grave was. At the entrance, a sign read: IT IS CATEGORICALLY PROHIBITED TO ENTER THE CEMETERY WITH DOGS. Just as functional was the heading on a large glass-covered panel: PLAN AND NUMERATION OF TOMBS. There were no names on the panel, only coldly neutral indications of areas like CHILDREN ONE and CHILDREN TWO. In any case, most of the names were unreadable because they were covered in condensation.

There was no one around to ask for directions. Both the pavilions were locked and shuttered. I wandered down a path, looking out not only for Tornay's name but also for a photograph that his family might have fixed to the headstone. Only a few yards from the gate, bold gold lettering caught my eye.

CÉDRIC TORNAY, and underneath: 24.07.74–04.05.98. The headstone was of russet-red stone streaked with white. It reminded me of the porphyry marble of some of the tombs in St. Peter's. There was no other inscription, no reference to how he had lived or died. But something else spoke volumes: screwed onto the headstone was a small dome-shaped panel of glass engraved with a full-length portrait of Tornay no taller than my hand.

He was dressed in his gala uniform, and stood in the position that training had turned into second nature for him: white-gloved hands clasped just below the buckle of his belt, feet at the proper angle, and sword hanging at his left side. The only hints of unorthodoxy were his embarrassed smile and the rakish angle of his big beret. The choice of the picture struck me as a show of defiance by Tornay's mother, who had wanted him remembered not with a black-and-white photograph of his face, as was the case with all the nearby tombs, but with the uniform that symbolized the proudest achievement of his short life— whatever the Vatican had to say.

A thin layer of ice covered a few wilted red roses placed on top of the grave. Next to them lay a small red heart in a transparent glass case, a stone statue of the Virgin with a robe of flaking blue paint, a plaque with the phrase AT THE BLESSED GROTTO, I PRAYED FOR YOU, and three stone carvings of a hedgehog, an owl, and a swan. Perhaps these carvings had belonged to him since childhood.

I left when an elderly couple, arm in arm for what struck me as both physical and moral support, walked slowly past me to lay some flowers at a nearby grave. A few yards away was a square plot of grass. It had been covered with piles of dead leaves, apparently by the grave digger, in an attempt to make sure the earth would not be too hard for his next job.

By the time I got back to Montreux, the mist over the lake had cleared, only to be replaced by thick low clouds that clung to the slopes on either side of the waters. Violetta had told me to look for "a girl with pretty short blond hair," on the Avenue des Alpes outside the railway station. But I hadn't expected a slight, tomboyish figure in a gray bomber jacket with a crew cut so short it would easily have passed muster with the Swiss Guard—had her hair not been dyed to look almost white.

We crossed the street to a restaurant that prided itself on its view of the lake. From our table inside, we could just glimpse a thin streak of silver-colored water beyond the windswept terrace, where benches had been piled high away from the puddles on the ground.

I studied her as she read the menu and ordered a salad. Her fragile face was pale, with sharply drawn, attractive features and high cheekbones. The pallor was heightened by dark eye shadow and by her lipstick, which looked black. A pair of sunglasses perched stylishly above her forehead. The daughter of Italian parents, she told me she'd been born in the same village as Tornay and had met him in a hotel bar in Saint-Maurice where she was working as a waitress. Tornay was on vacation at the time, his first trip back in Switzerland after signing up with the Guard six months earlier.

"Just one glance was enough," she said. "He was tall and handsome, with those deep blue eyes. He came up to me and he said: 'You're beautiful; you're a strange kind of girl. I'd like to get to know you.' I remember I replied quick as a flash: 'You don't know what you're taking on.' We went to a party together that evening. He was great fun, wonderful to be with."

I asked her when they had started going out together.

She was not at all embarrassed by the question: "That night. He had tremendous charm; I don't think any girl ever said no to him. We made love all night. We made love four or five times that first night. He was a great lover; I had a ball. Afterward I went home and slept for seven hours. He had to go back to Rome the day after we met."

"How often did you see him after that?"

"Not often enough. We kept in touch. He would call me all the time and write. He sent me letters from Rome and even from Mauritius when he went there to see his father. One Christmas he suddenly turned up at my house. I was ill in bed with bronchitis and a temperature of a hundred and three degrees, and he dropped by to surprise me. And then there were the ten days I spent in Rome, at the end."

"When was that?"

"April 1998, at the end of the month. I'd gotten pregnant by my boyfriend, Olivier. I felt that I couldn't tell Olivier because he was all shaken up over the divorce he was going through. And then one night—it was a Saturday—I dreamed that I was off to see Tornay. So on the following Monday I booked the night train to Rome, and I called Tornay twenty minutes before the train left. I told him: 'I'll be in Rome at ten o'clock tomorrow morning. Get organized and come and fetch me.' He found me a pensione, a cheap place right next to the Vatican."

"What happened when you told him about the pregnancy?"

"He'd guessed something was up even before I told him. He said: 'I don't know why you're here, but I get the feeling something's up.' I told him I thought I was pregnant, that I wasn't sure yet. I told him that if I was pregnant I wanted to lose the baby. He was the first person I told. He started saying I had no right to have an abortion, that the baby had not asked to be born, and that I'd created him. I told him to hold on, that it wasn't that simple."

"What did he want you to do?"

Violetta, who had been picking at her food with little appetite, pushed her plate aside and fished a pack of cigarettes from her small rucksack. She waved a waitress over to help her light one, pinched it hard with thin fingers, and took a long drag.

"He amazed me. He said he'd be finishing at the Swiss Guard in a month, and that he had a job lined up in Geneva. He said to me: 'Let's get married and I'll raise the kid.' I couldn't believe it, although I was sure he was sincere. I'm still sure he was sincere. I told him I was in a real fix, and here he was asking for my hand. He insisted. 'Keep the baby,' he kept saying. That evening we went for a long walk. He took me up the hill where there used to be a prison, to a park where all the lovers go. You can see all Rome from up there. You know the one I mean?"

"The Gianicolo Hill, near the Vatican," I said.

"That's right. He gave me a ring; he didn't say it was for our engagement, but that's what it meant. He said I had to keep it. The next day we went for a long walk; we went right around the Vatican walls. At one point he stopped and grabbed my hand. He put my hand flat against the wall and he said: 'Swear by these walls that I protect that you'll make an appointment with the doctor when you get back to Switzerland, and when you come out you'll call me.' I said yes, of course. I stayed in Rome for ten days, then I took the train home."

"And you called him?"

Violetta breathed out some smoke in a long sigh and cleared the air with her free hand. "Yes. I went to see my gynecologist the day I got back. He told me I was eight weeks pregnant. I called Tornay; he said that was fantastic. He said he'd come back to Switzerland soon and that I should wait for him. He said: 'I can't wait to get back, to hold you in my arms.' That was a Friday, and I put the scan result away because I wanted to give it to him. Three days later I found out that he was dead. I never did have the baby."

"Did he ever speak to you about Estermann?"

"Yes, but only on our last evening. He told me he had to be back at the Vatican by midnight because Estermann was breathing down his neck. Things were going really badly; Estermann was persecuting him. Tornay said he didn't want to risk screwing everything up a few weeks before he left Rome. He was really tense; you could see it in his face."

"Did Tornay mention the medal, the *benemerenti*?"

"No, not to me. What I remember him saying over and over again was that he couldn't wait to get home. But he wasn't a depressive like the Vatican made out. And I didn't see any sign of bronchitis, as the Vatican said. He would have had a temperature, or difficulty breathing or something. He was tense, but not ill. He still looked great in his uniform. He was so handsome." Her voice dropped to a tense whisper: "God, I love him, so much that sometimes I want to join him."

Violetta turned to look out over the lake, ashamed of her tears. The clouds were still hanging low over the water. She shook her head as if to clear her mind and chase the memories away. "I find it all so difficult to believe because he was so proud of his job. The way he said he was in the Papal Guard, you could hear the capital letters when he said it. Once, he said to me that his boss was not well and that he was worried. The pope was sick or something. It's funny, don't you think? I mean, how many people sympathize with their boss at work like that?"

"How do you think your visit, and the news that you might have been pregnant, affected Tornay?"

She made a face. Her tone was defensive. "It wouldn't have made him ruin everything. He treated me like a princess; he was very fatherly. We met often every day, but only for an hour or two because he was so busy. I spent most of my time in the pensione, because I knew deep down that I was pregnant: I could see it in my breasts and in my stomach. I was often in bed, or vomiting. One evening I really wanted an octopus salad. We walked around for ages until we found it in the old Trastevere quarter at ten-thirty. Tornay would go to the market to buy me fresh fennel; he'd take me for walks all over Rome. And he phoned me all the time; he even phoned me from just outside the pope's apartment."

Violetta refused to admit it, but it was clear that the dedication Tornay had shown in caring for her, combined with the pace of work and the tension with Estermann, had left him exhausted.

She suggested we go for a walk along the lakefront promenade. We came across an empty car whose roof had been shattered by a tree trunk. Police tape sealed off the area and snapped in the wind. I pointed it out to Violetta. She burst out laughing, the first time I had seen her do so. "It's a fake! An artist stuck it there for an open-air exhibition; it's supposed to recall a big storm we had some time ago. But no one thought of warning the locals. So they keep calling the fire department to have it removed. Not the kind of art exhibit you'd expect of tidy Switzerland, is it?"

I followed her to the quayside. The waters looked even less inviting from close up. We stood there in companionable silence, staring down.

Violetta broke the silence. "Tornay never mentioned death, or suicide. Only as a joke. He said that the day he became sexually impotent, he would kill himself. He was a nymphomaniac—or whatever the word is for a man. He never said no. I know some people have said he was gay, but that's impossible. Whenever he called me, he'd say that he wanted to see my breasts, and touch them. I don't think a homosexual would say these things to me. I still regret not making love with him the last night we saw each other. That night he told me: 'When I tell my mum that we're going to get married, she'll be happy.' I could feel his happiness. He was really close to his mum. He sent her a Valentine's card every year, and he sent her money, too, even though he wasn't earning much."

The pay at the Swiss Guard was so miserly that it was difficult to believe that the money Tornay sent his mother could have come out of his salary. But just as Violetta refused to believe that Tornay was bisexual, she could not conceive of his supplementing his wages with money earned with sexual favors—as the homosexual writer Lacchei had described to me. I could see no point in trying to persuade her otherwise, and any such attempt would only have upset her further. As we headed back toward the station where I had left my car, Violetta told me she had seen Tornay's tomb for the first time a few days earlier, with Kellenberger.

"I went only this morning," I said.

"Did you see the ring?" she asked me.

"What ring?"

"I left the ring Tornay gave me at his grave. I thought that was the right place for it. Did you see it?"

I didn't have the heart to tell her that the ring had already been stolen. "I didn't look very closely," I said.

She told me that when she had gone to the cemetery, the weather had looked as if it would snow, but it never did. Kellenberger brought two cans of beer along, and he poured one of them onto the grave. The ground was frozen so solid it took a long time for the foam to disappear. It was like dirty detergent water.

The grave didn't mean much to Violetta. She didn't feel that Tornay was there. She had a few good laughs with Kellenberger. They told each other Tornay anecdotes as they stood over the tomb. It had not seemed strange, laughing there. It had reminded them of Tornay's mother telling them that his death shouldn't stop them from cracking jokes or laughing with her as they had always done.

Kellenberger felt that Tornay had remained angry with him for leaving the Swiss Guard when he did. He and Violetta talked of going to Rome and walking through the Holy Door of St. Peter's because they'd heard that if you walk through it during the Holy Year and you think of someone as you cross the threshold, that person's soul goes straight to paradise. They could not believe that their meeting again after so many months had been just chance. They felt they should do something for Tornay, but they didn't know quite what. In the meantime, they'd think of Tornay as they entered the Basilica.

Violetta and I parted outside the station. She gave me a peck on the cheek, clasped my hand tightly, and held on to it. "I think Tornay isn't happy where he is now," she said. "He hasn't finished his mission. I think he's neither in hell nor in paradise, but somewhere in between. But if he came back to me today, the first thing I would do would be to punch him in the face. Then I'd tell him that I love him, and that I'd never had the courage to say it to him before." She released my hand and strode briskly away.

As I watched Violetta go, it struck me that there was something preventing her, and the friends of Tornay whom I had met, from properly mourning Tornay's passing and coming to terms with it. That something, I thought, was the Vatican's refusal to answer all the questions its version of events had left hanging.

CHAPTER TWENTY-FIVE

FROM MONTREUX, I called Gugelmann and told him I was back in Switzerland. He sounded apologetic: "I might have some trouble talking over the next few days because I'm going to have a stud pierced into my tongue. I'll be a bit sore after the operation."

I thought for a moment that he was telling me a lie to avoid seeing me. But the excuse—if it was one—sounded too far-fetched not to be true. And if it was true, the idea of a former Swiss Guard having his tongue pierced smacked of a rebellious spirit, which was welcome news to me. So I made a clean breast of it and told him why it was important for me that we meet: I was looking into Tornay's death, had met several of his friends, and was more than skeptical about the Vatican's version of events.

There was a long pause. "Ah. I thought that's what it might be." Another pause. "All right, I'll meet you. We could go for dinner. When you get to Payerne, ask for a place called La Rotonde. You won't have any problems finding it."

Payerne, a small market town on the other side of the lake of Neuchâtel from the Swiss-French border, had few notable features apart from the Romanesque abbey, whose various buildings, including a church with a turreted tower and a spire that twisted through the sky, looked haunting in the dusk.

La Rotonde, located on a roundabout on the main road into town, was indeed unmissable. It turned out to be a pizzeria, the outside daubed in a rendering of the Italian tricolor so garish the colors looked like those of artificially colored ice cream. Inside, strands of colored lights and bunches of oversize plastic grapes, lemons, and bananas hung from the rafters. Although it was early, most of the tables were already taken by men in the light blue shirts of the Swiss air force. Farmers, workers, and businessmen, they had all been called up to serve the regulation few weeks a year at the base outside the town, where they would report later that evening.

But for now there was nothing martial about them apart from their uniforms, and the atmosphere in the pizzeria was that of a rowdy party as they and the companions they saw only once a year caught up on one another's news. Stopping in front of a particularly merry table, a waitress wagged her finger: "Have a few drinks by all means, but mind you don't get drunk, otherwise you'll get us into trouble with the base." I found a table in one of the less noisy corners, but it was close to the pizza oven and the waiters were continually bustling past to collect the food.

Gugelmann arrived on time. He had the build of an amateur wrestler, and wore a tight-fitting gray T-shirt over his muscular torso. But he hardly looked like the archetypal warrior monk, and his manner was anything but brazen—he gave me a shy smile and sat down with his shoulders slightly hunched, as if bracing himself for an experience that he knew would be unpleasant but that for some reason he had decided to endure. He wore a shell necklace and three earrings in his left ear.

When I asked him about the piercing, he grinned, then stuck out his tongue, and a brand-new stud twinkled orange in the colored lights. He told me that his tongue had swollen to twice its normal size for a time. The pain was gone now, but he still had a faint lisp, and he could only manage liquids. He ordered a beer.

A carpenter by trade, he explained that it was the desire for a new experience rather than any strong religious faith that had taken him to Rome. "I just thought the Swiss Guard would look good on my CV. I'm not the kind who goes to Mass every day, never have been. Monsignor Jehle wanted us there every morning, but very few of us felt like going. We had no choice on Sundays, because they did a roll call outside the chapel to check that we were all there. But since I left Rome, I've never set foot in a church."

Not that religious piety had been uppermost in the minds of the officers who recruited him. He told me that the year he enlisted, 1997, the Swiss Guard was so short-staffed it had even accepted a volunteer who suffered from a twisted spine. The recruit was the right height, and that was all that mattered. He didn't last long. The pace was so grueling that Gugelmann often got only four hours' sleep and had no idea what time or even day it was. Often, time was defined only by the absence of meat in the canteen (on Fridays), the pope's weekly audience (Wednesdays), or the Angelus prayer in St. Peter's Square (Sundays).

Discipline was a mess. One noncommissioned officer had drawn his gun and pointed it at another guard to make him get out of bed. Promotion automatically rewarded not the best, but the longest serving. Gugelmann's most vivid memory was of the stormy nights he had spent on patrol, when lightning would illuminate the faces staring out of the frescoes in the Paoline Chapel of the Apostolic Palace. Some of the faces, he was convinced, had been painted in such a way that the eyes seemed to follow you everywhere you went.

As we talked about his time in Rome, Gugelmann fidgeted with his cell phone, which he had placed in front of him by his glass of beer. Every so often he would grab the phone and stare at it in the unlikely event that he had missed a call or a message. When they were not focused on the phone, his eyes darted across the room, following the waiters as they fetched the pizzas, or gazed at the plastic fruit above our heads. Praying silently that he would not get up and leave, I asked him to tell me what had happened on Tornay's last evening.

A long intake of breath. Gugelmann cast a last nervous glance into the distance, then his eyes finally settled on me. "I knew you'd get around to that," he said softly, a hangdog expression on his face.

I was relieved that he made no stronger protest, and yet felt sorry for him.

When he did speak, the words came rushing out. "That Monday, I meet Tornay in the barracks at about half-past seven in the evening. He's finished his afternoon shift at the synod of bishops, and he's still wearing his dress uniform. But I'm on the phone, so I'm not able to talk to him straightaway. Later, at about ten to eight, I go to Tornay's room together with another guard, a guy called Nicolas Beytrison. I open a bottle of red wine—Braghetto it was—sparkling stuff, and we start chatting about where we should go that evening. Dinner in the barracks and then out to a pub. We're on duty the next day, but that's not a problem. So far, so good. Then Beytrison says to Tornay: 'I didn't see your name on the list.' That's the list of those who get the medal; it's up in the canteen by the pigeonholes where we keep our cereal boxes and jam and things. It's news to Tornay. He takes it in, something clicks in his brain, and he puts his glass down. It's his first glass; he hasn't finished it. He says: 'I'm going to see for myself.' And he's off; he hasn't got much time left before the canteen closes."

"You don't follow him?"

Gugelmann gnawed at his index finger. "No, we don't. There's nothing to make us think we should. It's true he looked nervous when he got up, but he said to us: 'Don't move, I'll be right back.' We thought he'd be back soon."

I noticed his use of the word "we," as if he did not want to speak only for himself. Perhaps he was to blame in some way. But I let this slip for the time being. "Tell me more about the medal. How confident was Tornay about getting it?" I asked.

"Buchs, the previous commander, had promised Tornay that he'd get the medal at the swearing-in ceremony. Even Monsignor Jehle said Tornay's name would be on the list. And Tornay was hoping that his mother would be able to come to Rome to see him get the medal. But then Estermann was appointed, and Estermann decided otherwise. Basically everyone tells Tornay he's going to get the medal, and then at the last minute his name is not up there."

"So Tornay goes to see the list on his own. Does he come back to you afterward?"

"Yes, not much later. He comes up to my room. I'm still with Beytrison. I'm stretched out on the bed; we're listening to some music. I lived in the halberdiers' building, in a flat on the second floor that looked out onto the street. Tornay comes back in tears. He says he's not on the list for the medal and that he's on another list instead, the one for the detachment that escorts the new recruits at the ceremony. He says there's definitely a mistake because he's entitled to the medal after three years. Then he says: 'Don't move, I'm going to my room to write a letter.' We wait for a bit, and then Beytrison goes over to see what he's up to. He knocks on Tornay's door. The door is open, and Beytrison sees that Tornay is writing at his desk. Beytrison decides to leave him alone and goes back to his room."

"Is that all Tornay does, just write a letter? Doesn't he try to talk to someone?"

"He's desperate to ask someone about it, immediately. He wants to see Estermann and Jehle. I don't know whether he tries Estermann at that stage. All I know is that he tries Jehle and a warrant officer several times. Both are out. He also tries to phone Cardinal Schwéry. Anyway, that evening Tornay can't find anyone to talk to; all the doors are closed."

"And the letter for his mother? When does Tornay give it to you?"

"At about five minutes to nine. I'm chatting with Beytrison when Tornay comes in. He's not wearing his dress uniform anymore; he's changed into a pair of jeans and a black jacket. He tells me that he wants to talk to me, that he has something to give me. So I follow him out of the room and into the corridor, and then he gives me the letter in a sealed envelope. He's not calm about it; he's jumpy. And he says: 'Only to my mother.' I'm surprised. I ask him how I'm supposed to get it to her. He answers: 'Don't worry, you'll see her in the next few days.' That's it; that's all he says. Then he runs off."

I tried not to sound hectoring. "Surely this time you try to follow him?" I asked.

Gugelmann's face flushed. Again his hand darted to the mobile phone, as if it had the power to free him from the questions he must have asked himself hundreds of times. "Yes, yes, of course I do. But I have no shoes on, and it's raining outside. So I have to stop to put my shoes on, and then off I go. I'm running, but I have no idea where he's gone. My first thought is that he's driven off to a bar to get drunk, so I run to the parking lot by the Vatican Bank to see if his car is still there, and then farther up the hill to the other lot near the post office. That's when I hear the shots."

I looked away as Gugelmann wiped away a tear. I imagined him racing in the rain through the courtyard of the barracks, past the officers' mess and the door leading up to Estermann's apartment, which Tornay must have been about to enter at that precise moment—would three people still be alive if Gugelmann had guessed where his friend was?—through a passageway and a wrought-iron gate, to the foot of the tower of the Vatican Bank. He would have been just under Estermann's windows.

Then the dash around the base of the tower and a hundred yards on, straining to make out the car. Until the moment the noise of gunfire reached him, again and again.

I asked Gugelmann whether, once he had realized his mistake and made his way back to the barracks, he had been allowed to enter Estermann's apartment.

"No way. I wasn't even allowed up the stairs. A noncommissioned officer name Riedi, a lance corporal like Tornay, was the first to see all the bodies. A nun told him that she thought that Meza Romero had had a bad fall. I asked Riedi to let me go up. He told me not to; he said I wouldn't recognize any of them. I asked him to tell me at least if anyone was still alive. He wouldn't answer. That night, standing in the courtyard, it was like being outside a cinema. So many people were going up and down the stairs, but not me. Not just the Vatican ambulance people, but officers, priests, the spokesman Navarro-Valls. Talk about a crime scene being sealed off."

The pizzeria had emptied as we talked. Amid much toasting and slapping of backs, the men left to report for duty. Gugelmann relaxed as the place became quieter, and we moved on to a glass of grappa. He joked that it would disinfect his stud.

According to Gugelmann's account, Tornay must have been carrying his gun when he handed him the letter. "Did you see that Tornay had his weapon on him?" I asked.

"No. But he must have been hiding it in his jacket."

"Did Tornay ever say that he'd like to get even with Estermann, or anything like that?"

"He said that he'd like to bash Estermann's face in. But we all said that. Estermann had a real barracks mentality. He was very unpopular, and he just wouldn't listen. He was always waiting to check our uniforms and our haircuts when we had to go on duty. Once, he spotted tiny marks of sweat that my fingers had left on the golden handle of my sword, and he sent me back to clean it. That made me late and I got punished for it. Another time, I was just two minutes late, and I was given two hours of cutting up old uniforms—that chore is done to prevent anyone from stealing them. It would be faster to burn them. In any case, Tornay wasn't the only one bending the rules. In my last three months I never slept in barracks. I had an Italian girlfriend in Rome and I was always with her."

It was still unclear to me how Tornay's letter had fallen into the Vatican's hands. I asked Gugelmann why he had not given it to Tornay's mother as his friend had requested.

Gugelmann stuck his chest out, squared his shoulders, and spoke in a tone that mixed anger with injury. "I did give it to her, but the Vatican wanted a copy first. Not long after Tornay died, I spoke to Jehle about the letter. I told him I'd given my word; I asked what do I do now? But Jehle went straight to Judge Marrone, the investigator, and told him all about it. I was furious. Jehle shouldn't have told anyone. Okay, it's true we weren't in the confessional box, but for me, our talk had the same value. Jehle betrayed my trust. Jehle and Marrone called me into the commander's office, and they threatened to wreck my room if I didn't hand over the letter."

"So you handed it over."

"I didn't have any choice. I was given the third degree that night. I'd lost my friend, and they accused me of drawing straws with Tornay to decide who would go and shoot Estermann. I was so angry with Jehle that I had it out with him a few days afterward. I even grabbed hold of him, but luckily I didn't go any further."

"Jehle wasn't much loved by any of you, was he?"

"Correct. Jehle didn't want us to leave the barracks, even in the evenings. People like Jehle and Estermann didn't want us to get involved with any Italians; they thought it would be a bad influence on us. So we had to hide everything—the nightclubs, the girlfriends, even the fondue parties when we'd have fun using our halberds to mix the melted cheese."

A waitress came up to tell us that the pizzeria was closing. As we walked out into the cold night air, I asked Gugelmann why he had resigned a few months after the death of his friend.

"The way Tornay was treated, before and after his death, disgusted me. The way the Vatican dirtied his name. When people ask me whether they should sign up, I just stay mum."

◆

A FEW DAYS LATER, when I was back in Rome, Gugelmann wrote to me. He sent me a brief note—"Found it. Not very important but here it is"—along with a copy of his testimony to Marrone. Written in longhand by a Vatican clerk, the testimony was only just over two pages long—the Vatican had shown little interest in what such a key witness had to say.

Gugelmann had made a point of defending his friend's professional reputation, and did not hesitate to criticize Estermann in his evidence—a courageous stand given his audience. Tornay had good relations with all his colleagues, the testimony read, except for Estermann, "with whom a situation of incompatibility had developed, so much so that every time Tornay broke the rules he was punished more heavily than the others."

Still smarting from what he saw as Jehle's breach of trust, Gugelmann had insisted that the clerk take down for the record how he had been forced to hand over Tornay's letter. Gugelmann and Marrone had opened the sealed envelope together, and then Jehle had made a photocopy of the letter, which was handed to Marrone. The letter had been sealed again and handed by Gugelmann to Tornay's mother on her arrival in Rome on the afternoon of May 6.

She was given the letter a day after its contents had been leaked to the newspapers. It was beyond any doubt that the leak of an important piece of evidence, and the breach of the principle of judicial secrecy, had been committed not by Gugelmann, not by Tornay's mother, but by the Vatican.

CHAPTER TWENTY-SIX

ONLY ONE OTHER WITNESS could confirm Gugelmann's account of the last hour or so of Tornay's life: his fellow guard Nicolas Beytrison, who Gugelmann had told me was still serving in the Vatican. That Beytrison was still in Rome was bad news for me. He would feel less free to talk, given that he was still under the authority of Monsignor Jehle, the enforcer of the law of silence. I was reluctant to risk a curt refusal by telephoning him at the barracks.

But one May morning, information released by the Vatican's press office gave me an opportunity to approach Beytrison directly. Immediately after the annual swearing-in ceremony in St. Damasus Square by the Apostolic Palace, the press statement said, several members of the Swiss Guard would be awarded the *benemerenti* medal at a second function in the barracks. When I read through the list of names, I came across that of Lance Corporal Nicolas Beytrison.

If Beytrison spared a thought for his dead friend, it did not show on his round face when Colonel Segmuller, with other senior officers looking on approvingly, called his name in the drill yard of the barracks. *"Présent, mon colonel!"* Beytrison shouted in French before thrusting a stocky leg forward. Plump, with straw-blond hair, the most rustic looking of the guards I had seen, he kept any misgivings he might have had to himself as the medal was pinned to his barrel-like chest.

Later, when his companions had finished pumping his hand to congratulate him, I introduced myself and asked whether he would be willing to talk to me about his experiences in the Swiss Guard. A quizzical look crossed his rugged face, but he agreed more readily than I had expected.

One evening a few days later, we met on Borgo Pio, the street that runs from St. Anne's Gate toward the Castel St. Angelo and is the heart of a neighborhood nicknamed the Vatican Ghetto by locals. It was a rainy evening, and when I first caught sight of Beytrison ambling toward me down the empty alley of shuttered shops and cafés, the silhouetted towers and domes of the Vatican—God's citadel, which for centuries was designed to resist attacks and sieges—glistened darkly behind him like brooding giants trapped by dark clouds.

He suggested we go for a walk through the neighborhood, although he was exhausted after three hours on duty in St. Damasus Square, followed without a break by another three hours on the third loggia in the corridor leading to the pope's apartment.

I learned that he had started out as a plumber but decided to sign up "to see something else" after finding the work in his Alpine village too slow for his liking. "Not surprising, given that only six hundred people live there. Some plumbers make sure they don't repair things properly so that they create more work for themselves in future, but I'm not that kind of guy."

Beytrison didn't have a very high opinion of the plumbing in the Vatican, and he grumbled about a question in the examination that had followed his training: "What do you do if you see a puddle in a Vatican building?" The right answer, he explained, was not to touch anything and telephone the city-state's own fire brigade immediately.

He tut-tutted in disapproval. "What a waste of time. But then again, I suppose it's understandable. They're terrified that a leak will damage some fresco or other. I can tell you, on stormy days we're on the phone all the time. The Vatican is about as waterproof as the *Titanic*. It leaks all over the place. Up on the loggias, the caulking on the windows is crumbling to bits and the windowpanes beat against the iron frames and everything gets in, the wind and the rain."

I asked him when he had first sworn allegiance to the pope.

He abruptly plucked out the cigarette he had been savoring and stubbed it out with elaborate care in the soil of a potted plant we happened to be passing. "Ah, well. That was special. I was supposed to take the oath in May 1998. But the ceremony was shifted to a month after by events. I remember that year. The pope was weak and he had to sit down when he greeted us. We went up to him one by one with our parents. The previous years, he was strong enough to walk around the room."

The stare from his light blue eyes, which were set deep into his doughlike face, was as level as his tone of voice. Perhaps he realized he had given me an opportunity to broach the subject of what he had euphemistically called "events," the deaths that took place before the day set for the ceremony. "Do you known when Tornay found out that he was not getting the medal?" I asked.

Beytrison stopped to fumble in his pockets. His pudgy fingers trembled almost imperceptibly as he lit another cigarette. He walked for some moments in silence. He had been taking a series of right turns down the dark alleys, and I was uncertain how far we were from the

Vatican. "Tornay found out from us. I mean, me and a guy called Gugelmann. Tornay was so stunned. The year before he'd missed it, because he was two months short of the three years and the commander wouldn't make an exception. Tornay was so confident of getting it this time around that he'd organized a party to celebrate. Not getting the medal was the straw that broke the camel's back."

I decided not to mention that I had spoken to Gugelmann. "When did you see him for the last time?" I asked.

"At eight-fifty that evening, I saw him writing the letter to his mother. I was wet because of the rain, I'd gone to book a place for dinner right near here, and then I went up to find him to try to comfort him. But he was busy. Then a few minutes later I saw him hand the letter to Gugelmann. I couldn't hear what Tornay said; I was too far down the corridor. His black jacket was zipped up. Of course I had no idea at the time, but later I realized he must have had the gun in it."

"Did Gugelmann tell you what Tornay said to him?"

"Yes, but some time later. It was 'Only to my mother.' "

"So why didn't Gugelmann rush after him immediately? Surely he should have guessed that something terrible was about to happen?"

"You'd better ask Gugelmann that."

I didn't mention that I already had, and that Gugelmann had said he had wasted valuable time putting shoes on before running out into the rain. Instead I tried out Gugelmann's version on Beytrison: "Was Gugelmann not completely dressed or something; perhaps he had to put his shoes on?"

"No, no, he was completely dressed. And he had his shoes on. He just stood there like a bloody idiot."

One of the two was lying. It was probably Gugelmann, who I guessed had not come to terms with the guilt he must have felt at realizing that had he run after his friend sooner, three deaths might have been prevented.

It was still unclear to me what exactly Tornay had done in the time between seeing that his name was not on the list in the canteen and sitting at his desk to write the letter. The only certainty was that he had gone to see Monsignor Jehle. I asked Beytrison: "Did you find out what happened when Tornay went to see Jehle?"

"I asked Jehle about it. He told me that Tornay came to see him in the sacristy of Saint Martin's, the Guard's chapel, after evening Mass. It was about eight-fifteen. Jehle said Tornay did not want to talk."

"You believe that?"

Beytrison stopped and stroked the nape of his bull-like neck as if, I imagined, he were confronted by an awkward plumbing problem. He must have been weighing up how much to give away about a superior who could make a great deal of trouble for him. "Well, I just wonder why Tornay bothered to go and find him, if he didn't want to talk. I mean, what's the point? It's strange, isn't it? We only have Jehle's word for it. And Jehle was meeting some people for dinner soon after."

"How do you know that?"

"It was me and Gugelmann who saw him in a restaurant. Jehle had left the number for the restaurant with the duty officer, but when we called him, he refused to come back to the barracks. We insisted, but he wouldn't hear of it. And we weren't allowed to tell him what had happened over the phone. So we were sent to fetch him. It was about nine-fifteen P.M., not long after Tornay had died, and Jehle had already finished his meal. He was having his espresso."

The implication was that when a desperate Tornay had come up to him, Jehle had let nothing stand in the way of his dinner appointment and cold-shouldered the young guard. I admired Beytrison for being so plainspoken about his superior. But my regard for him quickly evaporated when I suddenly realized that Beytrison had steered me back toward the Vatican and that we were now within sight of St. Anne's Gate. I had been too concentrated on our talk, and his route too full of turns, for me to notice his stratagem. My time was running out.

I asked him again about Tornay's last hour: "But apart from the meeting with Jehle and making some phone calls, what else did Tornay do?"

"All I heard was that he was seen making his way to Saint Martha, the cardinals' residence, where he hoped to see Cardinal Schwéry. But the cardinal wasn't in, and Tornay came back in tears. All the Swiss French are very fond of Schwéry; he's a good sport and he doesn't talk down to us. He's such good fun that Jehle stopped putting his name down for our spiritual retreats, because he thought Schwéry got on too well with us and that undermined his authority."

Another barb directed at Jehle. I asked Beytrison why he hadn't resigned after the loss of his friend. So many others had done so.

Without stopping, Beytrison lifted a hand up as if to warn me off. "Those of us who decided to stay did it as a French-speaking contingent, to hold our ground."

"Against the Swiss Germans?"

"Making Tornay find out at the last minute that he wouldn't get the medal is typical of the things the Swiss Germans get up to."

To my dismay, we had reached St. Anne's Gate. Beytrison turned to me. "I talked to Tornay at lunchtime on the day he died, when he came back from the synod of bishops. I mentioned Estermann's appointment, and you know what Tornay said? He said: 'We can start making out our wills.'"

"How did you take that comment?"

"How was I supposed to take it? As a joke, of course. So I asked Tornay whether he'd leave me his espresso machine. He said okay. And that was that. I thought nothing more of it."

As I watched Beytrison dart back onto Vatican territory with a speed that was surprising given his bulk, a bored guard in navy-blue fatigues waving him through the wrought-iron gate with its imperial eagles, I thought about the many 'what-ifs' that could have changed the course of Tornay's evening. What if Gugelmann had restrained his friend; what if Jehle had given Tornay an opportunity to vent his indignation; and what if Tornay had found Cardinal Schwéry?

I had already spoken to Gugelmann. It was time to find Schwéry and Jehle.

CHAPTER TWENTY-SEVEN

THE GUARD ON DUTY at St. Anne's Gate smiled with pleasure when, a few days later, I asked for "His Eminence Cardinal Schwéry." His Eminence, who had agreed to see me during one of his frequent visits to Rome, was apparently well liked by his compatriots. The guard led me into the barracks. I thought I would find Schwéry in a grand office, dressed in the full scarlet regalia that befits a prince of the church with the power not only to elect the next pope, but also—on paper at least—to become the next pope.

I could not have been more mistaken. The guard turned into the officers' mess and gestured toward a rotund figure who was sitting on a wooden bench before his pre-lunch aperitif, a small pitcher of white wine. His Eminence was dressed not in flowing robes but in an unassuming gray suit and Roman dog collar. The only sign of his rank was the gold cardinal's ring on his right hand that the pope had given him on his appointment, with its engraving of the Crucifixion.

In his late sixties, the bespectacled Schwéry looked more like a genial country priest than a suave cardinal of the Curia. The heavy jowls that hung over the dog collar were slightly flushed, and there were broken capillaries on his nose. He had prominent ears, and dandruff speckled his shoulders. His dark brown eyes twinkled mischievously as he bantered with a white-haired orderly who was leaning on a cart loaded with soft drinks. The orderly explained that he was a veteran of the Swiss Guard and had volunteered to work for another few weeks in the barracks because of a shortage of fresh recruits.

"The first time I was here, it was under the *papa buono,* the good pope, John the Twenty-third. That was 1963," the orderly informed Schwéry.

"My, that was only yesterday," Schwéry joked with a wide grin and a wag of the finger.

"More like the day before yesterday," the orderly replied.

Schwéry offered me a drink, and I told him frankly that I was disappointed not to see him dressed in his brilliant vestments.

He gave a warm chuckle and lifted the flaps of his jacket, revealing a crucifix on a gold chain and a pair of suspenders. "I can do my job just as well dressed like this. Oh, that's not quite true, though. When I visit some drug addicts I look after, I have to get all my gear on—the robes, the biretta hat, the sash, and everything else—because they'd be most disappointed if I turned up dressed like this."

I learned that he had worked as a physics teacher at a school run by priests in his hometown of Sion before becoming, at the age of twenty-five, the youngest bishop in the Church. At the age of fifty-nine, he told me proudly, he had become "one of the six youngest cardinals in the world." The gathering of cardinals at his appointment in

St. Peter's Square had looked to him "like a field of tomatoes, and I was the baby carrot."

He knew the Vatican inside out, having sat on the ruling councils of a string of departments supervising its finances, the discipline of the sacrament, the clergy, and most recently the causes of saints— "we've had to split up into two groups to process all the candidates. This pope is so keen on them and we're naming new ones all the time."

He wagged a finger at me. "But don't mistake me. I am not of the Curia. You know, when I first came to Rome, my parish priest warned me: 'Watch out. You'll come back either more faithful to the pope, or a pagan.' You think the Vatican is ultrapure, but when you see a religious institution like the Vatican from close up, you see it's run by human beings, and well, that can be—how shall I put it?—discouraging. You have to struggle a bit not to lose your faith. I'd say that's one of the big disadvantages of joining the Swiss Guard."

He suggested we go for lunch nearby rather than eat in the mess. He hadn't come all the way to Rome to be fed a meal cooked by Swiss nuns, he said. Before we left, he pointed out a mural in the mess that showed a dying lion, a spear stuck in his flank.

"A Swiss Guard did that. It's a painting of the Lion Monument, a statue which is quite a popular spot back home in Lucerne. It's the symbol of the Swiss who gives his life for a noble cause. All the Swiss are born soldiers, you know. Even though I was planning to become a priest, I had to do my national service, and I took my weapon home and kept it there like everyone else."

Outside in the Borgo Pio street, the same one I had walked down with Beytrison, the café tables were full of tourists and pilgrims basking in the sunshine. But the heat felt somewhat oppressive, and some dark clouds were gathering north of the Vatican. I noticed that walking was an effort for Schwéry and asked him if he was all right.

"When I studied physics," he replied with a sad smile, "I learned that there's a lot of magma bubbling under our feet, and that there's just a thin crust protecting us from all that. So that's why I'm feeling a little poorly."

As we walked slowly down the street, I asked Schwéry how he tried to help out recruits from the Valais, his home region.

"It's not easy for them. There's a cultural conflict in the barracks. From the moment they set foot here, they have to obey orders which are given not in French, not in German, but in Swiss German, which is a language they can't make out at all. All they got at school was a smattering of German, so you can see they're thrown in at the deep end from the word 'go.' And then there's the mentality, which is completely different. The French speakers and the Swiss Germans don't laugh at the same time, and they laugh at different things."

Schwéry turned toward me and suddenly twisted his face into a clownlike mask: his eyes wide open, his bushy eyebrows arched, and his mouth shaped like an O. Then he snapped back to normal, smiling at my bafflement that a cardinal could make such a grimace.

"If an officer asks a French speaker to stand still at a guardpost for three hours, he'll do it because he thinks the discipline is good for him. But a Swiss German will do it without thinking; it's discipline for discipline's sake. If the officer isn't sensitive to the difference in mentality, the young boy gets confused. So I do what I can. I did a spiritual retreat for the French speakers at Ariccia, but I wouldn't dream of doing one for the Swiss Germans. I just wouldn't get through to them. I know I wouldn't."

We sat down under an awning on the crowded terrace of Il Mozzicone, a trattoria popular with both pilgrims and clergy. Across the narrow street, moth-eaten armchairs spilled out onto the pavement from an upholsterer's shop. We had barely started the meal, with Schwéry digging right into a hearty plate of spaghetti, tomato sauce, and hot *pepperoncino* without stopping to say grace, when he pointed his fork at me. "So tell me, why do you want to see me?"

I told him, and asked him what he could tell me about Tornay.

He took hold of the small glass bottle containing olive oil and twirled it as he thought about my request. He took his time reaching a decision. Eventually he smiled. "Tornay gave me his mobile-phone number. He said that it wasn't right that I carry my suitcases—as far as I know, I'm the only cardinal who carries his own suitcases in the Vatican—and he made me promise to call him whenever I was on my way in or out of the place. He said it would be a pleasure for him to carry them."

He gave the oil bottle another twirl. "One day I'm in Rome, I'm staying at Saint Martha, the cardinals' residence. There's no radio or TV there. I go down to breakfast, I'm all cheerful, and as usual I'm teasing the staff."

His Eminence flashed the clown's grimace again. "Anyway, some priests are just standing around; they've got really glum expressions. This monsignor from the Secretariat of State comes up to me, and he says: 'Apparently you don't know what has happened.' So I say tell me all about it. He tells me that Estermann and his wife have been killed by a guard who then took his own life. My Italian isn't brilliant, so I have to make him repeat it twice. And you know what I say? I say: 'My God, was it Cédric Tornay?' And the monsignor looks amazed; you could have knocked him over with a crucifix, and he asks me: 'How do you know?'"

Schwéry, who was lost in thought, did not notice drops of rain that fell on the tablecloth from a small gash in the awning above us.

"Well, how did you know?" I asked.

"I didn't. But if there was one guard who was going to do such a thing, it was him. Two months earlier I'd done my spiritual retreat, the one I told you about, for the French-speaking guards. I saw them both in class and in one-on-ones; I thought it would give them a chance to open up. Some of them did open up. Probably didn't do them much good. I wouldn't be surprised if they went back to their barracks afterward and thought: 'My God, why did I open myself to that old fogey?'"

"Is that what Tornay did? 'Opened up' to you?"

"Yes. I had him to myself, and let's say that for some time, he unburdened himself. He told me he was angry with Estermann, and with Monsignor Jehle. He hated the regulations; he thought they were ridiculous. And bear in mind that Tornay had been promoted to lance corporal, so he must have been doing something right."

"What did he tell you exactly?"

Schwéry reached up to his lined forehead and used his ring to trace a knobby vein across his temple. "It's a delicate matter, I'm sorry if my answers aren't as precise as I'd like them to be. I don't very much like talking about the dead. What I can say is that there had been no sign that he'd do what he did. I would never have guessed that he'd be willing to go to such lengths."

I wondered whether Tornay had mentioned his bisexuality, or even gone as far as to talk about his relationship with Estermann, but I realized there was no point in asking. "What did you make of Tornay's complaints? Did you do anything about them?"

"I have to be careful what I say here. I can tell you that after the retreat I went to see Estermann. I asked him whether he would take the job of commander if they offered it to him. He said yes. I said well, I won't have voted for you. I said it straight out, just like that. And I asked him to grant me just one thing: I said if you are appointed commander, please receive me for a cup of coffee and a talk. We must talk."

"What was it you wanted to talk to him about?"

"Several things."

Schwéry's affable manner was disappearing fast. "Like what?" I insisted.

"Well, for one thing, the cultural prejudice the French speakers were having to put up with."

"Anything else?"

Schwéry waved a hand dismissively but did not speak. Whether or not Tornay had mentioned his homosexuality, the cardinal was not saying.

I told him that Tornay had written about him in one of his letters, mentioning the spiritual retreat. He had written about Schwéry: "He's very friendly and what's more he makes us laugh."

Schwéry blushed with pleasure and leaned forward conspiratorially. "You want my opinion? I think that when he went up the staircase of the officers' building, he was out to get Jehle, not Estermann. Jehle wasn't at home, but I think he'd have gotten a bullet if he'd been in."

This cardinal was full of surprises, I thought. "But it was Estermann who refused to give the medal to Tornay, not Jehle," I objected.

"Even so. Many guards had complained to me about Jehle, but no one hated him as much as Tornay did. The newspapers said the medal was important, but in fact it wasn't that important. The main reason for Tornay doing what he did is everything he had experienced before, and the shock of seeing Estermann promoted."

A mandolin player in a shabby raincoat toured the tables, his head bent so close to the instrument that his ear hovered a fraction above the wood. Schwéry ignored the sweet sound as he had ignored the rain.

I thought it best not to remind Schwéry that the medal had been singled out as a key factor behind Tornay's last acts not only by the newspapers but also by Navarro-Valls, the Vatican's spokesman. Nevertheless, Schwéry's view of the reasons for Tornay's death were much closer to those of the young guard's comrades than to the Vatican version.

I poured him a little more wine. "I'm scared I'll start singing Vespers a little early," he quipped.

I asked him what he thought of Jehle's role in the Swiss Guard.

"Jehle's got his fingers in too many pies. There are these meetings at which the officers are supposed to assess the performance, the military capabilities, of the men. Jehle's on that. I ask myself why. All right, I know it's the Vatican, but this is a military body; it has a professional job to do, which is about security. Jehle's got nothing to do with that. Or rather, he shouldn't have. Did you know that Jehle's even got the power to approve or disapprove of marriages? If he doesn't like a guard's fiancée, that's it, the wedding's off. The chaplain should be on a level with, or under the authority of, the commander. Not above him. But Segmuller, the new commander, is an outsider and he doesn't know the ropes, so sometimes he gets caught out. I used to get mixed up with the Swiss Guard, but I quit some time ago."

He did not mention that it was Jehle who had forced him out, as Beytrison had told me. "Did you ever talk to Jehle about the problems of the French speakers?" I asked.

"Well, he realizes there's a problem, but he's got the Swiss-German mind-set. I don't think we'll ever see a French-speaking commander or chaplain. But there could be a French speaker among the senior officers. And it wouldn't be a bad idea to set a limit on the number of years a chaplain can remain in office."

I took this as a discreet way of saying that Jehle should be dismissed. "How would a time limit help?" I asked.

"Maybe it's my past life as a schoolteacher, but there's a law of physics called inertia. I ask people in the Vatican why they do things the way they do, and you know what they answer? 'Because we've always done it that way.' Some answer. But then I don't get the impression that God troubles His head about that kind of thing—apart from the fact that as far as I know, God doesn't have a head."

The bells of St. Peter's were ringing four o'clock when we got up to leave. The rain had stopped as abruptly as it had started, and the sun was already drying the cobblestones. Schwéry beamed with delight. "Ah. The power of the rain. It's purified everything, kicked away all that dust."

I left His Eminence washing his hands at a fountain in the street and staring with boy-like wonder at the way the water traced a perfect arc through the air, fascinated by what he hailed as "a marvelous law of physics."

✦

ONE THING PUZZLED ME about the talk Schwéry had had with Tornay in March. Although the cardinal had refused to go into much detail, it was clear that what Tornay had said had been serious enough to prompt the cardinal to take the highly unusual step of seeking out Estermann and reprimanding him, although despite his rank, he had no formal right to do so.

Seeking a clue to what Tornay could have had on his mind at the time, I looked back through my notes of the first press conference that Navarro-Valls, the Vatican spokesman, had given after the deaths. He mentioned that Tornay had failed to return to the barracks one night, and this had led Estermann to send him a letter on February 12, which Navarro-Valls described as "courteous and firm, but not harsh."

With the help of a former guard, I contacted a retired senior officer who agreed to talk to me on the condition that his name not be revealed. He told me that the Vatican had ordered him not to speak about the deaths, but for Tornay's sake, he was now ready to disobey. He told me he could throw some light on Tornay's grievances. He had befriended Tornay, and remembered a talk they'd had only a few days after Estermann had caught him out.

"Tornay was very depressed. He told me that Estermann had summoned him to his office and had detailed the punishment: three days confined to barracks, a day's leave canceled, and three hours of extra work. Tornay apologized, and that was that. Or so Tornay thought.

"But the next day, Tornay gets a letter from Estermann. Estermann confirmed the measures he had listed the previous day, but what really shocked Tornay was that there were two more sanctions—no *benemerenti* medal and immediate expulsion. Which is outrageous. You don't take those kinds of measures just because a guard spends a night away from the barracks.

"It would have destroyed Tornay's future, because any potential employer would have found out that he had been expelled. It was mean and narrow-minded, a pure vendetta on Estermann's part. Tornay protested, and a few days later Estermann backed down on the medal and the expulsion because otherwise the French-speaking contingent would have mutinied. But Tornay had made up his mind to leave in July. Basically, Estermann always had it in for Tornay. He kept Tornay in his sights."

The medal that the senior officer referred to was the same as the one that Estermann refused Tornay hours before his death. It was obvious that there was much more behind Tornay's violent reaction on that last day than simply the failure to receive this medal.

CHAPTER TWENTY-EIGHT

THE VATICAN HAD BEEN QUICK to dismiss Tornay's state of mind in the moments leading up to his death as "a fit of madness" brought on by the refusal to award him the medal. But according to Tornay's friends in Switzerland and in the Vatican, the diagnosis was too pat to be accurate. To find out, as far as was possible, what had been Tornay's real state of mind, and about the chain of events that shaped it, I needed the help of an outsider who could carry out a virtual post-mortem not on Tornay's body but on his mind—a forensic psychologist with no links to the Vatican.

Eventually, I found an authority who fit the bill: David Canter, a professor of investigative psychology and the leading British expert on the science of criminal profiling. Canter has had a fascinating career.

For more than a decade he has advised Scotland Yard, the FBI, and the U.S. Army on offender profiling—the science of making logical deductions about possible suspects based on the shared patterns of behavior among offenders.

His first big break occurred in the London "Railway Rapist" case, in which he drew up a profile of the likely culprit, which included details such as where he was likely to be living and the fact that he was a martial arts expert. The profile enabled police to catch a suspect who had previously ranked no higher than 1,505th on their list. One newspaper article compared Canter to a Sherlock Holmes character looking not for physical clues like dog bites on walking sticks but for intangible insights to read the mind of the offender.

Although sometimes controversial, his discipline is now part and parcel of criminal investigations, and is based on solid scientific techniques. I found a reference to his studies of how environment influences the circumstances of a crime and wondered what he would make of the Swiss Guard's barracks and the Vatican village.

When I telephoned Canter at his office at Liverpool University, he sounded bemused by my request but asked me to send him the Vatican statements, Tornay's last letter, and information I had gathered during my investigation. When I called again a couple of weeks later, it was clear that he was hooked—he had found the case "extremely intriguing" and was ready to discuss it.

I flew to London, drove up to Liverpool, and after spending a night in a hotel whose lobby played only music by the city's most famous export, the Beatles, walked into the offices of the university's department of psychology. I stopped to look at the students' bulletin board. There was a note from Canter asking for "students who have experienced mugging or assault" to volunteer as guinea pigs for a course in police interviewing techniques.

A tall thin figure in a brown jacket and blue corduroy shirt, Canter was awaiting me in an office so cluttered it looked as if he were in the middle of a move. Piles of books, box folders, loose-leaf papers, and newspaper clippings defied gravity like the Leaning Tower of Pisa and covered most of his desk, a table, and the carpet on which black rubbish bags also sprawled. On the desk, half a dozen dirty mugs competed for space with a transparent glass head of a boy. We had to lift papers off two armchairs before we could sit down. He looked at me expectantly with shrewd, piercing eyes.

I asked him what had struck him most about the case.

"The pressure which the investigators are evidently under. The fact that already at midnight, just a few hours after the deaths happened, they are explained in simple and direct terms, by Tornay's so-called fit of madness. That means the investigators aren't encouraged to look any further. In any case, in a closed community like the Vatican, it's extremely difficult to get beyond what some decided, and everyone agreed, very early on were the circumstances. That becomes the established—I was going to say God-given—truth."

"So what's your verdict? Was it a fit of madness, as the Vatican says?"

"Quite frankly, I don't know what the Vatican means by that expression; it's not a scientific phrase. It's wrong to assume that what Tornay did was irrational to him. In any case, I think you'd have a hard time finding any reference in any text on homicide to a fit of madness."

To prove his point, he rummaged on a bookshelf behind seven small statues of Walt Disney's dwarfs to pick out a hefty tome entitled *Homicide*. I noticed the book next to it was called *Lady-Killer*. He turned to the last pages of the book, glanced through them, and looked up with a satisfied expression.

"As I thought. Madness is not even in the index. What the Vatican seems to be saying is that because Tornay was mad, he committed this act. But madness means a lack of contact with reality, and there'd have to be evidence of that. In cases of what we call 'righteous slaughter'—and this is what Tornay's case is best described as—people think themselves into a situation where it's appropriate for them to be wildly angry. There's enormously heightened emotion due to a feeling of injustice, but there's also a logic to what they're doing. This is not uncontrolled rage. Here, Tornay has thought things out logically. And I don't see anything to back the Vatican's assertion that he was suffering from paranoid delusions either."

"What about the last letter Tornay wrote to his mother? Is it compatible with a 'fit of madness'?"

From a pile of papers at his elbow, Canter retrieved the copy of the letter I had sent him and read through it with a furrowed brow. "To me, the style of the letter is rather simple and formal. I find it curious, to say the least, that the Vatican thinks some sort of frenzy or rage could produce this really pretty formal note."

"What was Tornay thinking? Did he see himself as a martyr? In the letter, he says he's giving his life for the pope, that he's acting for the good of the Swiss Guard and of the Catholic Church."

"I think that's simply his style—rather pompous, almost operatic. Like the oath he had Violetta swear on the Vatican walls, making her promise to call him when she found out whether she was pregnant. Of course in the letter he wouldn't want to write that he was going to kill himself or somebody else."

"Why not?"

"Because someone might read it before he commits the murder or the suicide, and stop him."

I was skeptical. "He's thinking things out that clearly?"

Canter paused as his secretary brought us coffee. He looked around for a surface on which to rest the mug and casually placed it on top of a leaning pile of folders. "Tornay is part of a military culture in which there are secrets to be kept, and people are cautious about revealing things. So it's not necessarily something he would have to think about. It would come naturally to him to hold back on crucial details. And keeping his act enigmatic also gives the letter a grander flavor. By the way, had Tornay ever spoken before about death or suicide?"

"Tornay told a friend, Steve Kellenberger, that if he ever did commit suicide, he would have to make his death look like an accident so that his mother would benefit from his life-insurance policy," I replied.

"So. Tornay had thought about his own death, and he'd linked it to his mother. His relationship to his mother is clearly important to him. She's the last person he writes to. There are people in his life who could help him, but he's feeling extremely isolated. What's interesting here is what psychologists would call his coping mechanisms. Generally speaking, the more verbally fluent and intellectually capable people are, the more able they are to find ways of expressing their anger that are not violent. But Tornay was pretty average at school. Another thing to look out for are any events that affected him in his childhood, and particularly around the age of puberty—say, from the age of ten to fifteen. Those years are crucial for building up your sense of self, the idea that you are worthy of respect."

I described what Tornay's mother had revealed to me: the two divorces when he was three and twelve years old, his stepfather's violence, and how Tornay had to scramble out of the house to fetch help when the beatings started.

Canter thought for a moment. "The violence he saw in his stepfather means that to some extent he's learned to deal with the world through acts of anger and emotional response. What's more, he sees himself as an outsider in the Guard. He tries to demonstrate his independence and his qualities by doing things he's not allowed to do."

"And the man trying to stop him is Estermann," I offered.

Canter nodded. "Tornay sees his role in the Guard as defining everything that is possible for him, a new job and his return to Switzerland. What triggers it all is, on the one hand, Tornay's feeling that he isn't achieving, that his worth isn't recognized. He's promoted to lance corporal, but that's not enough. Violetta, the woman he wants to marry, is very probably pregnant by another man. That's also humiliating. And on the other hand, Estermann, the lover who jilted him, gets his promotion. Estermann is being hard on Tornay, very hurtful. So there's a tremendous feeling of not really having any significance, and that generates frustration and anger, and Tornay starts thinking how he can avenge that profound insult to himself. He's very clear that Estermann is the source of all his problems, and what's more, Estermann is close to Opus Dei, which Tornay is trying to investigate. Tornay really does believe that he has the right to kill Estermann, and weapons are easily available in a military setting like the barracks."

I asked Canter whether he had any idea what went through Tornay's mind when he shot Estermann and his wife, Meza Romero.

"A number of murderers I've spoken to blank out the moment of killing. They tell me that they sort of 'came to,' and there was blood all over their hands, and there in front of them was the body. But they will also tell me the detailed sequence of anger that led up to the point when the killing begins. In other words, the moment of killing is very strongly focused on the act itself, so much so that the individual cannot necessarily monitor what he is doing. And the psychological experience is of a separate identity, as when the murderer says he watched himself doing the killing. That's how many people feel in a car accident: they feel they are outside of it."

"What about immediately after Estermann and his wife had been shot? What could Tornay have been thinking before he shot himself?"

He read through Tornay's letter one more time, a detective seeking clues to his mind. "That's the hardest to reconstruct. He 'comes to'; he sees what he's done. It was all driven by his feeling of not being recognized. He has the gun in his hand. It's quite common for the murderer to commit suicide in such cases. There's the anger and the need for revenge, and once that's dealt with, a tremendous feeling of remorse and depression."

"But Tornay writes in the letter about sacrificing himself. Does that mean he's already decided to kill himself before setting out for Estermann's flat?"

"I always look to the roles people give themselves, and the narratives they are part of. So in a tradition where a soldier is ready to die for the pope, where dying is seen as an act of honor, Tornay has something to lock onto, something with which he can justify, at least to himself, committing suicide."

"Did anything strike you about the way he killed himself? The fact that first he knelt down before shooting himself in the mouth?"

"When people move into such an emotional condition, they lock onto habits which are the ingrained habits of a lifetime. You focus only on what you are about to do to yourself. All your other actions are dictated by habit because you have no time to think about them. I remember one suicide in which a chap took his shoes off, put them tidily to one side, then went to the balcony and jumped. That was his thing. He was a very tidy chap. In Tornay's case, my hunch would be that he was used to kneeling at important ritual moments, to pray during Mass, for example."

I was sure that Canter had hit the nail on the head. I told him about the special salute that guards had to make during Mass: they would face the altar, halberd in hand, when the host was consecrated, and drop to one knee. Perhaps Tornay wanted to show humility, or seek forgiveness, I said.

"It's possible. It's also possible that religious belief helped to make Tornay kill himself because he thought he would go to heaven. I've seen suicide letters from teenagers in which they say they're just interested in the afterlife. They kill themselves to see what it will be like afterward."

Canter had touched on a subject that was dear to him—the role that the wider context, or setting, can play in shaping a crime. "What about the Vatican as a backdrop to all this?" I asked.

Canter smiled with pleasure at the question. "Oh, that's a big one, isn't it? Some people would consider the Vatican a totalitarian state. What I'd like to know is what support and counseling system the Vatican's rulers have set up for people like Tornay. I wonder how much they believe the confessional is the cure to all ills. That was fine in the fourth century; it was quite a novel therapeutic process at the time. But if things haven't changed since, and there's no real attempt to give people in the Vatican other coping strategies apart from Hail Marys and rosaries, they're heading for trouble. For many, the Vatican becomes a mix of religious intensity and authoritarianism."

I thought of Monsignor Jehle as a "counseling system," the chaplain whom few trusted with their grievances, and who had to all appearances refused to hear out Tornay shortly before his death.

"It's very hard for the young men of the Swiss Guard," Canter continued. "Here they are, living in the Vatican, a theocracy, and the Roman friends they mix with when they go out in the evenings talk to them about alien things like contraception, abortion, and divorce. The guards have to cope with these very different worlds, and it's reflected in their work as soldiers, too. On the one hand, they're medieval mercenaries playing out an act. On the other, they've got to protect a very important figure from lethal threats. It's enough to turn their heads, and makes things very confusing. Especially if in addition to all that, you happen to be a guard who is forced to stifle your own homosexuality."

I filled Canter in on the many problems officers had with imposing discipline: the guns drawn to make guards get out of bed; the almost routine breaking of curfew rules; the clashes between the "saints" and the "killers," and between the Swiss German majority and the French-speaking minority.

Canter nodded. "That shows that these guards are not buying into the dominant culture. Their generation hasn't been brought up with a very strong commitment to the Roman Catholic religion. It makes holding on to the traditions and the discipline much harder. Coercion is necessary to keep the whole operation going, and the pressures of the workplace become enormous. And in Tornay's case, only his father is a Roman Catholic. His mother is a Protestant."

"So a single event, like the failure to get the medal, or Estermann's promotion, cannot explain Tornay's actions as the Vatican insists?"

"Absolutely not. A whole string of things comes together to give rise to this particular event. Tornay feels unfairly dealt with, he tries to change the system, but it's apparent that he's in a context in which pressures are allowed to build up, in which people do express their frustrations and their anger by breaking the rules. Because that's the only way they can express themselves. It strikes me that there is a lot of anger between Estermann and Tornay, and Estermann handled it totally inappropriately. It all gets out of control. I can see all the frustrations, the problems, coming together in a particularly vulnerable individual, and in a particularly unsupportive environment."

Canter's conclusions were completely at odds with the Vatican's, and what was more, they implied that the Vatican was at least partly to blame for the three deaths. "Could the deaths have been avoided?" I asked.

"Well, in any hierarchical organization in which individuals have to achieve certain standards and need awards to be promoted, any decent personnel officer wouldn't allow Tornay to discover by chance that he didn't get the key award he was hoping for. Estermann may have thought that a notice pinned to the wall was toughening and good for discipline, but it's putting terrible pressure on the young man who gets the message that he hasn't made it."

"What was the alternative?"

"The news should have been given to him in a meeting, so that he could either quietly discuss his future or rave and shout about it. And the timing could hardly have been worse—for the Swiss Guard it was a time of tension because of the swearing-in ceremony coming up and all that entailed: the rehearsals during what should have been spare time, the pressure to get it perfect."

After I left Canter, I thought of his doubts about there being anything more to the Vatican's counseling system than Hail Marys and rosaries. As had become increasingly clear to me, the only counseling system available to the likes of Tornay came down to a single individual, and I was impatient to tackle him. If anyone in Rome should perform a mea culpa for Tornay's death, it might well be the one figure within the Swiss Guard who was supposed to act as a confidant to the guards, and yet also represented the Vatican authorities that held sway over it: the chaplain, Monsignor Alois Jehle.

CHAPTER TWENTY-NINE

WHEN I FIRST TELEPHONED Monsignor Jehle, I was coldly sent packing. "I never give interviews" was the longest sentence I got out of him. It took the intervention of Colonel Segmuller, the commander of the Swiss Guard, to persuade the chaplain to grant me an audience. Only too aware that Jehle had gagged all the guards, I did not tell either Segmuller or Jehle that the three deaths were the reason for my request. I stuck to my story that I was writing a book on the Vatican and that the Swiss Guard would feature in it.

After Segmuller's intervention, I called Jehle again to arrange a meeting. He was less curt this time, and told me he could see me after the Mass he would celebrate for the guards at their chapel, St. Martin's, the following Sunday. Mass, he said, would be an opportunity for me to see the chapel, which he had just finished having restored. I sensed that this amounted to a summons to attend his service, and that a refusal would be taken as a personal offense. Jehle had another recommendation to make. He impressed upon me the need for "a smart turnout." I promised to wear a dark suit and tie, and he thanked me effusively.

Under a white sky, just before nine o'clock on a Sunday morning, St. Peter's Square was deserted and the only sounds hanging in the chill air were the splash of water in the fountains and the scrape of hooves against the cobblestones as the driver of a *carrozza* horse cab fed his animal out of a nose bag. With a feather duster, a souvenir seller flicked away the dirt which the Roman smog had deposited on his small plaster statues of the Basilica and the Colosseum.

At St. Anne's Gate, a guard wrapped in a thick blue cape stood idle, twirling a metal whistle on a string around his white-gloved hand. When I mentioned St. Martin's, he did not ask my name or for any proof of identity, but simply waved me up the slope toward the sinister Bastion of Nicholas V, which houses the Vatican Bank. Following his directions, I turned left in front of the tower and passed through an archway that led out onto the back of the colonnade that embraces St. Peter's Square. In the shadow of the Apostolic Palace, and directly beneath the windows of the pope's study, squatted Jehle's austere acid-yellow sanctum, the chapel of St. Martin's.

As I walked in, I faltered as I suddenly realized it was here that the three bodies had been laid out before the coffins were sealed. The inside of the tiny chapel was virtually bare, as welcoming and as spiritually uninspiring as a dentist's waiting room, the walls a clinical white since Jehle's "restoration" had stripped them of their delicate sixteenth-century frescoes. The tiny chapel was almost full: all wearing dark charcoal suits, young men with close cropped hair sat on the dozen wooden benches inscribed with the letters G.S.P., which stood for Pontifical Swiss Guard. I wondered how many of them were there simply to avoid punishment.

The door to the sacristy was suddenly flung open, and Jehle marched to the altar, his brilliant green-and-gold robe swishing down the short nave. His arms spread out, he adressed the congregation in his native Swiss German. Welcome, he said, to "the school of God." A bronze sun was affixed to the wall as part of the tabernacle behind his head, and its straggly pointed rays formed a jagged halo around his anemic-looking face. The positioning was too precise to be accidental.

Jehle was in his early forties, but a bald patch had already spread around the top of his skull and the bright lights of the bare chapel bounced off it whenever he looked up from the Bible, his eyes narrow slits behind small rimless lenses. Two deep creases ran like parentheses from his nose to the corners of his thin mouth.

We are all created as models, he preached, and this holds true not only for the pope, for bishops, and for the senior officers of the Guard, but "for all of us, even halberdiers." As soon as we strike up relations with other individuals, we become models for them, and we should be conscious of the heavy responsibility this brings, Jehle said.

After the service, I went up to him and he gave me a hasty, slippery handshake, then looked me up and down with a long stare. He told me this was the second Mass he had celebrated that day—the first had been at six o'clock—and there would be a third one later. That way, all guards would get a chance to attend, whatever their turns of duty.

While I waited, he changed into a black cassock, then led me to the barracks and up to his second-floor apartment, which was above both the commander's office and what had once been Estermann's home. On the landing, Jehle stopped to punch in a code and his door clicked open. His flat was the only one on the staircase equipped with such security—to protect him not from terrorists but from the very guards he was supposedly ministering to, I thought. Inside, a single dark corridor divided the entire length of the apartment. He showed me into the sitting room and gave a steely little bow. "My museum. I never use it, only for distinguished guests."

He disappeared noiselessly down the carpeted corridor. Soon afterward I heard the whine of an espresso machine.

The room certainly felt as musty as a museum. Judging by the glass cover that protected it, the prize exhibit was a dozen cigars, piled with maniacal precision to form a pyramid. A silver cigar cutter rested on top of the edifice. A stereo on the chest of drawers was also covered, by a frayed dustcover. In a corner, a crucifix crowned a tall pole. The floral print wallpaper and high-backed armchairs looked a little English in style, but the room felt as cozy as a used tea bag gone cold. On the wall, a large landscape painting was so darkened, the canvas split by age and neglect, it was impossible to make out the scenery.

I walked across to the window. Give or take a few yards, the view was the same as that from Estermann's home. It was cramped: the medieval Bastion of Nicholas V loomed so close I felt I could reach out and touch it, and just behind it, the east flank of the Apostolic Palace's high facade soared into the sky.

Jehle returned carrying dainty cups of coffee and sat down with his back as straight as a candle, his hands resting primly on his lap. I thought it best to start as gently as possible, and asked him how long he had been at the Vatican.

"Since 1999," he replied. But then he corrected himself: he had taken up the job in 1995, six years after his ordination. I wondered whether his mistake had been a Freudian slip, whether it betrayed how much he wanted to erase the memory of the three deaths that had occurred in May 1998.

I asked him to tell me about his duties.

He smiled tightly and gave a long, high-pitched wheeze, which was apparently the closest he came to a chuckle. "The chaplain is the 'mother,' so to speak, of the Swiss Guard. This is a family: the commander is the father, and the chaplain is the mother. The chaplain must be the friend, the guide. The chaplain must be the person to whom all can be told, like a mother. Without it causing a fuss. Without rumors spreading, and without a complaint leading to an official procedure."

"Like the secret of the confessional?" I asked. We had only just begun our conversation, and already I was irritated by him, because of his habit of speaking of himself in the third person.

"Yes, even a talk with a guard must have the same value as the confessional. The chaplain has to respect the guard's privacy. The chaplain is the person to whom you confide everything. The chaplain does not command; he guides."

"But I'm told you are more powerful than the commander." I didn't tell him my informant was Cardinal Schwéry.

"The chaplain is on a par with the commander. He is not below him in terms of influence."

I thought of the men, including Tornay, who refused to trust Jehle with their secrets because the confessional had taught Jehle the value of keeping only his own secrets, and of Gugelmann, who had felt betrayed when Jehle blurted out the news of Tornay's letter to his superiors. I found this particularly disconcerting given Jehle's duties as a priest. But it was too early to ask him directly about Tornay's death. I did not want to risk him cutting short our conversation. So, biding my time, I stuck to a more general tack. "How does the guidance begin? What are the first things you tell the recruits when they arrive?" I asked.

"The first thing I do is show them the place of worship. I take them to the chapel. That is where we as a community meet the Lord. I tell them they have two armories. The one where the guns are stored, and the Church and its Gospel. I call them spiritual weapons. To live properly, a guard must, *must* go to Mass every day and have a profound relationship with the Lord." His cup grated against the saucer each time he said the word "must."

"Every day?" I asked, mindful of the reluctance with which many guards went to Mass even once a week.

"It is advisable. But a guard must, *must* go every Sunday. You know, many people tell me that when they see a guard in uniform go down on his knee during the consecration, they think more deeply about what the consecration means. They realize the guard is kneeling before the mystical presence of Christ. And guards mustn't go out into Rome too much. I tell them they have to defend not only the person of the pope, but his ideals, too, and they will cut a poor figure if they meet people who attack His Holiness verbally and they don't have a clue what to reply."

"So the guards live isolated lives within the Vatican?"

"We live as Christians, and no one who lives his faith is isolated. And they can turn to the chaplain if they need help."

"What kinds of things do the guards worry about?" I asked.

Jehle steepled his fingers under his chin. "I don't want to confide to you what the guards tell me; that would be like a mother baring the souls of her own children. And you know, I tend to forget things. I forget what people tell me. Which is a good thing for a priest, believe me."

"But a recruit leaves his home and his family to come to Rome," I pressed. "Often he leaves a girlfriend behind, too. So what comfort can you give them when they complain that they feel homesick, or that they miss their girlfriend?"

"The guards have to be conscious of the fact that this is not just a military assignment, it is a vocation in the service of the Church. The best medicine apart from esprit de corps is going on pilgrimages. As for the girl, she must accept that she does not come first, that her boyfriend is ready to offer his life for His Holiness."

Jehle's use of the word "medicine" jarred on my nerves: he made homesickness, or missing a girlfriend, sound like diseases. "But apart from pilgrimages, surely you must offer the men words of comfort," I said.

"I tell them that the time spent here serves to purify their relationship with their girlfriend. Because when they are separated, they need more than eroticism to keep a relationship going; they need real love. And where the relationship is made of straw, then the straw burns and it's over. And that's just as well. Nothing you offer to the Lord is offered for nothing. Whatever sacrifice you make, He repays you a thousand times. Like the guard's promise to sacrifice his life for the pope. He's doing it for Jesus Christ Himself. The pope represents Christ, and so it becomes a heroic act. With the faith, the guard understands that his life is not the most important thing."

It was as good a time as any to try Jehle on what had undoubtedly been the worst day of his priesthood. "This readiness to sacrifice oneself for the pope," I said. "What did Tornay mean by—"

Jehle interrupted. His voice was tightly controlled. "No. We cannot talk about that. It is not the role of the chaplain to talk. You have to remember my duty of confidence, my duties toward the men."

In for a penny, in for a pound, I thought. "That is precisely what I would like to ask you about. I've been told that Tornay went to see you after Mass on that last evening, and apparently you refused to talk to him. He died not long afterward."

Jehle froze, save that his lower lip trembled. "Tornay didn't want to talk," he blurted out.

He stretched his arms out horizontally toward me, his clenched fists held tightly against each other as if by a pair of handcuffs. He leaned forward, his face so close I could make out the blotchy, open pores on a greasy patch around his nostrils.

I spoke for him. "You have your hands tied," I said.

The barest of nods, then a hoarse shout. "If I say anything, anything at all, I lose their trust!"

It was not clear to me whether he meant the trust of the guards under him or of the prelates above him. Or both. I pressed on. "But if Tornay had not wanted to talk, as you say, why then did he bother to seek you out?"

"I cannot speak," he said. I waited as he stared out of the window, his vacant gaze apparently seeing neither the Vatican Bank nor the Apostolic Palace.

Then he spoke again, the words coming quickly. "Tornay did come to see me, but he didn't want to talk. He just turned away."

"So you don't blame yourself at all for what happened?"

Jehle stared at the carpet and stroked his lower lip, as if comforting himself, for a long while. I worried that perhaps I had gone too far. Then he looked up: "I ask myself only this: Why did the Lord not give me a sign, just a small sign, that I should follow Tornay?"

I wondered whether that was the prayer Jehle had offered as he made his way to inform the pope on the night of the deaths.

"In any case, it was Estermann's fault," Jehle continued in a petulant tone. "He did wrong. You can't let Tornay know just two days before the ceremony that he won't get the medal he's been expecting. Estermann should have told him before. That was wrong."

I was astonished that Jehle could so blithely knock Estermann off his officially forged pedestal. After Cardinal Schwéry, Jehle was the second figure in a position of authority within the Vatican to dispute the official version of events.

"Do you blame Estermann for anything else?" I asked.

"There's a limit to what I can say about who was to blame. It was wrong to put the notice up on the wall. And now we've made some changes which mean that we can put people under observation. Before

Tornay's death, that was not the case, and that was wrong. There are other reforms that should have been made earlier, but I can't go into them."

I felt encouraged to raise the subject of Estermann's covert prose-lytizing on Vatican territory. "What about Estermann's links to Opus Dei? Is it true you told him off for trying to recruit guards into the movement?" I asked.

"Where did you hear that?" Jehle shot back.

I had no intention of telling him and tried to provoke him into answering me. "Are you a member of Opus Dei?" I asked.

"No. No, of course not. I am a priest, period. And I believe that the Swiss Guard must not become a breeding ground for Catholic move-ments, whether it is Opus Dei or anything else. The guards have their reli-gious representative and their guide, and that is the chaplain. The Swiss Guard cannot be abandoned to political battles. And you know, a com-mander who mentions 'the faith' every three sentences is out of line."

There it was again, another attack on Estermann. I took his reply as an implicit confirmation that he had indeed stepped in to stop Ester-mann's work for Opus Dei.

"What about Estermann's homosexual relationship with Tornay, and with the other guards—"

Jehle interrupted, and brought his right hand up to his mouth. He spoke from behind his fingers as he stroked his lower lip: "That's old hat. In any case, bear in mind that the Church tolerates homosexuals, as long as they are chaste."

I noticed he had failed to deny Estermann's affairs. "But did you take any steps—"

Again he interrupted me. "Enough," he said. With a glance at his watch, he stood up and asked me to follow him. I thought he was about to show me the door, but instead he led me down the gloomy corridor away from the entrance.

He stopped to make another tiny shot of coffee in the kitchen, where the refrigerator was empty save for a shelf full of plastic single-portion milk containers. Then he took me out onto his terrace, a jumble of wilting plants, a pair of stone angels, and a knee-high statue of the Virgin. Jehle pointed high above our heads at the Apostolic Palace. The windows of the pope's study were open.

A ripple of applause from St. Peter's Square reached us through the colonnade to our left, followed by the familiar stumbling and slurred voice on the loudspeakers. It was the pope's celebration of the Angelus, his noon greeting to pilgrims in the square. From where we stood to the side of the palace, all I could see of the pope was a flash of a white sleeve reflected in a pane of his window. Nor could I make out what he was saying, because his voice was too faint and the loudspeakers too far away.

But Jehle, who had struck an oddly debonair pose, with one foot resting on a flowerpot—arms akimbo, the fabric of his cassock stretched in ugly pleats across his stomach—was beaming smugly, pleased with his party trick featuring the supreme pontiff in the starring role. Again, the thin wheeze that indicated mirth. "Have you ever seen anything like this?" he asked, the proud sweep of his arm taking in both the facade of the Apostolic Palace and his shabby terrace.

I refused to be distracted. "If Tornay was as bad an element of the Swiss Guard as we were told, why wasn't he punished or even sacked much earlier?" I asked.

Jehle wiped the smile off his face with the sleeve of his cassock and looked peeved. I had spoiled his show and he replied in a sulky tone: "Both Estermann and I were in favor of Tornay's promotion because he had good qualities. We tried to offer him responsibility, but he took advantage of it. And he interpreted everything as a slight. He suffered from paranoia."

Perhaps worrying that he had been too indiscreet, Jehle had

returned to peddling the official line. It was with little hope of enlightenment that I asked him what lessons, if any, he had learned from the deaths.

He was in no hurry to answer. He took his small glasses off his nose and dangled them at me. He squinted at me shortsightedly and adopted the formal, ponderous tone of an old-fashioned preacher. "The people who look at the world through the wrong kind of glasses, what do they see? If you look for sex in everything, you will find it. If you look for bad things, you will find them. You should look for the good in people."

I bristled at the tone of condescension in his lecture. "So what was the good in those three deaths?" I asked.

Jehle jerked his head toward the Apostolic Palace. "The pope said he couldn't understand the deaths, and neither can I. It was a situation in which two worlds clashed. It was the work of the Devil. But a man of God does not despair. He cannot despair. God must have sown a seed in Tornay, but you cannot expect to see it sprout so quickly. That is the difficulty of our job: you sow and you don't see the result straightaway. But we continue to sow, not because it is reasonable, but because God tells us to. After all, it was from the worst crime in the world, from the death of His Son, that our salvation grew. In the end, the Lord will triumph, as long as we have faith."

The sermon was over, and so was our meeting. Nothing I could say would squeeze an Act of Contrition out of Jehle. The only apology I got from him was a mumble that he had other business to attend to, before he led me back down the corridor. As he walked briskly ahead of me, I made one last try. "Could the deaths have been avoided?" I asked.

From behind, I saw his shoulders stiffen, but he did not slow down. "Yes. But remember, I am not important. I am just a priest, a go-between. I answer to the Secretariat of State. And remember that the office of the pope was instituted by God. And the Swiss Guard serves His Holiness. So the Swiss Guard will last as long as the papacy lasts. And it has been promised to the Roman Catholic Church that it will live on until the end of the world."

By belittling his role, the self-proclaimed servant of the God of truth was granting himself absolution. I was given no opportunity to remind him that earlier in our conversation, he had described himself as the mother and guide of the guards, and as powerful as the commander himself. The slippery hand reached out for mine, and with a deft maneuver Jehle managed to shake my hand, steer, and almost push me out through the doorway all at the same time. A severe little bow, a curt good-bye, and the door clicked shut in my face.

I had just started down the stairs when I heard Jehle exclaim, loudly enough for the sound, and the irritation in his voice, to carry through his heavy wooden door: "Ach, people, people . . ."

CHAPTER THIRTY

THE WOMAN'S VOICE on my answering machine sounded familiar, but it took me a few moments to recognize it. I had never heard Tornay's mother, Muguette Baudat, speak with such a light tone of voice. "I'm sorry I haven't been in touch for so long. I know people think everything is slow in Switzerland, but that's not true. I've been so busy," her message said. I thought I could even hear a note of triumph as it concluded: "I wanted to tell you that we are going to hold a news conference in Martigny. At the Hotel du Parc, in two weeks' time. See you then."

Her message begged several questions. Who did "we" mean? And what had persuaded her to face the press now, after shunning the media for so long? I checked the calendar: it was Sunday, April 14, 2002, and in three weeks' time it would be the fourth anniversary of her son's death. I hadn't seen her for several months, and I was writing a book about my investigation.

When I called her back, there was no mistaking her mood: she was buoyant. She had been rushed off her feet the past few weeks, she said, such a rush that she had to install a fax in the café where she worked. But now things were looking up. She would be taking a backseat at the press conference—"It's not in my hands," as she put it—and her new lawyers, Jacques Vergès and Luc Brossollet, both French, would be doing all the talking.

They had been through the Vatican report into its inquiry with scrupulous care, she assured me, and would announce their conclusions at the conference she had organized herself. She had chosen to hold it in Martigny, the town where her son is buried. I asked her to tell me more, but she said she had to run because she had much work to do.

Later, I rummaged among some old boxes of mine and found what I was looking for: the file that I had kept on Vergès when I was doing research for my biography of Carlos the Jackal, the terrorist. When Carlos was on the run in the 1980s and 1990s, hunted by the CIA and every other Western intelligence service, it was Vergès who acted as his lawyer. Vergès was no stranger to high-profile trials: he had defended, among others, the Gestapo war criminal Klaus Barbie, and more recently Slobodan Milosevic, and had forged his reputation as "the Devil's advocate" with his eagerness to defend the indefensible. What, I wondered, could Tornay have in common with the likes of Carlos, Barbie, and Milosevic?

I arrived at the Hotel du Parc early on a Saturday afternoon. Baudat, Vergès, and Brossollet were still in the restaurant off the lobby. Baudat sat opposite them, flanked by two young women. I recognized the shy, dark-haired Mélinda, who had accompanied her mother to Rome so long ago, and guessed the fair-skinned blonde was her sister,

Sara. I had never seen Vergès in the flesh before, and sat down to study him from a table not too close.

I could see little of him apart from his silhouette, as behind him mountain-bright sunshine streamed through a windowpane that stretched from floor to ceiling. He was a graying seventy-eight-year-old, and his Eurasian features—he'd been born to a French father and a Thai mother—were intriguing. But it was his stillness, broken only by a few slow movements, that hypnotized me. He picked up his wineglass, tilted his head back as if in slow motion, his round glasses flashing, the liquid bloodred against the sun, and swallowed a mouthful. At the end of the meal he lit a fat cigar, the smoke swirling heavily over his head as if reluctant to leave his magnetic presence.

From what I could see of her, Baudat, too, was mesmerized by him. She stared at him often, paying more attention to him than to her food, which she picked at without interest, and spoke in a voice that was barely above a whisper. Her daughters were tongue-tied. Soon all three women were smoking Baudat's cigarettes.

An hour or so later, Vergès led the small party into a gray room off the hotel lobby where the news conference was about to start. Baudat, her rust-colored hair like a lion's mane around her sharply made-up face, sat behind the speakers' table, discreetly to one side. Mélinda and Sara—of the two, Mélinda looked more like their brother, with the same mouth and nose—again sat on either side of her, and as the conference began, Baudat slowly stretched her hands out to hold theirs under the table. There was a hunted look in her eyes, and she seemed to be dreading what lay ahead. Before her lay a sprig of lily of the valley someone had given her—the flower is called *muguet* in French, which is close to her first name, Muguette.

Clad in a black roll-neck polo, a gray-checked sport jacket, and green corduroy trousers, Vergès sat as immobile and enigmatic as a sphinx, and let the preppily dressed Brossollet do the talking.

"Mesdames et messieurs," Brossollet began, "we have invited you here today because Cédric Tornay is not a murderer, but a murder victim."

Brossollet's opening shot certainly had his audience hooked. Baudat stared fixedly at a point somewhere above the heads of the journalists sitting in front of her, all of whom scribbled furiously. For the following two hours, he explained how she and her lawyers had reached their conclusion.

They had started out by showing the results of Baudat's secret autopsy to several experts. These experts said that because the exit hole left by the bullet that pierced Tornay's skull was 7 millimeters wide, the bullet could not have been fired by Tornay's gun, since it fired bullets with a diameter of 9.41 millimeters. Nor could the gun have dropped from Tornay's grasp onto the floor as the Vatican said it had, just before he fell forward on top of it. The recoil from this gun was too strong for this to be possible, Brossollet said, and this again indicated that another gun had been used.

I listened to all this with increasing dismay. The points that Brossollet was making were those that had fueled conspiracy rumors from the outset. I had put them to Professor Bernard Knight, the leading forensic scientist, early on in my investigation, and he had exposed them as fallacies one by one. There was no room for doubt: Tornay had killed the Estermanns, and then shot himself.

I glanced at Baudat, but she was still staring into the middle distance. Of the three women, only Sara, the younger daughter, was staring at Brossollet. Mélinda sat with her head bent down. I saw Sara stiffen. Brossollet had gotten up to mime what he said were Tornay's last moments. He shaped his right hand into the form of a gun and brought the tip of the "barrel" to his lips. "Like this," he said. "Tornay must have had his head bent backward when the gun was fired. His two front teeth are fractured, and we have reason to believe that this is the result of the gun being introduced into his mouth."

Brossollet projected a slide onto a screen behind him. Twice natural size, three sketches of Tornay's skull, the gun a black mass close to his mouth, the bullet's supposed trajectory inked in red, hovered over the heads of Baudat and her daughters. Baudat glanced at them briefly, then reached into her bag, pulled out a handkerchief, and dabbed quickly at her eyes.

Her relief, and that of her daughters, was palpable when Brossollet switched off the slide projector. He started reading out Tornay's last letter, the one he wrote to his mother. Then he set the text aside and announced: "We've hired an expert graphologist to study the handwriting of this letter. We've looked into how this letter came to be published. We've analyzed its content. This letter is a forgery, written by a forger close to the Vatican whose mother tongue is Italian."

Brossollet made no attempt to explain away the fact that the letter had been handed by Tornay himself to his fellow guardsman Gugelmann shortly before his death.

"Cédric Tornay's innocence is manifest," Brossollet concluded. "We demand that the Vatican reopen its investigation. And that the mysterious deacon, Yvon Bertorello, who told Tornay's mother that he had written proof that her son was murdered, be interrogated. Did he play a role in the tragedy? We don't know whether he did, but he is hiding something."

Vergès, who until then had remained virtually immobile save for a moment when he chewed first his upper lip and then his lower one, then picked up a pen to take a couple of notes, spoke at last. He was brief, but he spoke with the theatrical pauses of a lawyer pleading his client's case before a jury.

"Why was this murder committed? One thing we do know: Estermann was an agent of the Stasi. It is not we who say so but Markus Wolf," he said.

I noticed that Vergès did not bother to point out that Wolf, the former Stasi spymaster, had been quoted as saying this in an interview with a Polish newspaper, and that both Wolf and the journalist who interviewed him later shot the story to pieces, saying they had not talked about Estermann. I was surprised to see that Vergès was taking for granted a report that, as I had found out in Berlin, was based on nothing more than an anonymous letter.

Vergès ended with a plea which he said was addressed to the pope himself: "If we are here today, it is not to arm-wrestle with the Vatican, but to appeal for an investigation which in any democratic country would automatically allow all parties in the case to be heard, with the Vatican showing respect for the family's grief instead of slandering them. This is not a lost cause, but it is a difficult one because of the wall of silence we are up against."

Neither Baudat nor her daughters spoke during the news conference. When it was finished, Sara handed out copies of a photograph of her brother. His eyes were a bright gray blue, but there were deep lines underneath them and his smile was tight. I asked Sara when the picture was taken. She smiled shyly. "Five or six months before," she answered.

That evening I had dinner with Baudat in a restaurant just off a hairpin bend on the road that snaked up the mountainside from Martigny. On the way up, she told me that the seats of her red Nissan were covered in dog hairs because her daughters had given her a Doberman pinscher as a pet. "They have both left home. I am on my own now," she said. "Sometimes I think that's why they gave me the dog. They don't want me to feel lonely." Mélinda was working in a bakery, and Sara had found a job as a dentist's assistant after finishing her apprenticeship "right at the worst time for us."

Baudat took her time choosing a bottle of the local Dôle red wine and seemed determined to enjoy herself—the day's events had obviously given a great lift to her spirits. I noticed she smoked less than the previous times we had met, and told her so.

"Today wasn't easy," she replied. "I warned the girls this morning: 'If one of you starts to cry, whatever you do, don't look at each other because you'll both break down.' In the end I was the one who got tearful during the press conference—twice—but they held my hands. Once when I felt bad, Mélinda said to me: 'Take my hand; I'll give you my strength.' But from now on the lawyers will do the work: I'm going to let myself be guided for once. It's taken a long time to get this far, but it's been worth the effort because in the end it's the result that counts."

I was pleased to see that she was beginning to take pleasure in life once again, but it struck me that she was clinging to the illusion that her son had not killed anyone, and that his death was no suicide. It was her way of dealing with his death, but I wondered how long it would be before she could face the truth. And for the moment her lawyers, perhaps for their own purposes, were keeping her illusions alive.

Had she really no suspicion that her son had pressed the trigger at any time? I wondered. "Do you now rule out that your son could have killed the Estermanns and then himself?" I asked.

"Yes, I do rule it out. And now I don't feel alone anymore in that belief."

I thought of challenging this belief of hers, and telling her the details of my own investigation then and there. I decided against it. Today was the wrong day to do this, I told myself. And in any case I would achieve little by doing so. She was so convinced that her fabrication was true that she would simply not be able to give me a fair hearing. Perhaps I was simply not courageous enough to confront her, but I decided the best way to tell her what I had found out was to wait until she could read the whole story of my research. I felt more than a twinge of guilt at not making a clean breast of it in the restaurant.

"How come Vergès took on the case?" I asked. "You know he's

defended people like Carlos the Jackal and Milosevic? Surely Cédric doesn't have much in common with people like that?"

Baudat's eyes flitted across the room before she answered. When she spoke, her tone sounded defensive. "Well, I do trust Vergès. And he doesn't need me to get publicity for himself. He's getting on, he's at the end of his career, I don't think he wants to hit out at the Vatican because it's about the only state left that he hasn't attacked. I believe he really is outraged at the way the Vatican has handled the whole thing, and I'm sure he's convinced that Cédric is innocent."

I was struck by the fact that Baudat had used her son's first name. The first time we met, she had told me that she preferred to call him "Tornay" because "Cédric" was too painful to her. Perhaps she was, after all, beginning to come to terms with his loss.

I still wanted to know how she had come to be convinced that Tornay was murdered. "Who did most of the research that we heard about today? Who got the experts' opinions and so on?" I asked.

"I did."

"Did you ask the forensic scientist who carried out the autopsy you commissioned what his conclusions were on the cause of death?"

She replied in a listless monotone. "I didn't ask him about the causes of death."

"Why not? Seems an obvious question to me," I insisted.

"Because I'm worried about outside pressures. You know, even people who are very eminent can be influenced by others. I just asked him to say what he saw on the body, and I passed that information on to several doctors."

"Yes, but why not ask him at least for an opinion?"

"I didn't want to put all my eggs in one basket."

The answer was feeble and I knew she was trying to hide something from me. On my flight to Switzerland, I had been through the notes I had taken at our last meeting. She had told me then that the expert who carried out the autopsy had indeed talked about the cause of death. If Tornay had been murdered, he had said, the killer would have had to completely incapacitate him beforehand, and there were no signs of such an occurrence.

Toward the end of the meal, Baudat's mobile phone rang. It was Sara, who had found a report on the day's news conference on a Swiss newspaper's Web site. Baudat nodded and smiled as her daughter read it. "Good, that's good," she said as she listened.

"You were great today," Baudat said to Sara when she finished. "You're okay now? So you'll sleep well tonight? Good, bye-bye, then. Good night."

Baudat put the phone away in her handbag and turned back to me. "Sara's the one who suffered the most. She was alone at home when the news came, and for two hours she had to cope with it on her own. For months afterward she lived in fear; she'd look under her bed every night before going to sleep. Once I saw her standing in the kitchen, there was something odd about her, her whole body looked wrong, and she said to me: 'Mummy, it's coming back.' I knew that 'it' meant the fear."

As we left the restaurant, a full moon hung low over the ridge of the mountain on the far side of the valley, illuminating Martigny far below us. At the foot of the mountainside, in a patch that the moon's rays did not reach, was the cemetery where Tornay lay.

She drove me to the train station and kindly got out of the car to say good-bye. The sprig of lily of the valley was poking limply out of her handbag. She kissed me three times on the cheeks. Her last words to me were: "I feel as if I've been in a tunnel for such a long time, and now at last I can make out the light at the end of it."

EPILOGUE

AS MY TRAIN ROLLED through the clear night after I left Baudat, the moon darting in and out among the peaks high above Lake Geneva, I thought about her manner that day. Although she had been more lively and self-confident than she'd been at our previous meetings, I was sure that her newfound self-assurance was only skin-deep and that she was in fact more fragile and vulnerable than ever. She was clutching at straws. I was convinced that the Vatican's whole approach to the murders and its refusal to grant her access to the files of its inquiry was prolonging her mourning for Tornay, just as families whose loved ones disappear without a trace have their grief suspended in time.

Although Baudat refuses to accept it, the truth is that her son,

Cédric Tornay, did indeed kill his commander, and his commander's wife, before turning the gun on himself. But his last moments were not those of a madman, as the Vatican would have us believe.

Tornay had come to the Eternal City believing that his mission was to protect the pope, and ready to sacrifice his own life if necessary. But soon he discovered that the Swiss Guard was stuck in a time warp, so archaic, and so incompetently run, that any determined assassin could easily break through its flimsy defenses.

He was not the only one to see its glaring ineptitude, but when others remained silent, he was brave enough to suggest reform, only to be slapped down at every turn. He was persecuted by his superiors and by the Swiss Germans, who were the majority contingent in the Guard and whose mentality was completely alien to him.

The man he turned to for affection embodied that mind-set more than anyone else in the Guard: Alois Estermann. Their affair remains a riddle to me. Perhaps Tornay saw in him the authoritative, or rather authoritarian, father figure that he never had. Perhaps Tornay admired Estermann as the most ambitious and most quickly promoted officer in the Guard, an officer who claimed to enjoy the personal trust of the pope himself.

One thing is certain: No one shattered Tornay's illusions as devastatingly as Estermann. Their relationship deteriorated into acrimony as Tornay realized that Estermann had betrayed him with another guard. From then on, Tornay had little hesitation in standing up to Estermann on professional grounds—always the only guard who dared to do so. In response, Estermann enforced his authority with more determination than ever.

Further wrecking their relationship was the fact that any respect Tornay felt for Estermann must have vanished when he investigated his links to Opus Dei, a sect with a passion for self-flagellation. Tornay could not accept his commander's wish to link the Swiss Guard to such a sect, and he might well have been thinking of this when he wrote in his last letter that he would die for the sake of his fellow guards and of the Catholic Church.

Although nothing of what happened to Tornay can be seen as an excuse for what he did, Baudat would be more than justified in pointing an accusatory finger at the Holy City, which must take blame for nurturing her son's disillusion, solitude, and distress, and which did nothing to pull him back from the brink to which it had helped drive him.

There were plenty of reasons why it was imperative for the powers that be in the Vatican to prevent the sordid story behind the deaths of May 4, 1998, from ever becoming known outside its walls. The need for silence over an event that was a damning indictment of the twilight of John Paul's papacy was paramount. As Cardinal Sodano, the Vatican's prime minister, said at the Estermanns' funeral in St. Peter's Basilica: "In times like these we feel above all the need to be silent." It was on his orders that Tornay's comrades-in-arms were sworn to silence. Even today, the conspiracy of silence and the refusal to admit any responsibility prevails: although the three victims have long been buried, and the Vatican's inquiry—a shoddy affair that lied by omission—remains closed, the files of that inquiry are still locked away.

When the Vatican did break its law of silence to speak about the deaths, it was to effectively excommunicate Tornay. The young guard was reviled from every pulpit with a virulence worthy of the Holy Inquisition, and dismissed as a drugged paranoiac. The Vatican even violated subjudice rules to leak key evidence—Tornay's last letter—when this suited its purpose.

From the moment the bodies were found in the Estermann apartment, the Vatican's conduct was dictated by genuflection to "reasons of state"—a euphemistic phrase that served to give personal ambition, intrigue, secrets, and lies a thin veneer of dignity. And yet, no mea culpa has ever been pronounced by anyone in the Vatican. None of those involved in the events that led to the three deaths has been called to account for his actions. The same is true of those who fabricated an official version in order to prevent the truth from emerging.

Cardinal Sodano remained at his post. When the pope celebrated the fiftieth anniversary of Sodano's priesthood, he paid tribute to the cardinal's "well-proven wisdom in assessing human vicissitudes." The Vatican village whispered that the text of the pope's message had been drafted by Sodano himself. Navarro-Valls, the pope's spokesman, and Jehle, the chaplain, are both still at their posts. Even Opus Dei received a new seal of approval from the pope himself when he ordered the canonization of its founder.

Any sins these men may have committed have been either ignored or pardoned by the pope. But no such Christian mercy has ever been shown to Cédric Tornay. The only time the pope commented on Tornay's fate in public was at his weekly Angelus, three days after the lance corporal's death. Tornay, the pope said, was now before the judgment of God, "to whose mercy I entrust him."

Seventeen years earlier, John Paul II had been far kinder to a man who tried to assassinate him in St. Peter's Square, and almost succeeded: the Turkish gunman Mehmet Ali Agca. When the pope regained consciousness after losing 60 percent of his blood and undergoing five hours and twenty minutes of surgery, among the first remarks he made to Dziwisz, the secretary waiting at his bedside, was a pardon for the man who had shot him. Almost two years later, the pope visited Ali Agca in his prison cell, and as they huddled so close to each other that their knees were almost touching, the pope assured his would-be assassin that he need not be scared of divine reprisals. Have no fear, the pope said. The Virgin Mary loves everyone, and there is no reason to be afraid.

Throughout my investigation, an image stuck in my mind: Tornay, dressed not in his picturesque uniform but in a somber leather jacket, falling to his knees, his back to the window and to the Apostolic Palace, looking at the mayhem before he presses the muzzle of his weapon into his mouth. If he knelt because he was praying for forgiveness, that prayer has yet to be answered.

ACKNOWLEDGMENTS

MANY PEOPLE HELPED ME to carry out the investigation that led to this book. My debt to those mentioned in the text is clear, but there are several who cannot be named for various reasons—in most cases, because they fear that their cooperation with me, if it were made public, would affect their standing in the Vatican. To them, my special thanks.

I also owe much to the following, with the proviso that my interpretation of the events that led up to the Swiss Guard deaths, and of those that followed, is mine alone: Massimo Bachella; Patrick Barman; Bruno Bartoloni; Mirko Basso; Pierre Berset; Giovanni Bianconi; Marco Biasetti; Jürek Blaser; Kristian Boos; Father Giorgio Bruni; Francesco Bruno; Cornelia Buell; Maria Antonietta Calabrò; Yvan

Clerc; Fabio Croce; Domenico Del Rio; Josip Duiella; Robert Estermann; Michele Figus-Diaz; Terry Gander; Marie Giantomaso; Daniel and Sophie Greco; Matteo Guidelli; Laurent Guillet; Daniel Harvey; Peter Hertel; Roland Huber; Robert Hutchison; Markus Imhof; Judge Ferdinando Imposimato; Giampaolo Iorio; Father Peter Jacobs; Roger Juillerat; Johannes Legner; Massimo Lulli; Gian Marco Chiocci; Sandro Magister; Monsignor Luigi Marinelli; Enrico Marinelli; Judge Gianluigi Marrone; Massimo Martinelli; André Marty; Admiral Fulvio Martini; Michael Meier; Gerald O'Collins; Joan O'Sullivan; Stéphane Penouel; Christian Perrat; Fabien Piller; Judge Rosario Priore; Judge Adele Rando; Stephanie Rappaz; Mario Reggio; Fabrizio Roncone; Father Giampaolo Salvini; Heinrich Suter; Laurent Theys; Wolfgang Tietze; Sarah Weatherley; Nigel West.

I am also grateful to the following organizations and institutions: the AGI and ANSA news agencies; APTV; the Archdiocese of Westminster; Civiltà Cattolica; *Corriere della Sera*; Editions Golias; Famiglia Cristiana; the Forensic Science Service; Istituto di Sostenimento del Clero; *Jane's Infantry Weapons; L'Espresso; L'Illustré; Le Matin; Le Monde Diplomatique; L'Osservatore Romano; National Catholic Reporter;* Radio Suisse Romande; *La Repubblica;* Procura di Roma; RaiDue TV; SIG Arms AC; Vatican Radio; the Venezuelan Embassy to the Holy See.

The book owes much to the encouragement of John Cornwell: very early on, over a meal in a Rome trattoria, I mentioned to him what was then only a vague idea. He urged me to go ahead, and gave me precious advice. Clare Alexander, my agent, helped to resolve my doubts as the investigation took shape. Michael Morrison, my publisher, and Claire Wachtel, my editor, were supportive from the outset—including, in Claire's case, when I outlined my progress to her during a nighttime visit to St. Peter's Square.

Writing is said to be a lonely business, but this book was in part a family affair. Thanks to my parents for accompanying me during research trips in Paris and London, to my mother for her suggestions on the first draft of the manuscript, and to my sisters Martine and Katy for their ideas. As ever, my wife Rita was a patient and understanding companion when the demands of the book grew heaviest, and heard me out many, many times. For all those and other times, thank you.

—JOHN FOLLAIN

Rome, January 2003

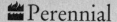 Perennial

Books by John Follain:

CITY OF SECRETS
The Startling Truth Behind the Vatican Murders
ISBN 0-06-093513-8 (paperback)

A chilling look inside the Vatican: *City of Secrets* exposes the greed, hypocrisy, and corruption in the court surrounding the Pope and addresses the cover-up of the infamous Swiss Guard murders of May 4, 1998. *City of Secrets* is not only the story of a gruesome crime on holy territory; it is also an exposé of the shameful efforts by men of the cloth—including a would-be successor to John Paul II and one of the Pope's most trusted servants—to obstruct the course of justice, vilify the character of Tornay (who had fallen victim to barrack mobbing), stifle a potential scandal over homosexual affairs within the Guard, and hide fatal failings that make the force unfit to protect the Pope.

"Follain's judicious inquiry pushes all buttons of true-crime popularity: mystery, spies, lust, and death . . . Follain's is journalism of high quality." —*Booklist*

ZOYA'S STORY
An Afghan Woman's Struggle for Freedom
ISBN 0-06-009783-3 (paperback) • ISBN 0-06-050223-1 (audio)
BY ZOYA, WITH JOHN FOLLAIN AND RITA CRISTOFARI

Devastated by the murder of her parents by Muslim fundamentalists and the destruction of war, Zoya fled Kabul with her grandmother and started a new life in exile in Pakistan. She joined the Revolutionary Association of the Women of Afghanistan (RAWA), which challenged the crushing edicts of the Taliban government. She made dangerous journeys back to her homeland to help the women oppressed by a system that forced them to wear the stifling *burqa*, that condoned public stoning or whipping if they ventured out without a male chaperone, and that forbade them from working.

In this chilling book, Zoya is our guide and our witness to the horrors perpetrated by the Taliban and the Mujaheddin "holy warriors" who defeated the Russian occupiers.

"A tale of struggle and suffering . . . from a courageous freedom fighter who has become an international spokesperson for the Afghan people. . . . Timely and sobering." —*Kirkus Reviews*